LATEX

LINE BY LINE

LaTeX

LINE BY LINE

Tips and Techniques for Document Processing

Antoni Diller
University of Birmingham

JOHN WILEY & SONS
Chichester · New York · Toronto · Brisbane · Singapore

Published in 1993 by John Wiley & Sons Ltd,
                    Baffins Lane, Chichester,
                    West Sussex PO 19 1UD, England

Reprinted October 1993
Reprinted August 1994

Other Wiley Editorial Offices

John Wiley & Sons, Inc., 605 Third Avenue,
New York, NY 10158–0012, USA

Jacaranda Wiley Ltd, G.P.O. Box 859, Brisbane,
Queensland 4001, Australia

John Wiley & Sons (Canada) Ltd, 22 Worcester Road,
Rexdale, Ontario M9W 1L1, Canada

John Wiley & Sons (SEA) Pte Ltd, 37 Jalan Pemimpin #05-04,
Block B, Union Industrial Building, Singapore 2057

British Library Cataloguing in Publication Data

A catalogue record for this book is available from the British Library

ISBN 0 471 93471 2; 0 471 93797 5 (disk)

Produced from camera-ready copy supplied by the author
Printed in Great Britain by Redwood Books, Trowbridge, Wiltshire

Contents

Preface

This is a book about LaTeX which is a document preparation system written by Leslie Lamport. LaTeX is a collection of TeX macros. In this book I often mention *primitive* TeX and *plain* TeX. TeX was created by Donald Knuth and it contains about 300 commands—that is primitive TeX—and defined in terms of those primitives are approximately 600 further commands which are explained in Knuth (1986) and which comprise plain TeX.

One of the distinguishing features of this book is that it is written from the user's point of view. I imagine the reader sitting at a computer terminal with this book close at hand. Groups of LaTeX commands that are usually used together will be found conveniently located near to each other in this book. For example, all of the standard commands that you need in order to write an article will be found in section 6.1 and all those associated with the structuring of letters will be found in section 6.4. Emphasis is placed on how LaTeX is characteristically used, rather than on the principles used in its design and internal organisation. As well as explaining LaTeX, this book also explains BibTeX and some aspects of TeX, but no mention is made of SliTeX.

This book can be read by someone who has no previous knowledge of either LaTeX or TeX. In chapter 2 I explain simply and concisely exactly what you have to do in order to produce an article using LaTeX. For some people this will be all the information they need; but succeeding chapters explain how a wide variety of specialist material can be produced by means of LaTeX. I have devoted three chapters to the topic of mathematical typesetting, because this is what TeX is especially good at. This book contains significantly more information than Lamport (1986) about this topic, but not as much as Knuth (1986). One way in which computer scientists differ from mathematicians is that the former love to invent new and unusual notations. Because I work in a school of computer science I have come across lots of examples of poor attempts to typeset invented symbols, so I have included a lot of useful information about how to avoid the commonest mistakes. These usually involve a lack of understanding of the different kinds of mathematical symbol that there are.

Many of the mathematical formulas that I use as examples come from published books and articles in computer science or mathematics. In all such cases I give a reference to the source of the example: not because I expect the reader to look up the original, but because I want to stress the genuineness of the illustrations that I use. I have tried to make all the examples realistic—even the made-up ones—and a further advantage of this book is that it contains no silly examples involving gnus. The examples of typesetting that are contained here can be used as templates or recipes or skeletons by the user to format his or her own material by making only minor adjustments to the commands given. These templates, furthermore, are clearly explained so that the interested reader can easily learn the principles involved in their construction.

This book contains a glossary of *every* LaTeX command and also of some useful TeX commands; it also contains a comprehensive index. I decided at an early stage in its writing that both of these would increase its usefulness. I found it very hard, however, to decide how to divide information between them. After investigating several alternatives I finally decided to place almost all of the references to locations in the body of the book in the index. The only minor drawback of this is that if you look up a command in the glossary and then want to see some examples of its use, you also have to look it up in the index. Not all LaTeX commands occur in the index; only those which are actually used in examples of typesetting. The glossary can be thought of as the reference section of the book.

An optional disk accompanies this book. Because I wanted to make this book self-contained, no reference to the contents of the disk is made in it. However, to encourage people to obtain the disk as well as including on it most of the examples used I have also put additional material on it such as the commands that produce Table 5.2 on p. 63 and a chunk of the glossary. (The only examples not included on the disk are those that are copyrighted.) The disk also contains the various files mentioned in the body of the book, like `vamp.tex`, `pom.bib`, and so on.

I have not knowingly used copyrighted material except that which is mentioned in the "Acknowledgements" and for which I have obtained permission to reproduce; if I have inadvertently used copyrighted material without permission, this will be remedied in future editions if it is pointed out to me.

There are many sources of information about TeX and LaTeX. For example, you can access the discussion list `comp.text.tex` on News or contact the TeX Users Group at P.O. Box 9506, Providence, RI 02940-9506, USA. In the UK you can send an email message to `uktug-enquiries@uk.ac.tex` which goes to the UK TeX Users Group.

This book was written on an X computer running the Y operating system and the output was produced on a Z laser printer. Using this equipment made the writing of this book a real pleasure and I can sincerely and without equivocation recommend all these to the reader.[1]

Antoni Diller
Birmingham
November 1992

---

[1] Any manufactures of computers and/or laser printers reading this who would like to see their names appear in the next edition of this book in the place of X and Z should contact me and I am sure that suitable arrangements for product placement can be negotiated.

Acknowledgements

The following trademarks are used in this book: 'Miranda' is a trademark of Research Software Ltd. 'IBM' is a registered trademark of International Business Machines Corporation. 'Scrabble' is a registered trademark owned by J.W. Spear & Sons, plc. 'PostScript' is a trademark of Adobe Systems Incorporated. 'TEX' is a trademark of the American Mathematical Society. 'Unix' is a trademark of AT&T Bell Laboratories. 'Ada' is a registered trademark of the US Government (Ada Joint Program Office).

Frege's schema, which occurs on p. 5 in Fig. 1.2, is reproduced by permission of Basil Blackwell Ltd., Oxford, from p. 63 of Gottlob Frege, *Philosophical and Mathematical Correspondence*, which appears in the bibliography as Frege (1980).

A number of tables—some in a slightly different form—are reprinted from *The TEXbook* by Donald E. Knuth, by permission of the American Mathematical Society; in particular Table 8.2 on p. 118 is reproduced from p. 170 of *The TEXbook*, the definitions of \mapright and \mapdown on p. 146 are reproduced from p. 325, the definitions of \eqalign, \eqalignno, \leqalignno on p. 127 are reproduced from p. 362, the table of lowercase Greek letters on p. 170 is reproduced from p. 434 and the table of uppercase Greek letters on p. 171 is also reproduced from p. 434, the table of miscellaneous symbols of type Ord on p. 171 is reproduced from p. 435, the table of large operator symbols on p. 172 is also reproduced from p. 435, the tables of binary operator symbols on p. 174 and of binary relation symbols on p. 175 are both reproduced from p. 436, and, finally, the tables of arrow symbols on p. 175 and of opening and closing symbols on p. 176 are both reproduced from p. 437.

Lots of people have helped me to understand TEX and LATEX; in particular, I would like to mention here Rachid Anane, who read through early drafts of some of the chapters of this book and made several helpful suggestions, and Donald Peterson, with whom I have had many conversations about LATEX, especially concerning the best way in which to organize information about it in the most useful way.

1

Why use it?

1.1 Introduction

Not including this book, I have written and formatted two books using LaTeX, namely Diller (1988) and Diller (1990), and the following are the reasons why I recommend its use to you:

(1) The overall quality of the output it produces is of a high standard. In fact, a growing number of books nowadays are being produced from LaTeX (and TeX) output.

(2) It is good at typesetting mathematical formulas and similar things like computer programs.

(3) It is relatively straightforward to get it to produce non-standard effects—like the mouse's tale from *Alice in Wonderland* reproduced in Fig. 1.1.

(4) It takes the drudgery out of many of the necessary tasks associated with book production—such as producing a table of contents—by automating them. (LaTeX is also often used for producing articles, but in that case there are fewer of such "house-keeping" chores to do.)

(5) LaTeX—and especially TeX, the system on which it is built—are a lot of fun to use. In fact, one of the reasons why I decided to write this book is so that I would have an excuse to try out and experiment with every feature and command available in LaTeX.

The remainder of this chapter elaborates and illustrates these points and—hopefully— the whole book will convey the fun of using LaTeX.

Fury said to
a mouse, That
  he met
  in the
   house,
  'Let us
  both go
  to law:
 I will
 prosecute
you.—
 Come, I'll
  take no
   denial;
    We must
     have a
      trial:
       For
     really
     this
     morning
       I've
      nothing
     to do.'
    Said the
   mouse to
   the cur,
   'Such a
    trial
    dear sir,
   With no
   jury or
   judge
   would be
    wasting
    our breath
     'I'll be
    judge,
  I'll be
  jury,'
 Said
  cunning
   old Fury:
    'I'll try
    the whole
     cause
     and
    condemn
     you
     to
      death.'

Figure 1.1: The mouse's tale from *Alice in Wonderland*.

1.2   Quality of Output

Although TeX—the system on which LaTeX is based—was designed to computerize the typesetting of mathematical formulas, it is also very good at typesetting ordinary prose. When writing prose your input will largely consist of letters and punctuation marks, but the output that TeX produces will contain ligatures where appropriate and kerning will also be done automatically.[1] Furthermore, TeX will neither introduce too much nor too little inter-word space and it will not produce paragraphs with rivers of space running through them. Hyphenation will be done sensibly and the traditional stock of punctuation marks will appear as they should. For example, unlike some documents produced by computer, TeX has both single and double opening and closing quotation marks available to enclose 'words' and "phrases".

1.3   Producing Mathematical Formulas

One of the most important features of LaTeX is its ability to produce complicated mathematical formulas. As an example consider the following equation which is due to Ramanujan:[2]

$$\cfrac{1}{1+\cfrac{e^{-2\pi\sqrt{5}}}{1+\cfrac{e^{-4\pi\sqrt{5}}}{1+\cfrac{e^{-6\pi\sqrt{5}}}{1+\;\cdots}}}} = \left(\cfrac{\sqrt{5}}{1+\sqrt[5]{5^{3/4}\left(\frac{\sqrt{5}-1}{2}\right)^{5/2}-1}} - \frac{\sqrt{5}+1}{2}\right)e^{2\pi/\sqrt{5}}.$$

In order to get LaTeX to produce this you just have to tell it the logical structure of the formula and it will typeset it. Some formulas have to be hand-tweaked, but most do not. It is not surprising that LaTeX is good at typesetting mathematics as TeX— the program on which it is based—was commissioned by the American Mathematical Society for the very purpose of producing mathematical formulas by computer, and Donald Knuth—TeX's creator—has done a very good job indeed.

As well as typesetting mathematical formulas LaTeX—if told to do so—will also number them automatically and allow you to refer to them. So that, for example, if you write an article containing 20 numbered formulas and then realize that you need to add an extra numbered formula between formulas (3) and (4), then LaTeX

---

[1] A ligature is a symbol made up by joining two or three letters. The English ligatures are: ff, fi, fl, ffi and ffl. Note that ligatures vary from language to language and by default TeX only produces English ligatures. It is also possible to get TeX to produce the vowel-ligatures: æ, œ, Æ and Œ, but these are not produced automatically as they are only used in special circumstances. Kerning refers to the amount of space that is placed between letters in a single word. Compare, for example, 'TAVERN' with 'TAVERN': the second of these has not been kerned.

[2] This formula is displayed in Hofstadter (1979), p. 563, and the TeX commands that produced it are given on p. 103 below.

will automatically renumber all the formulas from (4) to (20) and will also alter all your cross-references automatically. Such an operation—if done manually—is highly error-prone. Similarly, if you are writing a book or paper with various numbered theorems, definitions, lemmas, propositions, and so on, then LaTeX will number them automatically for you (and you can tell it to do the numbering in a variety of ways). Furthermore, if you realize at some stage that you have inadvertently left out a numbered definition or lemma near the beginning of your book or paper, then when you insert it LaTeX will automatically renumber all the previous definitions and lemmas accordingly.

1.4   Producing Unusual Material

There are quite a few book which contain unusual, non-standard and—perhaps—one-off typesetting requirements. One example of the sort of thing that I am thinking of is emblematic or figured verse, a famous example of which is the mouse's tale from chapter III—entitled "A Caucus-race and a Long Tale"—of Lewis Carroll's *Alice in Wonderland*, as shown in Fig. 1.1.[3] Although the production of the mouse's tale involves quite a bit of input from the user, it makes use of standard LaTeX ideas and features and it is easy to understand conceptually what is going on as will become apparent when I explain how it was achieved on p. 25 below.

Another example of a one-off typesetting problem is found in the published version of Frege's letter to Husserl dated 24 May 1891—found in Frege (1980), p. 63—and reproduced in Fig. 1.2. This is again produced using standard ideas and techniques, though it is more difficult to achieve than more usual typesetting structures like quotations or enumerated lists. In this case Frege's schema was produced using some ideas of Knuth's on how to typeset commutative diagrams in mathematics and this is explained on p. 147 below.

Whereas the mouse's tale from *Alice in Wonderland* and Frege's schema present one-off typesetting problems, a book on contract bridge is likely to contain lots of diagrams similar to that shown in Fig. 1.3. This illustrates a further advantage of LaTeX over comparable packages in that it would be possible in LaTeX to define a (parameterized) command or macro for producing such diagrams. This would ensure consistency of presentation of bridge diagrams throughout a book (or even a series of books). What a user-defined LaTeX command is is explained in section 2.6 below and many illustrations of the use of such macros or commands are given throughout this book. In section 10.6 below I explain how the diagram that occurs in Fig. 1.3 was produced.

---

[3] In one of his marginal notes to Carroll (1970) Gardner writes on p. 51, 'The American logician and philosopher Charles Peirce was much interested in the visual analogue of poetic onomatopoeia. Among his unpublished papers there is a copy of Poe's *The Raven*, written with a technique that Peirce called "art chirography," the words formed so as to convey a visual impression of the poem's ideas.' I would have liked to include an example of Peirce's art chirography in this book, but I was unable to track down any examples.

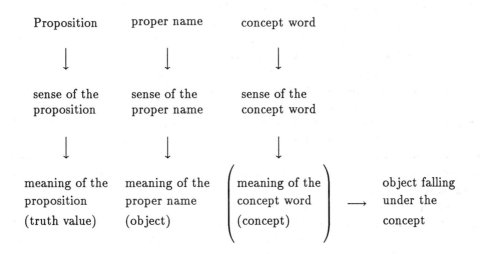

Figure 1.2: Frege's schema.

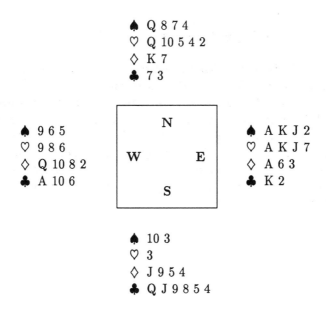

Figure 1.3: A contract bridge diagram.

1.5   Decreasing Drudgery

When the creative part of writing a book—and this is especially true of non-fiction books—is finished or is nearing completion, then a number of necessary or desirable but tedious tasks have to be done. For example, a table of contents needs to be prepared and if your book contains a significant number of tables or figures or both, then it is desirable to have a list of figures or a list of tables or both. LaTeX will generate these automatically for you (as explained in subsection 6.2.2 below). LaTeX automatically generates chapter and section numbers (but this can be suppressed if desired) and if you decide to alter the structure of your book by moving chapters or sections, then LaTeX will automatically renumber all the chapters and sections appropriately and produce an updated and correct table of contents. And if your book contains cross-references to chapters, sections or pages, then all this cross-referencing information will be automatically updated as well.

Similarly, LaTeX automatically numbers footnotes consecutively with Arabic numbers (but it is possible to alter this default handling of footnotes if so desired) and if, for example, when your book is nearing completion you decide to add or delete a few footnotes, then LaTeX will automatically renumber all the others. LaTeX also helps with the production of an index, but this is not fully automated in the standard system. However, the facilities available in standard LaTeX take much of the drudgery out of producing an index and additional packages are widely available that fully automate the process.

1.6   LaTeX and TeX are Fun to Use

While it cannot be denied that a fair amount of new ideas need to be acquired before LaTeX can be used well, the effort needed to master it will be amply rewarded because it is such a flexible, versatile and enjoyable system to use. This is even more true of TeX than LaTeX; in fact what many people do is to use LaTeX's facilities for the large-scale organization of a document—such as splitting it into chapters, sections and so on—and for its drudgery-decreasing and cross-referencing features, while using the less sophisticated commands of (plain) TeX for interesting typesetting problems such as the production of tree-proofs in a logical system or the production of Frege's schema shown in Fig. 1.2.

2

Getting Started and Basic Principles

2.1 Introduction

To begin this chapter I explain the overall process of document production using LaTeX. This is quite different from standard wordprocessing systems. LaTeX is definitely not a WYSIWYG system.[1] You start by creating a text or ASCII file using your favourite text editor. Apart from end-of-line characters (and an end-of-file character inserted by the operating system), this will only contain visible characters—and that includes the space character—drawn from the following:[2]

```
a b c d e f g h i j k l m n o p q r s t u v w x y z
A B C D E F G H I J K L M N O P Q R S T U V W X Y Z
0 1 2 3 4 5 6 7 8 9
!  "  #  $  %  &  '  (  )  *  +  ,  -  .  /  :
;  <  =  >  ?  @  [  \  ]  ^  _  '  {  |  }  ~
```

An example of the contents of such a LaTeX *input* file is given in Fig. 2.1. In most operating systems names of files consist of two parts, namely a *base name* and a *file extension*.[3] For example, the file that contains what is shown in Fig. 2.1 could be called `vamp.tex` with `vamp` being the base name and `tex` the file extension, the two parts of the name being separated by a full stop (or period). If you are reading this book near to a computer terminal, it would be a good idea to create a file called `vamp.tex` containing what is shown in Fig. 2.1.[4] The meaning of the various things that appear in that file will be explained in due course; all that I want to get across at present is the overall picture of how you use LaTeX to produce a document. Here, I will just say that

---

[1] WYSIWYG is an acronym for 'what you see is what you get', sometimes described as 'what you see is *all* you've got'.

[2] Throughout this book typewriter type is usually used to indicate LaTeX input, though—on a small number of occasions—it is used to indicate operating system commands or external file names.

[3] Sometimes the base name is called a *first name* and the file extension is known as a *suffix*.

[4] For more information about Vlad the Impaler see Florescu and McNally (1989) and Wilson (1984), pp. 400ff.

```
\documentstyle[11pt]{article}
\title{The Historical Dracula?}
\author{Antoni Diller}
\begin{document}
\maketitle
\noindent
There is growing evidence that Bram Stoker's Count Dracula
was based on the historical figure of Vlad III \c Tepe\c{s}
(1431--1476) of Wallachia, which is south-east of
Transylvania.  This prince is more commonly known as Vlad the
Impaler, because of a penchant for a particularly unpleasant
form of capital punishment whose precise details are perhaps
best left to the reader's imagination.  In present-day
Romania he is revered as a national hero.

Vlad's father was a member of the Order of the Dragon---one
of several semi-military and religious orders of knights then
in existence---and came to be called `Dracul'.  The word {\it
drac\/} in Romanian means {\it dragon\/} (but it can also
mean {\it devil\/}) and the ending {\it ul\/} is simply the
definite article.  Vlad the Impaler thus came to be called
`Dracula'.  The final letter {\it a\/} in {\it dracula\/} is
a diminutive and the whole thing just means {\it son of
dracul}.
\end{document}
```

Figure 2.1: The contents of the input file `vamp.tex`.

the way you indicate to TEX that you want to start a new paragraph is by leaving a blank line in your input file; furthermore, TEX treats any number of consecutive spaces as a single space and a single carriage return (or end-of-line character) is treated like an ordinary space. Thus, the way your input file is organized into lines bears little relation to the way in which the output is organized into lines.

Having created the file `vamp.tex` you then need to process it or run LATEX on it. The way you do this may vary from one operating system to another, but on many systems you would issue the operating system command `latex vamp` or `latex vamp.tex`; LATEX input files usually have the extension `tex` and some operating systems will assume this if you just type your input file's base name.[5] Various messages will

---

[5] Note that LATEX input files can have any extension, but if this is not `tex`, then it has to be explicitly included when you invoke LATEX.

The Historical Dracula?

Antoni Diller

February 14, 1992

There is growing evidence that Bram Stoker's Count Dracula was based on the historical figure of Vlad III Ţepeş (1431–1476) of Wallachia, which is south-east of Transylvania. This prince is more commonly known as Vlad the Impaler, because of a penchant for a particularly unpleasant form of capital punishment whose precise details are perhaps best left to the reader's imagination. In present-day Romania he is revered as a national hero.

Vlad's father was a member of the Order of the Dragon—one of several semi-military and religious orders of knights then in existence—and came to be called 'Dracul'. The word *drac* in Romanian means *dragon* (but it can also mean *devil*) and the ending *ul* is simply the definite article. Vlad the Impaler thus came to be called 'Dracula'. The final letter *a* in *dracula* is a diminutive and the whole thing just means *son of dracul.*

Figure 2.2: "The Historical Dracula?"

be written to your terminal and—assuming that LaTeX discovered no errors when processing your file—you will find that when LaTeX has completed its processing it has created three additional files, namely **vamp.aux**, **vamp.dvi** and **vamp.log**. The **aux** (or auxiliary) file contains various cross-referencing information and the **log** file contains everything that appeared on your terminal when you ran LaTeX and additional information as well. The **dvi** (or device independent) file is the most important one. In order to produce a document you need to run another program on the **dvi** file. For example, if the printer you are using understands PostScript, then you need to run a program which converts the **dvi** file into a PostScript file. Such a program is often called something like **dvi2ps**, **dvitops** or **dvips**. Once you have a PostScript file, this can then be sent to the printer which will produce the final output. Hopefully, this will look something like what is shown in Fig. 2.2. The date shown on your output will, however, be different.

2.2   LATEX Commands

2.2.1   Special Characters and Control Sequences

TEX treats the following ten characters as special characters:

$ % & \ ^ _ { } ~

(This is a complete list of such characters.) The character %, for example, signals that everything that follows it on the line on which it occurs is a comment. Everything that occurs between the character % and the next occurring end-of-line character (including that end-of-line character) is ignored by TEX and does not appear in the final document produced by LATEX. The two characters { and } are used for grouping purposes and they should always be matched. The character \ is the escape character.[6] The meaning of the other special characters will be explained in those contexts where it is most appropriate to do so. (If you want to include one of these special characters—except the backslash, caret and tilde symbols—in your output document, then you have to precede it with the escape character. Thus, to produce & you type \& and to produce $ you type \$. To produce the backslash, however, you need to type \backslash; but this is only available in math mode.)

Every LATEX command starts with the escape character and is followed by either one or more letters or by a single non-alphanumeric character. Such commands are known—in TEX—as *control sequences*. Control sequences consisting of the escape character followed by one or more letters are known as *control words* and control sequences consisting of the escape character followed by a single non-alphanumeric character are known as *control symbols*. For example, \noindent, \it and \c are control words and \/ is a control symbol. Note that TEX is case-sensitive and so \eg and \Eg, for example, are two different control words. Note that in a control word *only* letters can occur and not also numerals. Control words are terminated either by a space or by any character which is not a letter. If terminated by a space, then that space is ignored; TEX does not treat it as a real space. Furthermore, TEX treats a sequence of any number of spaces as a single space.

2.2.2   Environments

Certain patterns of commands in LATEX are called *environments*. For example, in Fig. 2.1 there occurs one instance of the document environment. Its general form looks like this:

\begin{document} *text* \end{document}

In describing the general structure of LATEX commands words and symbols that appear in typewriter-style type represent characters that can actually occur in an input file; whereas words that appear in italics indicate places in the input file where the user

---

[6] This has nothing to do with the escape *key* on a computer terminal.

decides what is to occur. The `document` environment is slightly unusual in that only *one* instance of it can occur in any input file; normally, several instances of the same environment can occur in an input file and they can also be nested within other environments. A typical example of an environment is the `quotation` environment which is used for including quotations in your documents. For example, the commands:

```
\begin{quotation}
\noindent
The plot of a typical narrative movie is a set of transformations
which operate on a series of disequilibriums with the net result
that some sort of narrative equilibrium emerges.  Heath writes:
%
\begin{quotation}
\noindent
A narrative action is a series of elements held in a relation of
transformation such that their consecution---the movement of the
transformation from the ones to the others---determines a state
$S'$ different to an initial state $S$ \ldots
\end{quotation}

One of Heath's presiding metaphors in describing the work of
movie narrative is ''getting things back into place.''
\end{quotation}
```

produce the following piece of indented text:[7]

The plot of a typical narrative movie is a set of transformations which operate on a series of disequilibriums with the net result that some sort of narrative equilibrium emerges. Heath writes:

> A narrative action is a series of elements held in a relation of transformation such that their consecution—the movement of the transformation from the ones to the others—determines a state S' different to an initial state S ...

One of Heath's presiding metaphors in describing the work of movie narrative is "getting things back into place."

The dollar signs that occur in the input that produced this quotation are used to signal to TeX that what they enclose is to be typeset as a mathematical formula

---

[7] The quotation is from Carroll (1988), p. 161, where he quotes Heath (1981), p. 136. When there is a danger of the LaTeX-generated output of some input commands being confused with my explanatory text, then horizontal rules are used to demarcate the illustrative output.

and the command \ldots produces the three full stops of an ellipsis. By default the first line inside the quotation environment is indented, but this indentation can be inhibited by the use of a \noindent command.

The general format of an environment is:

\begin{env} *text* \end{env}

where *env* is the name of the environment. Such names normally consist entirely of letters, though some environment names end in an asterisk *. Environment names cannot contain any characters other than letters and the asterisk.

2.2.3   Declaration

A *declaration* in LaTeX is a command which does not produce any output—there is no text or symbol in the document produced corresponding to a declaration in your input file—but it affects the appearance of the output in some way.[8] For example, in the input shown in Fig. 2.1 there are several occurrences of the \it declaration. This declaration tells LaTeX to process what follows it in such a way that it will appear in the output in *italic* type. The *scope* of the type-changing \it declaration is delimited by curly braces. In Fig. 2.1 note the presence of the *italic correction* control symbol \/ when italic type is followed by Roman type. This control symbol adds additional inter-word space. To see why this is needed compare '*dead* beat' with '*dead* beat'; the first was produced by the input {\it dead} beat in which no italic correction was present, whereas the second quoted expression was produced by the input {\it dead\/} beat in which italic correction was present.

2.3   General Structure of an Input File

Every LaTeX input file has the following general form:

\documentstyle[*opt-list*]{*doc-style*}
   dec-seq
\begin{document}
   text
\end{document}

For example, in the file vamp.tex the first command is:[9]

\documentstyle[11pt]{article}

---

[8] Computer scientists—and maybe others as well—are likely to be confused by this characterization of the category of declarations as it includes assignments; it is more common in computing to think of the category of declarations and that of commands—which includes assignments—as being disjoint.

[9] Only a very small number of commands can precede the \documentstyle command in the input file; among them are \batchmode, \errorstopmode, \nonstopmode and \scrollmode. These run mode commands are explained in the glossary in appendix C.

This means that the style of the document you are producing is that of an article. The standard alternatives are `report`, `book` and `letter`; but further possibilities may be available on your system. One and only one of these can take the place of *doc-style*.

In the first command in the file `vamp.tex` the `11pt` option has been chosen. This relates to the size of the type that will appear in the final document. The letters `pt` here are short for 'point', which is a unit of length. One inch is equal to 72.27 points. A large number of units are used in TEX and LATEX, but the important ones are point (`pt`), inch (`in`) and millimetre (`mm`).[10] (TEX regards one inch as being exactly equivalent to 25.4 millimetres.) Some other possible options are `12pt`, `draft`, `fleqn`, `leqno`, `openbib`, `titlepage`, `twocolumn` and `twoside`. If no options are chosen, then you also leave out the square brackets, like this:

    \documentstyle{article}

Usually in LATEX mandatory arguments to commands are enclosed in curly braces, whereas optional arguments are enclosed in square brackets; the major exceptions to this occur in some commands relating to the `picture` environment.

You can have two or more options and if you do this, then the options you choose should be separated by commas; but be careful not to include any spaces inside the square brackets as this will cause strange things to happen. In other words, *opt-list* is a sequence of one or more options separated by commas and not containing any spaces. If you make a copy of the file `vamp.tex` and call the copy `vamp2.tex` and then change the first command in that file to the following:

    \documentstyle[11pt,twocolumn]{article}

and also include the command `\newpage` before the blank line and just after the concluding words of the first paragraph and then process it as explained in section 2.1 above, then the result will look something like what is shown in Fig. 2.3.

That part of a LATEX input file that occurs between the `\documentstyle` command and the opening of the `document` environment is known as the *preamble*.[11] I have represented it as *dec-seq* because it consists of a—possibly empty—sequence of declarations that affect the final appearance of the output document. In the case of the file `vamp.tex` it contains the two declarations:

    \title{The Historical Dracula?}
    \author{Antoni Diller}

These, by themselves, do not produce any output; the first of them declares The Historical Dracula? to be the title of the article and the second declares Antoni Diller to be the author of the article. The actual title of the article—and also the name of the author and the date—are produced by the `\maketitle` command that occurs within the `document` environment.

---

[10] All of the length units recognized by TEX are discussed in section B.1 and the important notion of a *length parameter* is explained there as well.

[11] Rather confusingly, Lamport (1986) includes the `\documentstyle` command in the preamble on p. 21, but excludes it on p. 35; I have consistently *excluded* it from forming part of the preamble.

The Historical Dracula?

Antoni Diller

February 14, 1992

There is growing evidence that Bram Stoker's Count Dracula was based on the historical figure of Vlad III Ţepeş (1431–1476) of Wallachia, which is south-east of Transylvania. This prince is more commonly known as Vlad the Impaler, because of a penchant for a particularly unpleasant form of capital punishment whose precise details are perhaps best left to the reader's imagination. In present-day Romania he is revered as a national hero.

Vlad's father was a member of the Order of the Dragon—one of several semi-military and religious orders of knights then in existence—and came to be called 'Dracul'. The word *drac* in Romanian means *dragon* (but it can also mean *devil*) and the ending *ul* is simply the definite article. Vlad the Impaler thus came to be called 'Dracula'. The final letter *a* in *dracula* is a diminutive and the whole thing just means *son of dracul.*

Figure 2.3: "The Historical Dracula?" in two columns.

2.4   Modes

When processing an input file LaTeX is in one of three modes, namely paragraph mode, math mode or LR mode (left-to-right mode). If you ever use the `picture` environment, then picture mode is used, but this is just a restricted form of LR mode.

2.4.1   Paragraph Mode

LaTeX is in *paragraph mode* when it is processing ordinary prose. TeX contains very sophisticated algorithms for formatting paragraphs and for deciding where to break lines and hyphenate words. One consequence of this is that there is a maximum limit on the size of the paragraphs that your document can contain. It is about 1,900 words. It is possible to fool TeX and get around this problem. If you insist in having paragraphs of over 1,900 words, then insert `{\parfillskip=0pt\par\parskip=0pt\noindent}` in random places every 50 lines or so of text. There is no need to understand these commands in order to use them, but when you do understand them you will be well on the way to becoming a real TeXpert. (The explanation is in Knuth (1986), p. 315, where it is the solution to exercise 14.15.)

To indicate to LaTeX that you want to start a new paragraph just leave a single empty line, that is to say, two consecutive carriage returns; alternatively, the control word or command `\par` forces what follows it to begin a new paragraph. By default, paragraphs are indicated in output produced by TeX by being indented slightly from the left margin. The amount of indentation is stored in the *length parameter* `\parindent` and can be changed—to half an inch, say—by the assignment `\parindent=0.5in` which can occur anywhere in your input file, but is best placed in the preamble.[12] To prevent TeX from indenting the first line of a paragraph use the command `\noindent`. The amount of vertical space that TeX inserts between paragraphs—in addition to the normal amout of vertical space that it puts between lines—is "stored" in the length parameter `\parskip`.

2.4.2 Math Mode

The great advantage of both TeX and LaTeX over comparable programs is in typesetting mathematics. To produce a mathematical formula or expression as part of a paragraph you are writing enclose it in dollar signs. So, `$x - y > 3$` results in $x - y > 3$. There are two alternative ways of producing this in LaTeX, namely `\(x - y > 3\)` and `\begin{math}x - y > 3\end{math}`, but it is difficult to think of a sensible reason to ever use these since they are more complicated that the straightforward dollar signs.

Between the single dollar signs TeX is in *math mode* (and it processes any formulas there in text style). Spacing inside math mode is done differently from how it is done in paragraph mode—see section 8.2 for more information—and the inclusion of spaces in math mode does not affect what TeX does; the only place where they have to occur is after a control word that is followed by a letter, that is to say, to indicate the ending of a control word.

To cause a mathematical formula to be displayed enclose it between double dollar signs. So, the sequence of symbols `$$x - y > 3$$` results in:

$$x - y > 3.$$

There are two alternative ways of producing this in LaTeX, namely `\[x - y > 3\]` and `\begin{displaymath}x - y > 3\end{displaymath}`. A slight difference between the use of double dollar signs to produce displayed equations and the other two methods is that if you choose the `fleqn` option to the `\documentstyle` command, displayed formulas produced by either the `displaymath` environment or the pair of commands `\[` and `\]` will not be centred on the page—they will be indented from the left margin by the distance contained in the `\mathindent` length parameter—whereas displayed formulas produced by using double dollar signs will continue to be centred. So, if you intend to use the `fleqn` option to the `\documentstyle` command, then use the commands `\[` and `\]` to produce displayed formulas. Within the `displaymath` environ-

---

[12] This assignment is, therefore, in the language of LaTeX a *declaration*; note that the equals sign is optional. See subsection B.1.2 for more information about length parameters.

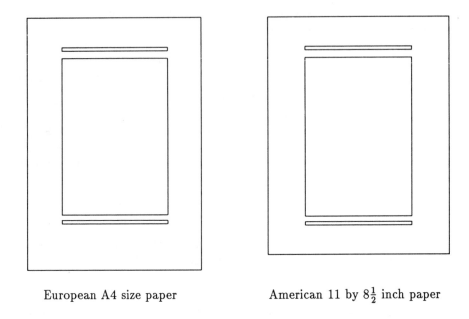

European A4 size paper   American 11 by $8\frac{1}{2}$ inch paper

Figure 2.4: The location of the head, the body and the foot.

ment, between the commands \[and \] and between double dollar signs TEX is in *math mode* (and it processes the formulas that occur there in display style).

In math mode LATEX ignores spaces altogether and typesets the formula as mathematics. When writing mathematics do not forget to include the correct punctuation; one of the most annoying things about many books—especially those written by some computer scientists—is their incorrect punctuation of mathematical formulas. There are a large number of mathematical symbols available in LATEX; see appendix A for more information. In chapters 7, 8 and 9 I explain how to do more sophisticated mathematical typesetting using TEX and LATEX.

2.4.3   LR Mode

LR mode is basically a way of keeping a piece of text together on one line. Some people, for example, do not want names of computer programs hyphenated. In order to ensure that they are not enclose them like this \mbox{ProgramName}. This is also useful to ensure that mathematical formulas or expressions are not broken across lines. For example, writing \mbox{$x - y > 3$} will ensure that the formula $x - y > 3$ will appear on a single line. Inside the argument to the \mbox command LATEX is in LR mode. The \mbox—make box—command produces a *box*, which in TEXese is a block of material that is treated as a unit and which will not under any circumstances be broken up into its constituents.

2.5   Altering the Size of the Output Page

When producing a page of output LaTeX can put text in three distinct regions on the page, namely the head, the body and the foot. If running heads are being produced, then they and the current page number go into the head region; but if running heads are not being produced, then the page number is placed in the centre of the foot region. Note that footnotes—if present—go into the *body* region of the output page. Assuming the `article` document style and either the `10pt` or the `11pt` option, the locations of these three regions on a sheet of 11 by $8\frac{1}{2}$ inch paper and a sheet of A4 size paper are shown in Fig. 2.4.[13] In these diagrams the outer rectangle—in both cases—is the physical piece of paper and the three inner rectangles, from the top down, are the head, the body and the foot. Note that the body of the text area is not centred on A4 size paper. This is because TeX and LaTeX assume that you going to print your output on standard American size paper rather than on A4 size paper, which is a European standard. There are commands to position the body of the text differently on the physical page and also to alter its size. The distance, for example, from the top edge of the physical piece of paper to the top of the head region is one inch plus the value of the LaTeX length parameter `\topmargin`. This can be altered by means of an assignment of the form `\topmargin=0.25in`. Note that altering the value of `\topmargin` has the result of shifting the head, body and foot regions either up or down, since they are regarded as a unit. The distance from the left edge of the physical piece of paper to the left-hand edge of the body region is one inch plus the value of the rigid length parameter `\oddsidemargin`.[14] You can also alter the size of the body of the text by changing the values of the LaTeX length parameters `\textheight` and `\textwidth`. The following assignments achieve this:

```
\textheight=8.5in
\textwidth=6in
```

These assignments do not alter the left-hand margin or the top margin. Note that the lengths used in these assignments are for illustrative purposes only and are not meant to be meaningful. (There are several other length parameters that affect the appearance of the output page and all of them—and their effect—are shown in Fig. C.4 on p. 258.)

2.6   Defining your own Commands

According to Spivak (1986), p. 120, one reason to define your own commands—also known in TeXese as *macros*—is to save yourself some typing. This is not as useful as

---

[13] A sheet of A4 paper is 297 by 210 millimetres. The `article` document style is a *one-sided* style. In one-sided document styles all pages are (conceptually) right-handed and odd-numbered ones. This means that the head, body and foot of both odd- and even-numbered pages are positioned in the same place on the physical piece of paper relative to the left and top edges of the paper.

[14] When two-sided printing is in effect the length parameter `\oddsidemargin` affects the width of the left-hand margin on odd-numbered pages and the length parameter `\evensidemargin` affects the width of the left-hand margin on even-numbered pages; when one-sided printing is in effect only `\oddsidemargin` has any effect.

it may at first sight appear, but I do use the following definitions:

```
\def\eg{for example}
\def\Eg{For example}
\def\ie{that is to say}
\def\Ie{That is to say}
```

With these in force putting, for example, \ie in your input file produces 'that is to say' in the output document.

Note that these definitions use the primitive TeX command \def; the LaTeX command for defining macros is \newcommand and—using this—the definitions given above would look like this:

```
\newcommand{\eg}{for example}
\newcommand{\Eg}{For example}
\newcommand{\ie}{that is to say}
\newcommand{\Ie}{That is to say}
```

One of the main differences between \def and \newcommand is that \newcommand checks to see if the command you are trying to define already exists; if it does, then your attempted definition is rejected. The command \def, by contrast, will happily redefine an existing command.[15] Some people—such as Snow (1992), pp. 56–57—regard this as an advantage of the LaTeX \newcommand declaration because there is no possibility of accidentally redefining an important TeX or LaTeX command. Snow points out that accidentally redefining some primitive TeX command may cause dramatic changes in the output produced because that command may be used in the definition of many additional commands. I prefer, however, the TeX definition mechanism because it is more flexible. To avoid the danger of accidentally redefining an existing command I *use* any command that I intend to define *before* I actually include its definition in my input file; then I run LaTeX on my input file and if I get an error message saying that the command is not defined, I know that it is not currently being used by either TeX or LaTeX. I can then include its definition knowing for certain that there is no danger of an important TeX or LaTeX command being redefined accidentally.

It is possible to have local definitions in your input file—their scope being delimited by the use of curly braces—as the following example illustrates:

```
\def\wendy{James}
{\def\wendy{Wendy} Tom loves \wendy\ and}
Mary loves \wendy.
```

These definitions produce the following text:

Tom loves Wendy and Mary loves James.

---

[15] The LaTeX mechanism for redefining already existing commands is \renewcommand.

And it also possible to have parameterized commands as the following example illustrates:

```
\def\loves#1#2{#1 loves #2}
\loves{Jack}{Jill} and \loves{Jill}{Jack}.
```

This produces the following text:

Jack loves Jill and Jill loves Jack.

Be careful not to leave any space between the name of the command that you are defining and the argument list, nor between the elements of the list, nor between the last member of this list and the curly brace that is followed by the definition.[16] The curly braces following the argument list are part of the syntax of the \def command and do not delimit the scope of any declarations that might occur in the definition. Thus, if you declare \def\B{\bf B}—where \bf is a declaration that makes the output appear in boldface type—then when you use the command \B everything that follows this use of the command will be in bold; by contrast, the declaration \def\B{{\bf B}} will ensure that when the command \B is used only the letter B it produces will be in bold. A similar point applies to the LaTeX macro-defining mechanism.

Definitions introduced by either \def, \newcommand or \renewcommand can occur anywhere in your input file, but if you are going to be using LaTeX a lot, it would be a good idea to set up your own style file. This can have any first or base name, but its extension must be sty. For illustrative purposes I shall assume that your style file is called own.sty. In this you should put—at least—all your non-local definitions and then to ensure that these definitions are loaded when you use LaTeX you should include the first or base name of your style file amongst the list of options *opt-list* to the \documentstyle command, like this:

```
\documentstyle[11pt,own]{article}
```

Whereas any commands that you define in your input file must have names consisting entirely of letters, names of commands defined in a style file can also include the commercial at-sign @; thus, \@lqq and \@rqq are acceptable as names of commands defined in a style file. Such commands cannot, however, be used outside of a style file; though, such a command defined in one style file can be used in another.

As already mentioned, a local definition is one whose scope is delimited by curly braces; a *global* declaration, by contrast, is one whose scope is not so delimited. If you want to include a global definition within curly braces, then you have to precede the \def command with a \global command as illustrated in this example input:

```
{\global\def\toyah{Toyah}
Robert Fripp} married \toyah\ Willcox.
```

---

[16] The reason for this is that the \def command is much more subtle and complicated than here explained—see, for example, chapter 11 of Eijkhout (1992) for a very good discussion of macros in TeX—but if you use it as I have explained, you will not experience any problems with it. A fuller account of the \def command is to be found in the glossary to this book in appendix C.

which produces the text:

Robert Fripp married Toyah Willcox.

Whereas, an attempt to process the input:

```
{\def\toyah{Toyah}
Robert Fripp} married \toyah\ Willcox.
```

will result in an error message informing you that the command \toyah is undefined. One disadvantage of the LaTeX \newcommand and \renewcommand definition mechanisms is that they always produce *non-global* definitions.

2.7   Coping with Errors

When people first start to use LaTeX one of the commonest mistakes is to incorrectly input the name of some command. To show you what happens when you do this, change the command \maketitle in the file vamp.tex to \maketitel and then process it using LaTeX; the processing of your file will be aborted and something like the following will appear on your terminal:

```
This is TeX, C Version 3.14t3
(vamp.tex
LaTeX Version 2.09 <7 Dec 1989>
(/bham/tex/inputs/article.sty
Document Style 'article' <16 Mar 88>.
(/bham/tex/inputs/art11.sty)) (vamp.aux)
! Undefined control sequence.
l.5 \maketitel

?
```

(You will not see exactly this because some of the information it contains is peculiar to the system on which I use LaTeX, in particular the path names of the files article.sty and art11.sty.) If you now type a lowercase letter e in response to the prompt, you should find yourself in a text editor with the cursor positioned at the start of the line in which the misspelt command name occurs. You can also type h in response to the prompt and then LaTeX or TeX will usually give you additional information about what went wrong. Sometimes you may experience difficulties in exiting LaTeX; in this case inputting I\stop in response to the prompt should get you out. There are quite a few TeX and LaTeX error messages that you might get, but most of them are self-explanatory and so will not be explained here. If you want to know what they are consult chapter 6 of Lamport (1986).

Something else that happens a lot when processing LaTeX files is to get an Overfull \hbox warning message. To illustrate this, add the declaration \textwidth=4.5in to the preamble of the file `vamp.tex`—after changing `\maketitel` back to `\maketitle`—and then run LaTeX on it. You will see something like the following:

```
This is TeX, C Version 3.14t3
(vamp.tex
LaTeX Version 2.09 <7 Dec 1989>
(/bham/tex/inputs/article.sty
Document Style 'article' <16 Mar 88>.
(/bham/tex/inputs/art11.sty)) (vamp.aux)
Overfull \hbox (6.54004pt too wide) in paragraph at lines 16--24
\elvrm sev-eral semi-military and re-li-gious or-ders of knights
then in existence---
[1] (vamp.aux) )
(see the transcript file for additional information)
Output written on vamp.dvi (1 page, 1624 bytes).
Transcript written on vamp.log.
```

This warning message means that some text sticks out into the right-hand margin of the page. The best way to resolve this problem is to rewrite the sentence that caused the problem. Alternatively, you could tell TeX explicitly where it can insert a hyphen. Part of the above message is:

```
\elvrm sev-eral semi-military and re-li-gious or-ders of knights
then in existence---
```

The command `\elvrm` here just indicates that TeX is producing 11 point Roman type output; what follows this is the actual line whose end juts out into the right-hand margin. The single hyphens in this are the places where TeX can hyphenate a word. The control sequence `\-` is known as the *discretionary hyphen* and it allows TeX to hyphenate a word where it occurs; the hyphen only appears if the word is broken across lines. You could try to remedy the problem under discussion by changing `existence` in `vamp.tex` into `exis\-tence` and seeing what happens when you process your input using LaTeX. The commands `\hyphenate`, `\sloppy` and `\linebreak` can also be used to try and resolve this problem; they are all explained in the glossary in appendix C.

3

Fancy Prose (and Poetry)

3.1 Accents

In the file `vamp.tex` shown in Fig. 2.1 on p. 8 there occurs the input `\c Tepe\c{s}` which produces as output the text 'Ţepeş'. This illustrates one of TEX's commands for making accents. All of these are shown in the following table:

result	command	name
á	`\'a`	acute
b̆	`\u b`	breve
ĉ	`\^c`	circumflex
d̈	`\"d`	dieresis (umlaut)
ė	`\.e`	dot
f̀	`\`f`	grave
ğ	`\v g`	háček
h̋	`\H h`	long Hungarian umlaut
ī	`\=\i`	macron
j̃	`\~\j`	tilde
ḳ	`\b k`	bar-under
ļ	`\c l`	cedilla
ṃ	`\d m`	dot-under
ño	`\t no`	tie-after accent

All of these commands—except `\t`—produce an accent either over or under the next single following character; hence, there is no need to enclose that character in curly braces, but there is no harm in doing this. Note that the commands `\i` and `\j` produce a dotless i and j, respectively, which are used when an accent is placed over either of them.

3.2   Type-changing Declarations

There are seven declarations in LaTeX that alter the kind of type being used and these are illustrated in the following table:

result	command	name
Once upon a time ...	{\bf Once upon a time ...}	bold
Once upon a time ...	{\it Once upon a time ...}	italic
Once upon a time ...	{\rm Once upon a time ...}	Roman
Once upon a time ...	{\sc Once upon a time ...}	small capitals
Once upon a time ...	{\sf Once upon a time ...}	sans serif
Once upon a time ...	{\sl Once upon a time ...}	slanted
Once upon a time ...	{\tt Once upon a time ...}	typewriter

There is a further type-changing declaration that behaves differently from those shown and that is \em. The effect of this depends on the context in which it occurs:

output	input
I *hate* **you.**	{\bf I {\em hate\/} you.}
I hate *you.*	{\it I\/ {\em hate} you.}
I *hate* you.	{\rm I {\em hate\/} you.}
I *hate* you.	{\sc I {\em hate\/} you.}
I *hate* you.	{\sf I {\em hate\/} you.}
I hate *you.*	{\sl I\/ {\em hate} you.}
I *hate* you.	{\tt I {\em hate\/} you.}

Note that italic correction should always be included when italic or slanted type is followed by type that is neither italic nor slanted; if you are not sure what \em will do, then put in the italic correction as it has no effect unless italic or slanted type is followed by type that is neither.

3.3   Declarations that Change the Size of Type

There are ten declarations in LaTeX for altering the size of type being used and these are shown in order—with the smallest coming first—in the table that follows; note that the local command \temp is defined here like this: \def\temp{Once upon a time \ldots}, where \ldots produces an ellipsis consisting of three full stops.

output	input
Once upon a time ...	`\tiny\temp`
Once upon a time ...	`\scriptsize\temp`
Once upon a time ...	`\footnotesize\temp`
Once upon a time ...	`\small\temp`
Once upon a time ...	`\normalsize\temp`
Once upon a time ...	`\large\temp`
Once upon a time ...	`\Large\temp`
Once upon a time ...	`\LARGE\temp`
Once upon a time ...	`\huge\temp`
Once upon a time ...	`\Huge\temp`

As well as changing the size of type being used these commands also select the Roman style of type. Thus, if you want LARGE boldface type, you need to input `{\LARGE\bf ...}`. Note that LaTeX does not have every style of type in every size.[1] Furthermore, because the fonts that LaTeX uses take up a lot of its memory, not all the available fonts are always loaded. For example, if you have chosen the `11pt` option to the `\documentstyle` command, then the LARGE sans serif font is only loaded on demand; so, if you make use of the LARGE sans serif font in your input file, when you process it using LaTeX you will get a warning message like this:

```
LaTeX Warning: No \sf typeface in this size, using \rm.
```

This can be remedied by including a `\load{`*size*`}{`*style*`}` command in your input file. This command loads a font whose size is given by *size* and whose style is given by *style*, where *size* is one of `\tiny`, `\scriptsize`, `\footnotesize`, `\small`, `\normalsize`, `\large`, `\Large`, `\LARGE`, `\huge` or `\Huge`; and *style* is one of `\bf`, `\it`, `\sc`, `\sf`, `\sl` or `\tt`.

The following commands are part of what I used to produce the mouse's tale displayed in Fig.1.1 on p. 2:[2]

```
{\parskip=-1.5pt

{\large
\setlength{\parindent}{1in}
\addtolength{\parindent}{1em}\par        Fury said to
\addtolength{\parindent}{4em}\par        a mouse, That
\addtolength{\parindent}{.5em}\par       he met
\addtolength{\parindent}{0.5em}\par      in the
                                         house,\par}
```

---

[1] Buerger (1990), pp. 39 and 41, has tables showing which styles of type are standardly available in which sizes.
[2] LaTeX has a `verse` environment for typesetting normal poetry.

```
{\normalsize                                    'Let us
\setlength{\parindent}{1.9in}                   both go
\addtolength{\parindent}{-1.5em}\par            to law:
\addtolength{\parindent}{-.5em}\par             {\it I\/} will
\addtolength{\parindent}{-1em}\par              prosecute
\addtolength{\parindent}{-1em}\par              {\it you\/}.---\par}}
\addtolength{\parindent}{-.5em}\par
```

There are probably other and better ways of doing this in TEX and LATEX, but in this method each line is in a paragraph all by itself. The length parameter \parskip is the addditional vertical space that TEX puts between paragraphs; additional, that is to say, to \baselineskip which is the normal distance between baselines.[3] The length parameter \parindent is the amount of indentation that marks the first line of every paragraph. The command \setlength{*cmd*}{*len*} assigns the length *len* to *cmd*—which must begin with an initial backslash—and is an alternative way of representing the assignment *cmd=len*. The command \addtolength{*cmd*}{*len*} adds *len* to the current value of *cmd* and puts the result in *cmd*. In both \setlength and \addtolength *len* can be any valid TEX length or it can be another length parameter (or user-defined length command) which can be multiplied by some floating-point number, thus: \addtolength{\parindent}{-1.5\parindent} is a valid use of the \addlength command.

3.4   Punctuation Marks

Dashes

Four distinct types of dashes are used by typesetters, namely the em-dash, the en-dash, the hyphen and the minus sign.[4] The minus sign only occurs in math mode and so will be discussed later on in this book. Here I will look at the three other kinds of dashes, namely the em-dash (—), the en-dash (–) and the hyphen (-).

The Em-dash   To produce the em-rule you need three consecutive minus signs in LR or paragraph mode. Em dashes are often used in pairs to indicate that the text that occurs between them is to be read parenthetically.

The En-dash   To produce the en-rule you need two consecutive minus signs in LR or paragraph mode. It is used in number ranges, like 'pp. 33–35' or 'the 1939–1945 holocaust', between place names that are linked in some way, for example, 'the

---

[3] The *baseline* in TEX is the imaginary line on which letters "sit"; some letters—like 'g' and 'y'—have parts that descend below the baseline on which they "sit".

[4] The em- and en-dashes are sometimes known as the em- and en-*rules*. 'Em' and 'en', as well as being very useful words to know in Scrabble, are also the names of units of length used in typesetting. See section B.1 for more information about units of length and length parameters in LATEX.

Rome–Berlin axis' and between names of joint authors to avoid confusion with double-barrelled names, for example, 'the Church–Rosser theorem'. It is also used instead of a hyphen in a compound adjective at least one of whose components consists of a hyphenated word or of two words. For example, 'the New York–Amsterdam flight' and 'a quasi-public–quasi-judicial body'.

Hyphen The dash that occurs in hyphenated words, like 'semi-standard', is produced by typing a single minus sign in LR or paragraph mode.

Quotation Marks

To enclose a word or phrase in single quotation marks enclose it with an apostrophe and quotation mark. So, 'death' is produced by typing `'death'`. To enclose a word or phrase in double quotation marks enclose it in two apostrophes and two quotation marks. So, "death" is produced by typing `''death''`. Books and articles published in Britain use—on the whole—single quotation marks for direct speech and for mentioning words and phrases, whereas American books usually use double quotation marks. The following table illustrates this:[5]

	output	input
American	"I heard 'Go away' being shouted," she said.	`''I heard 'Go away' being shouted,'' she said.`
British	'I heard "Go away" being shouted,' she said.	`'I heard ''Go away'' being shouted,' she said.`

If the nested quotation marks occur next to each other, then a thin amount of space—produced by the command `\,`—should be inserted between them:

	output	input
American	John said, "James said, 'Janet said, "Yes." ' "	`John said, ''James said, 'Janet said, ''Yes.''\,'\,''`
British	John said, 'James said, "Janet said, 'Yes.' " '	`John said, 'James said, ''Janet said, 'Yes.'\,''\,'`

The thin space introduced here is also useful in other contexts. A Biblical reference like 'Isaiah 30 : 22' is produced by the input `Isaiah~30\,:\,22` and a musical reference like 'Op. 59' is produced by the input `Op.\,59`.[6] Note that the tilde ~ just produces an

---

[5] See Quirk, Greenbaum, Leech and Svartvik (1985), pp. 1630–1631, for more information.
[6] See Knuth (1986), pp. 311 and 409.

inter-word space, but TEX will never break a line at the place in your input file where it occurs.

A further difference between American and British English emerges when quotation marks are used to indicate the title of books, articles, films, plays and so on, and these interact with punctuation marks.

	output	input
American	Coppola has directed the films "Apocalypse Now," "The Conversation," "The Godfather," "One from the Heart" and others.	`Coppola has directed the films ''Apocalypse Now,'' ''The Conversation,'' ''The Godfather,'' ''One from the Heart'' and others.`
British	Coppola has directed the films 'Apocalypse Now', 'The Conversation', 'The Godfather', 'One from the Heart' and others.	`Coppola has directed the films 'Apocalypse Now', 'The Conversation', 'The Godfather', 'One from the Heart' and others.`

Spacing

TEX by default puts more space after a full stop, question mark and exclamation mark than it normally puts between words, except when any of these follow a capital letter. This creates two problems, namely when one of these punctuation marks is preceded by a capital letter when it ends a sentence and when one of these punctuation marks does not end a sentence when it is not preceded by a capital letter, and these problems are resolved as follows:

output	input
Warner Bros. is a film production company.	`Warner Bros.\ is a film production company.`
He was from the UK. In fact, he was from Scotland.	`He was from the UK\@.  In fact, he was from Scotland.`

The control sequence \␣ inserts normal inter-word space where it occurs. Note that more space is placed after a full stop, question mark and exclamation mark even if these are followed by quotation marks or parentheses; the above remedies work in these cases as well.

4

Displaying Information

4.1 Itemized Lists

An itemized list in LaTeX looks like this:

- Computer science is the mathematical study of algorithms.

- A programming language is a notation for expressing algorithms.

- The way in which programming languages are studied is based on the way in which logical systems are studied.

This was produced by means of the commands:

```
\begin{itemize}
\item
Computer science is the mathematical study of algorithms.
\item
A programming language is a notation for expressing algorithms.
\item
The way in which programming languages are studied is based
on the way in which logical systems are studied.
\end{itemize}
```

Only four levels of nesting are permitted and by default the labels are the symbols: • ($\bullet$), − ({\bf --}), * ($\ast$) and · ($\cdot$). These symbols are "stored" in the four commands \labelitemi, \labelitemii, \labelitemiii and \labelitemiv, respectively. So, if you want to use ♠, for example, instead of • as a label at the top level you have to redefine the \labelitemi command by means of either of the following two equivalent declarations:

```
\def\labelitemi{$\spadesuit$}
\renewcommand{\labelitemi}{$spadesuit$}
```

These can appear anywhere in your input file. (In the file that produced the chapter you are now reading the first of these was used and it appeared just before the next itemized list.)

♠ Computer science is the mathematical study of algorithms.

♠ A programming language is a notation for expressing algorithms.

♠ The way in which programming languages are studied is based on the way in which logical systems are studied.

It is also possible to have different labels at the same level of nesting by giving an additional argument to the \item commands within the itemize environment. Consider, for example, the following list:

♡ Computer science is the mathematical study of algorithms.

◇ A programming language is a notation for expressing algorithms.

♣ The way in which programming languages are studied is based on the way in which logical systems are studied.

This was produced by means of these commands:

```
\begin{itemize}
\item[$\heartsuit$]
Computer science is the mathematical study of algorithms.
\item[$\diamondsuit$]
A programming language is a notation for expressing algorithms.
\item[$\clubsuit$]
The way in which programming languages are studied is based
on the way in which logical systems are studied.
\end{itemize}
```

4.2 Enumerated Lists

Enumerated lists in LaTeX look like this:

---

1. Prove the following sequents from the propositional calculus:

    (a) $Q \Rightarrow R \vdash (P \lor Q) \Rightarrow (P \lor R)$.

    (b) $\vdash ((P \Rightarrow Q) \Rightarrow P) \Rightarrow P$.

2. Prove the following predicate calculus sequents:

    (a) $(\forall x)(Px \Rightarrow Qx) \vdash (\forall x)Px \Rightarrow (\forall x)Qx$.

    (b) $(\exists x)(\forall y)Pxy \vdash (\forall y)(\exists x)Pxy$.

This list was produced by the following commands:

```
\begin{enumerate}
\item
Prove the following sequents from the propositional calculus:
%
\begin{enumerate}
\item
$Q \Rightarrow R \vdash (P \lor Q) \Rightarrow (P \lor R)$.
\item
\label{PEIRCE}
$\vdash ((P \Rightarrow Q) \Rightarrow P) \Rightarrow P$.
\end{enumerate}
%
\item
Prove the following predicate calculus sequents:
%
\begin{enumerate}
\item
$(\forall x) (Px \Rightarrow Qx)
\vdash (\forall x) Px \Rightarrow (\forall x) Qx$.
\item
$(\exists x)(\forall y) Pxy \vdash (\forall y)(\exists x) Pxy$.
\end{enumerate}
%
\end{enumerate}
```

Only four levels of nesting are allowed. The outermost items are labelled 1., 2., and so on; items in the next level of nesting are labelled as (a), (b), and so on; in the next level they are i., ii., and so on; and in the fourth level the labels appear as A., B., and so on. The labels are generated automatically and the four counters enumi, enumii, enumiii and enumiv are used for this purpose.[1] It is possible to use a \label command inside an enumerate environment—as the above example illustrates—and the command \ref{PEIRCE} yields '1b'. (The formula $((P \Rightarrow Q) \Rightarrow P) \Rightarrow P$ is known as Peirce's law.) If you want to refer to the page on which this occurrence of Peirce's law appears, then you need to use the command \pageref{PEIRCE}. Thus, the input p.~\pageref{PEIRCE} yields 'p. 31'; note the use of the tilde which prevents a line break happening at the point where it occurs.

It is also possible to give optional arguments to the \item commands that occur inside an enumerate environment. So, for example, the commands:

```
\begin{enumerate}
\item[(1)]
$Q \Rightarrow R \vdash (P \lor Q) \Rightarrow (P \lor R)$.
\item[(2)]
$\vdash ((P \Rightarrow Q) \Rightarrow P) \Rightarrow P$.
\end{enumerate}
```

produce the following enumerated list:

---

(1) $Q \Rightarrow R \vdash (P \lor Q) \Rightarrow (P \lor R)$.

(2) $\vdash ((P \Rightarrow Q) \Rightarrow P) \Rightarrow P$.

If an optional argument is given to the \item command, then this also has the effect that the relevant counter is not incremented.

4.3   The description Environment

The description environment is usually used to produce glossaries. For example, these commands:

```
\begin{description}
\item[lamplighter]
A provider of such support services
as surveillance and minding.
\item[finger man]
```

---

[1] A *counter* in LaTeX is an integer-valued variable; for more information about counters see section B.3.

An agent whose job it is to kill specified people.
\item[wrangler]
An operative whose job it is to break codes.
\end{description}

produce the following mini-glossary of some of John le Carré's jargon:

---

lamplighter A provider of such support services as surveillance and minding.

finger man An agent whose job it is to kill specified people.

wrangler An operative whose job it is to break codes.

Note that although the words being defined are given as optional arguments to the
\item commands here if they are omitted, then the result produced by LaTeX will look
very odd. By default the optional argument to the \item command appears in bold
type in the output, but this can be altered by including a type-changing declaration
inside the square brackets, thus:

    \begin{description}
    \item[\tt chapter]
    Counter used by \LaTeX\ to number chapters.
    \item[${[x]}X$]
    Used to represent bracket abstraction in combinatory logic.
    \item[\it leg theory]
    Type of bowling in which the leg stump is
    attacked by a fast bowler.
    \end{description}

These commands produce the following result:

`chapter` Counter used by LaTeX to number chapters.

$[x]X$ Used to represent bracket abstraction in combinatory logic.

leg theory Type of bowling in which the leg stump is attacked by a fast bowler.

Note the presence of curly braces in \item[${[x]}X$]; these are needed to prevent
LaTeX getting confused between the square brackets that enclose the optional argument
and the square brackets that are to appear in the output. If you want to get something
like \par in your output you need to include either {\tt \char92par} or \verb+\par+
in your input file; both the commands \verb and \char are explained in the glossary.

4.4   The flushleft, center and flushright Environments

The following output:

Time-travel is impossible and yet science fiction writers from H.G. Wells onwards
have been fascinated by the idea the fecundity of which has once again been shown
by the recent success of the *Back to the Future* and the *Terminator* series of films.
One narrative paradigm that has had several incarnations involves the time-traveller
being an art historian who is interested in discovering more about a famous
artist—in some versions a painter and in others a sculptor—who ...

---

was produced by means of this input:

```
\begin{flushright}
Time-travel is impossible and yet science fiction writers
from H.G.~Wells onwards have been fascinated by the idea the
fecundity of which has once again been shown by the recent
success of the {\it Back to the Future\/} and the
{\it Terminator\/} series of films.
One narrative paradigm that has had several incarnations
involves the time-traveller being an art historian who is
interested in discovering more about a famous artist---in some
versions a painter and in others a sculptor---who \ldots
\end{flushright}
```

If the environment is changed from **flushright** to **center**, then the output will look
like this:

Time-travel is impossible and yet science fiction writers from H.G. Wells onwards
have been fascinated by the idea the fecundity of which has once again been shown
by the recent success of the *Back to the Future* and the *Terminator* series of films.
One narrative paradigm that has had several incarnations involves the time-traveller
being an art historian who is interested in discovering more about a famous
artist—in some versions a painter and in others a sculptor—who ...

And if the environment is changed from **flushright** to **flushleft**, then the output
will look like this:

Time-travel is impossible and yet science fiction writers from H.G. Wells onwards
have been fascinated by the idea the fecundity of which has once again been shown
by the recent success of the *Back to the Future* and the *Terminator* series of films.
One narrative paradigm that has had several incarnations involves the time-traveller
being an art historian who is interested in discovering more about a famous
artist—in some versions a painter and in others a sculptor—who ...

In each of these environments it is possible to use an end-of-line command \\ in order
to force the termination of a line; do not confuse the end-of-line command \\ with the
end-of-line or carriage return character that ends lines in your input file and which
TeX treats as an ordinary space.

It is possible to use the \raggedright declaration instead of the flushleft environment, the \centering declaration instead of the center environment and the
\raggedleft declaration instead of the flushright environment. One difference,
however, is that when an environment is used a vertical amount of space separates its
output from the preceding text whose value is given either by the sum of the length parameters \topsep and \parskip—if neither a blank line nor a \par command precedes
the environment—or by the sum of the three length parameters \topsep, \parskip
and \partopsep—if either a blank line or a \par command does precede the use of
the environment.[2]

4.5   Boxes

A *box* is something that TeX treats as a unit and it will not, therefore, be broken
across lines or pages. The \framebox command produces a box with a frame—made
up out of horizontal and vertical rules—drawn around it. Its general format is:[3]

   \framebox[*len*][*pos*]{*text*}

The effect of the optional arguments *len* and *pos* are shown in Fig. 4.1. The value of
the length parameter \fboxrule gives the width of the rules that make up the frame
and the value of the length parameter \fboxsep is the amount of space that separates
the frame from the result of processing *text* (which is processed in LR mode).

The \makebox command is similar to the \framebox one except that no frame is
drawn around the result of processing *text*; its general format is:

   \makebox[*len*][*pos*]{*text*}

---

[2] This amount of space is inserted before all the list-like environments, that is to say, the environments center,
description, enumerate, flushleft, flushright, itemize, quotation, quote, thebibliography, verse and
all environments created by means of the \newtheorem declaration.

[3] Note that the \framebox, \makebox and \savebox commands described in this section behave differently inside
the picture environment, where they even take different arguments.

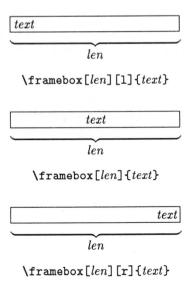

$\backslash$framebox[*len*][l]{*text*}

$\backslash$framebox[*len*]{*text*}

$\backslash$framebox[*len*][r]{*text*}

Figure 4.1: The effect of the *pos* argument in the $\backslash$framebox command.

where the arguments *len*, *pos* and *text* have exactly the same meaning as in the $\backslash$framebox command.

The $\backslash$savebox command is similar to the $\backslash$makebox command except that no output is produced; the box produced is rather placed into a *storage bin* and the $\backslash$usebox command can then be used to actually output the stored box. This is particularly useful for things that you want to include several times in a document and which take a lot of processing; using the commands $\backslash$savebox and $\backslash$usebox ensures that the processing only takes place once. The general format of these two commands is:

$\backslash$savebox{*cmd*}[*len*][*pos*]{*text*}
$\backslash$usebox{*cmd*}

In the $\backslash$savebox command the arguments *len*, *pos* and *text* have exactly the same meaning as for the $\backslash$makebox command and the argument *cmd*—in both commands— is the name of a storage bin which must start with an initial backslash and which must previously have been introduced by means of a $\backslash$newsavebox{*cmd*} command.[4]

There are variants of the $\backslash$framebox, $\backslash$makebox and $\backslash$savebox commands that take fewer arguments and they are shown in this table:

---

[4] An example of the use of the $\backslash$newsavebox, $\backslash$savebox and $\backslash$usebox commands is given in section 10.8.

$\backslash$framebox[*len*][*pos*]{*text*} $\backslash$fbox{*text*}

$\backslash$makebox[*len*][*pos*]{*text*} $\backslash$mbox{*text*}

$\backslash$savebox{*cmd*}[*len*][*pos*]{*text*} $\backslash$sbox{*cmd*}{*text*}

4.6 Footnotes

Footnotes are produced by means of the \footnote{*text*} command; this places *text* at the bottom of the page with a number as the footnote mark and the same footnote mark is placed in the body of the page as a superscript. Footnotes are numbered automatically by LaTeX with the first one being numbered 1; the counter footnote is used for this purpose. This is initialized to zero at the start of each chapter in the report and book document styles and at the beginning of the document in the article document style. Note that the counter is incremented before the footnote mark is produced. (Inside the minipage environment alphabetical footnote marks are produced starting with *a* and the counter used is mpfootnote.)

There are certain contexts in which the \footnote command will not work, namely those that produce a box. (The only exception to this is the minipage environment.) There you should use \footnotemark inside the box-making command to produce the footnote mark in the text as a superscript and just outside the box-making command you should use a \footnotetext{*text*} command to place *text* as a footnote at the bottom of the page; note that the \footnotemark command increments the footnote counter.[5]

4.7 The minipage Environment and \parbox

Whereas the \framebox, \makebox and \savebox commands process their *text* arguments in LR mode, the minipage environment and the \parbox command process their *text* arguments in paragraph mode. The boxes they produce are, thus, known as *parboxes*. The following commands:

```
\begin{center}
\begin{minipage}{4in}
Time-travel is impossible and yet science fiction writers
from H.G.~Wells onwards have been fascinated by the idea the
fecundity of which has once again been shown by the recent
success of the {\it Back to the Future\/} and the
{\it Terminator\/} series of films.\footnote{For more
information about time-travel see Lem's ``The Time-travel
Story'' and Gardner's ``Time Travel''.}
```

---

[5] These commands can all take an additional optional argument whose effect is explained in the glossary.

```
One narrative paradigm that has had several incarnations
involves the time-traveller being an art historian who is
interested in discovering more about a famous artist---in some
versions a painter and in others a sculptor---who \ldots
\end{minipage}
\end{center}
```

produce the following output:

Time-travel is impossible and yet science fiction writers from
H.G. Wells onwards have been fascinated by the idea the
fecundity of which has once again been shown by the recent
success of the *Back to the Future* and the *Terminator* series
of films.[a]

One narrative paradigm that has had several incarnations
involves the time-traveller being an art historian who is interested in discovering more about a famous artist—in some
versions a painter and in others a sculptor—who ...

[a] For more information about time-travel see Lem's "The Time-travel Story"
and Gardner's "Time Travel".

Note that paragraphs are not indented inside the `minipage` environment, but slightly
more vertical space than is normally placed between lines is inserted between paragraphs.

The `\parbox` command has a similar effect to the `minipage` environment and the
general formats of both reveal these similarities:

```
\begin{minipage}[pos]{len} text \end{minipage}
\parbox[pos]{len}{text}
```

The *len* argument specifies the width of the parbox produced and the optional *pos*
argument specifies its alignment: a t option aligns the baseline of the first line with
the baseline of the current line, a b option aligns the baseline of the last line with the
baseline of the current line, and the default is to centre the parbox vertically.

4.8   The tabular **Environment**

4.8.1   Basic Principles

LaTeX's tabular environment is used to produce the following sort of table:[6]

Category	Intuitive meaning	Typical element
Nml	numerals	N
UnOps	unary operators	α
BinOps	binary operators	ω
Ide	identifiers	I
Exp	expressions	E
Cmd	commands	C

In fact, this table was produced by the following commands:

```
\begin{center}
\begin{tabular}{|c|c|c|} \hline
Category        & Intuitive meaning & Typical
                                      element   \\ \hline\hline
${\it Nml}$     & numerals          & $N$      \\ \hline
${\it UnOps}$   & unary operators   & $\alpha$ \\ \hline
${\it BinOps}$  & binary operators  & $\omega$ \\ \hline
${\it Ide}$     & identifiers       & $I$      \\ \hline
${\it Exp}$     & expressions       & $E$      \\ \hline
${\it Cmd}$     & commands          & $C$      \\ \hline
\end{tabular}
\end{center}
```

The enclosing center environment is just used to centre the resulting table on the page; if it was absent, then the table would be set flush left on the page.[7] The tabular environment can occur in any mode and its general form is:

\begin{tabular}[*pos*]{*preamble*} *row-list* \end{tabular}

The optional *pos* parameter controls the vertical positioning of the box produced. By default alignment is on the centre of the box, but a t option aligns on the top row and a b option aligns on the bottom row. The *preamble* specifies how the columns of the table are going to be formatted. In the example just given the *preamble* is

---

[6] The tabular environment is very similar to the array environment, but that can only occur in math mode; in fact, any valid array preamble is also a valid tabular preamble, so everything that I say about array preambles in section 7.6 is also applicable here.

[7] Note that if the first item in the *preamble* is neither | nor an @-expression, then the table is not set flush left on the page; horizontal blank space equal to the value of the length parameter \tabcolsep is inserted before the box produced. The same amount of space is inserted after the box produced if the *preamble* does not end with | or an @-expression. If this space causes any problems use @{} at the start or end of the *preamble* to remove it.

inference rules	
proper	improper
∧-introduction	
∧-elimination	
∨-introduction	∨-elimination
⇒-elimination	⇒-introduction
¬-elimination	¬-introduction
¬¬-elimination	
#-elimination	
∀-elimination	∀-introduction
∃-introduction	∃-elimination

Table 4.1: Proper and improper natural deduction inference rules.

|c|c|c|. The three occurrences of the letter c indicate that this table will consist of three columns and that the material in each column will be centred in that column. (The c comes from 'centre' and not 'column'.) Instead of a c you can use l for left-aligning items or r for right-aligning them. A line | in the *preamble* causes a vertical line to be produced which separates columns; usually this extends from the top to the bottom of the resulting box. You can have two or more lines next to one another in the *preamble*, like ||. This causes two vertical lines to be produced which separate adjacent columns. The distance between the two vertical lines is given by the rigid length parameter \doublerulesep. The width of the lines produced is given by the rigid length parameter \arrayrulewidth. To change either of these you need to include assignments of the form \doublerulesep=5mm or \arrayrulewidth=2pt in your input file; the scope of these assignments can be controlled by using curly braces. The *preamble* |c|c|c| has exactly the same effect as the *preamble* |*{3}{c|}. The element *{i}{*pre*} is equivalent to i copies of *pre* where i is any positive whole number and *pre* is any valid preamble. In fact, *pre* here can itself contain *-expressions.

Following the opening of the environment in the example above there is a \hline command. This causes a horizontal line to be produced across the entire width of the resulting box.

The *row-list* element in a tabular environment consists of one or more *row* components which are separated by \\ commands. Each *row* will usually contain $i - 1$ ampersands where i is the number of columns that the table contains. (Note that if a row contains some \multicolumn commands, then fewer ampersands may be required.)

Following a \\ command you can include one or more \hline commands. If two \hline commands occur next to one another, then the vertical space separating them is given by the rigid length parameter \doublerulesep. Note that vertical lines produced by | expressions in the *preamble* do not appear in the space between the horizontal lines produced by two adjacent \hline commands. If you want a line to appear at the bottom of your table, then the final \hline command must be preceded by a \\ command; but the \\ command should be left out if not followed by a \hline command.

4.8.2 The \multicolumn Command

The table shown in Table 4.1 was produced by the following commands:[8]

```
\begin{center}
\begin{tabular}{|c|c|} \hline
\multicolumn{2}{|c|}{inference rules}            \\ \hline\hline
proper                    & improper           \\ \hline\hline
$\land$-introduction      &                    \\
$\land$-elimination       &                    \\
$\lor$-introduction       & $\lor$-elimination \\
$\implies$-elimination & $\implies$-introduction \\
$\neg$-elimination        & $\neg$-introduction \\
$\neg\neg$-elimination &                       \\
$\absurd$-elimination     &                    \\
$\forall$-elimination     & $\forall$-introduction \\
$\exists$-introduction & $\exists$-elimination   \\ \hline
\end{tabular}
\end{center}
```

The tabular environment here again occurs within a center environment. One new feature of the tabular environment is introduced here and that is the \multicolumn command whose general form is \multicolumn{i}{pre}{$text$} where i is a positive whole number, *pre* is similar to the preamble of the tabular environment except that fewer expressions are allowed and *text* is what is to appear. A \multicolumn command must either begin a *row* or immediately follow an ampersand. In the example given there occurs \multicolumn{2}{|c|}{inference rules}. This means that the *text* inference rules is to span two columns of the table produced and |c| means that it will be centred with vertical lines occurring at the start of the first column and at the end of the second column. The presence of a \multicolumn command suppresses any vertical lines or positioning expressions which occur in the tabular environment's *preamble*.

The \multicolumn command can also be used in the array environment and examples of its use in that context can be found in Fig. 9.1 on p. 142. All the examples of the use of the \multicolumn command given in this chapter inside the tabular environment can be used within the array environment.

---

[8] The information contained in this table relates to the classification of inference rules given by Prawitz (1965), pp. 16–21.

	Atypical vampire story	*Invasion of the Body Snatchers* (1956, Siegel)
onset	A mysterious stranger arrives in a small town and both the mortality rate and the number of anaema cases goes up.	The doctor in a small community notices that some of its members are behaving strangely.
discovery	The heroine begins to suspect that there is a vampire about, but no one believes her—not even her fiancé.	He stumbles across a pod and realises that people are being replaced by aliens, but he never manages to get absolute proof.
confirmation	The heroine's fiancé becomes anaemic and the local doctor and priest see the characteristic puncture marks of the nosferatu on his throat and believe.	A truck carrying pods out of the community provides the required proof.
confrontation	The priest, the heroine, her fiancé and his doctor seek out the vampire's coffin, drive a stake through her heart and cut off her head.	Absent.

Table 4.2: The confrontation plot structure.

```
{ % open scope for temporary local definitions

\def\temphead{Atypical vampire story}
\def\tempon{A mysterious stranger arrives in a small town and
both the mortality rate and the number of anaema cases goes up.}
\def\tempdisc{The heroine begins to suspect that there is a
vampire about, but no one believes her---not even her fianc\'e.}
\def\tempfirm{The heroine's fianc\'e becomes anaemic and the local
doctor and priest see the characteristic puncture marks of the
nosferatu on his throat and believe.}
\def\tempfront{The priest, the heroine, her fianc\'e and his
doctor seek out the vampire's coffin,
drive a stake through her heart and cut off her head.}

\def\TempHead{{\it Invasion of the Body Snatchers} (1956, Siegel)}
\def\TempOn{The doctor in a small community notices that some of
its members are behaving strangely.}
\def\TempDisc{He stumbles across a pod and realises that people
are being replaced by aliens,
but he never manages to get absolute proof.}
\def\TempFirm{A truck carrying pods out of the community
provides the required proof.}
\def\TempFront{Absent.}

\tabcolsep=4mm
\def\arraystretch{2.5}

\begin{tabular}{lp{4.4cm}p{4.4cm}}
                    & \temphead  & \TempHead \\
\bf onset           & \tempon    & \TempOn \\
\bf discovery       & \tempdisc  & \TempDisc \\
\bf confirmation    & \tempfirm  & \TempFirm \\
\bf confrontation   & \tempfront & \TempFront
\end{tabular}
} % close scope of temporary definitions
```

Figure 4.2: Commands used for producing Table 4.2.

4.8.3   Using the \shortstack Command

To produce the table shown in Table 4.3 you need these commands:

```
\begin{center}
\def\temp#1{\multicolumn{1}{|r|}{#1}}
\begin{tabular}{r|c|c|c|c|} \cline{2-5}
 & \shortstack{D\\a\\v\\i\\s}
 & \shortstack{H\\e\\n\\d\\r\\y}
 & \shortstack{\rule{0mm}{1mm}\\P\\a\\r\\r\\o\\t\\t}
 & \shortstack{W\\h\\i\\t\\e} \\ \hline
\temp{Steve Davis}     & $\times$ & 23 & 19 &  0 \\ \hline
\temp{Stephen Hendry}  & 34 & $\times$ &  0 &  4 \\ \hline
\temp{John Parrott}    & 22 &  0 & $\times$ & 18 \\ \hline
\temp{Jimmy White}     &  0 & 10 & 11 & $\times$ \\ \hline
\end{tabular}
\end{center}
```

Several new ideas are introduced here. The first is the command \cline{2-5} which is similar to \hline, except that the horizontal rule that is produced only extends between columns 2 to 5 inclusive; the \cline command can occur anywhere that the \hline command can occur. It is possible to use the \cline command to draw a horizontal rule spanning just a single column, but you still need two column numbers and a hyphen; thus, the command \cline{*i-i*} draws a line spanning the *i*th column.

The \shortstack command is a bit like a single column tabular environment and is used—as its name suggests—for stacking letters or other material. There is less inter-row space, however, than if a tabular environment had been used. The \rule command is usually used to produce rectangular blobs of ink, but here it is used to produce an invisible strut whose purpose is to ensure that the topmost horizontal rule is not too close vertically to the letter 'P' of 'Parrott'.

Note that the scope of the command \temp is delimited by the center environment, that is to say, it is a local command to that environment. This is, in fact, true in general; definitions that occur inside environments are local to those environments.

4.8.4   Including Parboxes

To produce the spatial arrangement of text displayed in Table 4.2 on p. 42 you need to include the commands shown in Fig. 4.2 on p. 43.[9] The rigid length parameter \tabcolsep is half the amount of horizontal space left between the columns produced by a tabular (or tabular*) environment. The command \arraystretch has a value which is a floating-point number. It controls the amount of vertical space that occurs between the rows produced in a tabular (or tabular* or array) environment by multiplying the default width. Its default value is 1 and changing it to 1.25, say, by

---

[9] For more information about the structure of horror narratives see chapter 3 of Carroll (1990).

	Davis	Hendry	Parrott	White
Steve Davis	×	23	19	0
Stephen Hendry	34	×	0	4
John Parrott	22	0	×	18
Jimmy White	0	10	11	×

Table 4.3: Results—in frames—between the top four snooker players in ranking tournaments during the 1990–1991 season.

the \renewcommand or \def declaration makes the rows produced one and a quarter times further apart.

The *preamble* of the tabular environment in Fig. 4.2 is lp{4.4cm}p{4.4cm}. This means that the resulting table will have three columns; the material in the first column will be placed flush with the left-hand edge of the column. The text in the next two columns will be treated similarly to each other; what occurs in an entry in the tabular environment will be typeset in a parbox of width 4.4 centimetres; in effect, each such entry will be typeset as if it were the argument *text* of a \parbox[t]{4.4cm}{*text*} command.

4.9 Floats

A *float* in LaTeX is a box the relative position of whose input is not usually mirrored in the relative position of its output. Two environments produce floats and those are the figure and the table ones. (There are also *-versions of these two environments, namely figure* and table*, but they behave exactly like the figure and table environments, respectively, except when the twocolumn option to the \documentstyle command has been chosen.) The general format of the figure and table environments is as follows:

    \begin{figure}[*pos*] *text* \end{figure}
    \begin{table}[*pos*] *text* \end{table}

The only difference between these appears when you include a \caption command inside them: in the case of the figure environment the word 'Figure' is produced by LaTeX and in the case of the table environment the word 'Table' is automatically generated by LaTeX. The *text* argument is processed in paragraph mode and a parbox of width \textwidth is produced. The optional parameter *pos* is a sequence of between one and four different letters chosen from b, h, p and t. It affects the position where the float may appear as follows:

b The float may appear at the bottom of a text page.

h The float may be placed in the output in the same relative position to its neighbours as it occurs in the input.

p The float may appear on a floats-only page.

t The float may appear at the top of a text page.

The default value of *pos* is tbp.

To see how the table environment works look at Table 4.4 which was produced by the following commands:

```
\begin{table}
\begin{center}
\begin{tabular}{cp{2in}p{2in}}
& \multicolumn{1}{c}{\it ponens}
& \multicolumn{1}{c}{\it tollens} \\
\it ponendo &
If Jack snores, then Maxine hallucinates;
but Jack does snore;
{\it therefore}, Maxine hallucinates.
&
It is not the case that both
Jack snores and Maxine hallucinates;
but Jack does snore;
{\it therefore}, Maxine does not hallucinate. \\
\it tollendo &
Either Jack snores or Maxine hallucinates;
but Maxine does not hallucinate;
{\it therefore}, Jack snores.
&
If Jack snores, then Maxine hallucinates;
but Maxine does not hallucinate;
{\it therefore}, Jack does not snore.
\end{tabular}
\end{center}
\caption{The family {\it modus}.}
\label{MODUS}
\end{table}
```

The \caption command is used to produce a caption to the table or figure produced. Its general format is \caption[*entry*]{*heading*} and it produces a numbered

	ponens	*tollens*
ponendo	If Jack snores, then Maxine hallucinates; but Jack does snore; *therefore*, Maxine hallucinates.	It is not the case that both Jack snores and Maxine hallucinates; but Jack does snore; *therefore*, Maxine does not hallucinate.
tollendo	Either Jack snores or Maxine hallucinates; but Maxine does not hallucinate; *therefore*, Jack snores.	If Jack snores, then Maxine hallucinates; but Maxine does not hallucinate; *therefore*, Jack does not snore.

Table 4.4: The family *modus*.

caption. (If you want to refer to a captioned figure or table, then you need to include a \label command either somewhere in *heading* or else following the \caption command but within the body of the environment.) If a list of figures or a list of tables is produced by means of either the \listoffigures or the \listoftables command, then *heading* is the text that will appear in the list of figures or the list of tables produced; except if the argument *entry* is present in which case *entry* is the text that will appear in any list of figures or tables produced by a \listoffigures or a \listoftables command.

There are a number of parameters that affect the placement of floats. First, I will look at the counters that affect the placement of floats:

bottomnumber is the maximum number of floats that can occur at the bottom of each page which contains both text and floats.

totalnumber is the maximum number of floats that can occur on a page.

topnumber is the maximum number of floats that can occur at the top of each page which contains both text and floats.

Next, I look at some parameters whose values are floating-point numbers between 0 and 1 that affect the placement of floats:

\topfraction is the fraction of each page that can be occupied by floats at its top (if it also contains text).

\bottomfraction is the fraction of the page that can be occupied by floats at its bottom (if it also contains text).

\textfraction is the minimum fraction of a page, containing both text and floats, that has to be occupied by text.

\floatpageraction is the minimum fraction of a floats-only page that can be taken up by floats.

Finally, I look at some length parameters that affect the appearance of floats:[10]

\floatsep is the amount of vertical space left between floats that appear on the same text page.

\intextsep is the amount of vertical space placed above and below a float that occurs in the middle of a text page because the h location option has been chosen.

\textfloatsep is the amount of vertical space left between a float and the text either below or above it, if the float appears at either the top or the bottom of a page that contains both text and floats.

4.10   Including Encapsulated PostScript Files

On many systems there exists a non-standard option to the \documentstyle command which allows you to include encapsulated PostScript files in your LaTeX-generated document; the option is called epsf and the macros in the corresponding style file were written by Tomas Rokicki and revised by Donald Knuth. To use this option you first need to create an encapsulated PostScript file using some such utility program as xfig; for illustrative purposes I shall assume that this PostScript file is called frege.ps. Including the following commands in your input file:

```
\begin{figure}
\begin{center}
\leavevmode
\hbox{%
\epsfxsize=4.5in
\epsffile{frege.ps}}
\end{center}
\caption{Fragment of Frege's conceptual system.}
\label{FREGE}
\end{figure}
```

produces the diagram shown in Fig. 4.3.[11] The command \epsffile{*file*} (or equivalently \epsfbox{*file*}) actually includes the encapsulated PostScript file in your dvi file; the rigid length parameters \epsfxsize and \epsfysize can be used to scale the diagram that you want to include—use only one of them at most—and the \leavevmode and \hbox commands are necessary in order to successfully centre the diagram on the page.

---

[10] Note that these are all *rubber* length parameters; for more information about what these are see subsection B.1.2.

[11] This way of presenting conceptual schemes is adapted from Thagard (1992), for example, Fig. 3.6 on p. 47; for a book called *Conceptual Revolutions* it is surprising that—in my opinion—it is so riddled with conceptual confusions.

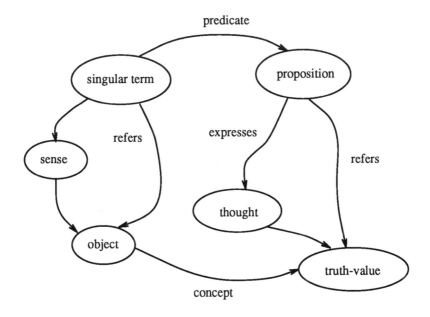

Figure 4.3: Fragment of Frege's conceptual system.

4.11 The `list` Environment

> LaTeX's `list` environment is a flexible mechanism for displaying information sequentially with the option of labelling each individual piece of information in a variety of ways.
>
> Diller (1997), p. 382.

The fictional quotation that opens this section was produced by the following commands:

```
\begin{list}{}{\leftmargin=7em \rightmargin=0em}\item[]
\LaTeX's {\tt list} environment is a flexible mechanism for
displaying information sequentially with the option of
labelling each individual piece of information in a
variety of ways.
\begin{flushright}
Diller (1997), p.~382.
\end{flushright}
\end{list}
```

The `list` environment used here is a multi-purpose and flexible list-making mechanism; several of LaTeX's list-like environments are defined by means of it, namely `center`, `description`, `enumerate`, `flushleft`, `flushright`, `itemize`, `quotation`, `quote`, `thebibliography` and `verse`. Its general format is:

> `\begin{list}{`*text₁*`}{`*dec-list*`}` *text₂* `\end{list}`

where *text₁* is what will be generated by an `\item` command which does not have an optional argument, *dec-list* is a sequence of assignments to some of the length parameters that appear in Fig. C.3—any length parameter that is not given a value in this way is initialized by an assignment in one of the `@listi`, ..., `@listv` or `@listvi` (the choice depends on the level of nesting) which is carried out before *dec-list*—and *text₂* is the information to be displayed; one or more `\item` commands can occur in *text₂*.

Often you want to use the same list-like structure several times in the same document. For example, you may want to have several quotations like the one that begins this section. In that case it would be a good idea to make the structure into an environment by using the `\newenvironment` command. The following achieves this; it is called **popper** after Popper because I first saw this kind of quotation in Popper (1973) and Popper (1974):

```
\newenvironment{popper}
{\begin{list}{}{\leftmargin=7em \rightmargin=0em}\item[]}
{\end{list}}
```

You use this environment with `\begin{popper}` and `\end{popper}` commands as for the built-in environments. The following commands, therefore, would also produce the quotation that opened this section:

```
\begin{popper}
\LaTeX's {\tt list} environment is a flexible mechanism for
displaying information sequentially with the option of
labelling each individual piece of information
in a variety of ways.
\begin{flushright}
Diller (1997), p.~382.
\end{flushright}
\end{popper}
```

The general form of the `\newenvironment` command is explained in the glossary as is the `\renewenvironment` command used for redefining existing environments.

In Fig. 5.1 on p. 56 I simulate the output produced by the `thebibliography` environment. This was achieved by the following commands:

```
\newcounter{eee}
\newlength{\ee}
\settowidth{\ee}{[1]}
\begin{list}%
```

```
{[\arabic{eee}]}%
{\usecounter{eee}%
\setlength{\labelwidth}{\ee}%
\setlength{\leftmargin}{\ee}%
\addtolength{\leftmargin}{\labelsep}}
\item
Michael Hallett,
''Towards a Theory of Mathematical Research Programmes (I)'',
{\it British Journal for the Philosophy of Science},
vol.~30 (1979), pp.~1--25.
\item
Imre Lakatos,
{\it Proofs and Refutations:
The Logic of Mathematical Discovery},
[Cambridge, Cambridge University Press, 1976].
\end{list}
```

If you want the list produced to be numbered automatically in some way by LaTeX, then you need to define a counter and employ the \usecounter command. The \settowidth{*cmd*}{*text*} command assigns to the length command *cmd* the natural width of the result of processing *text* in LR mode and the \setlength{*cmd*}{*len*} command assigns to the length command *cmd* the value *len*. The function of an \addtolength{*cmd*}{*len*} command is to assign to the length command *cmd* the result of adding *len* to its current value.

The simulation of the output produced by the thebibliography environment shown in Fig. 5.2 on p. 57 was produced by the following commands:

```
\settowidth{\ee}{[Lakatos 76]}
\begin{list}%
{\setlength{\labelwidth}{\ee}%
\setlength{\leftmargin}{\ee}%
\addtolength{\leftmargin}{\labelsep}}
\item[{[\rm Hallett 79]}\hfill]
Michael Hallett,
''Towards a Theory of Mathematical Research Programmes (I)'',
{\it British Journal for the Philosophy of Science},
vol.~30 (1979), pp.~1--25.
\item[{[\rm Lakatos 76]}]
Imre Lakatos,
{\it Proofs and Refutations:
The Logic of Mathematical Discovery},
[Cambridge, Cambridge University Press, 1976].
\end{list}
```

The command \hfill inserts horizontal space where it occurs that expands to fill all the available space; its effect here is to push the "label" '[Hallett 79]' to the left, making it flush with the left-hand edge of the enclosing box.

4.12   The tabbing Environment

The tabbing environment is used to present information in which certain items are aligned vertically. The basic idea is conveyed by the following simple example:

```
                       \begin{tabbing}
    one                123\=456\=789\=\kill
                       \>       one \\
    two                \>       two \\
        three          \>\>     three \\
        four           \>\>     four \\
            five       \>\>\> five \\
            six        \>\>\> six \\
        seven          \>\>     seven \\
        eight          \>\>     eight \\
    nine               \>       nine \\
    ten                \>       ten \\
                       \end{tabbing}
```

The first line inside the tabbing environment here sets the tab positions—rather like tab positions on a typewriter—and the \kill command just tells LaTeX not to produce any output corresponding to this line. The commands \= actually set the tab positions. Note that outside the tabbing environment \= produces a macron accent over the next following single character; if you need a macron accent inside the tabbing environment use \a=. Note also that in the Computer Modern fonts designed by Knuth all the digits are half an em wide. The command \> actually moves the following text to be aligned on the next tab stop.[12]

Inside the tabbing environment LaTeX maintains two variables, namely *next-tab-stop* and *left-margin-tab*, whose values are non-negative whole numbers. The tab positions are, in effect, imaginary vertical lines along which text is aligned; each such line is numbered starting with 0 and usually they are numbered consecutively as you move to the right. In the above example three tabs are set and they are numbered 0, 1 and 2. Initially, the value of *left-margin-tab* is set to 0 and it is positioned at the current left margin and initially the value of *next-tab-stop* is set to 1. The command \> aligns text on line *i*—if *i* is the value of *next-tab-stop*—and it increments *next-tab-stop* by 1. (Note that the end-of-line command \\ resets *next-tab-stop* to 1 + *left-margin-tab* as well as terminating the current line; it has no effect on *left-margin-tab*.)

The above output can also be produced in the following two ways:

---

[12] Note that in plain TeX \> can only be used in math mode where it produces a medium amount of space; for that in LaTeX use \: but only in math mode.

```
\begin{tabbing}                    \begin{tabbing}
123\=456\=789\=\kill               123\=456\=789\=\kill
\+ \\                              \+ \\
     one \\                        one \\
     two \\                        two \+ \\
\>   three \\                      three \\
\>   four \\                       four \+ \\
\>\> five \\                       five \\
\>\> six \\                        six \- \\
\>   seven \\                      seven  \\
\>   eight \\                      eight \- \\
     nine \\                       nine \\
     ten                          ten
\end{tabbing}                      \end{tabbing}
```

The command \+ increments the value of *left-margin-tab* by 1 and \- decreases its value by 1. Note that outside the tabbing environment \- is the discretionary hyphen.

Some further features of the tabbing environment are illustrated by the following example:

```
                                   \begin{minipage}{1.75in}
                                   \begin{tabbing}
                                   123\=456\=789\=\kill
                                   \+ \\
   one                             one \\
   two                             two \+ \\
       three                       three \\
       four                        four \+ \\
   five                            five \' \\
           six                     six \- \\
                    seven          \' seven  \\
       eight                       eight \- \\
   nine                            nine \\
   ten                             ten
                                   \end{tabbing}
                                   \end{minipage}
```

The command \' is a bit like \hfill except that it pushes text leftwards towards the imaginary alignment line numbered by the value of *left-margin-tab* leaving a distance between the line and the text which is given by the rigid length parameter \tabbingsep, and \` is also a bit like \hfill pushing text rightwards. Note that outside the tabbing environment \' produces an acute accent and \` produces a grave accent; to get these inside the tabbing environment use \a' and \a`, respectively. The minipage environment is included here to show the effect of the \' command.

Some further commands available inside the `tabbing` environment are illustrated in section 9.1 below.

4.13   The `verbatim` Environment

When all else fails you can use the `verbatim` environment to output text exactly as it appears in your input file. For example, the input:

```
\begin{quote}
\begin{verbatim}
Jardine was one of the most controversial English cricket
captains that there has ever been.  Australians, especially,
usually regard him as the embodiment of the antithesis of
sportsmanship; but is this reputation deserved?
\end{verbatim}
\end{quote}
```

produces the following output, in typewriter style:

```
Jardine was one of the most controversial English cricket
captains that there has ever been.  Australians, especially,
usually regard him as the embodiment of the antithesis of
sportsmanship; but is this reputation deserved?
```

Note that in the ending of the environment `\end{verbatim}` no spaces can occur between `\end` and `{verbatim}`. A `verbatim` environment cannot occur in the argument to any other command, but it can occur inside another environment. There is also a `\verb` command for outputting short input exactly as it appears; see the glossary for more information.

5

Bibliographies and Indexes

5.1 Introduction

In this chapter I look at the commands and environments that are available in LaTeX
for producing bibliographies, indexes and glossaries. There are several ways of making
a bibliography in LaTeX and I explain two of them here:[1] the first of these makes use
of the thebibliography environment and the second employs an additional system
known as BibTeX. My recommendation would be for you to use BibTeX if it is available
on your computer or network; in the long run it saves a lot of time, effort and space.
The bulk of the chapter is taken up with explaining various features of BibTeX. And
briefly—at the end of the chapter—I say how LaTeX can format an index and I say
something about the various "glossary" commands that are available in it.

5.2 Using the thebibliography Environment to Create a Bibliography

An example of the use of the thebibliography environment is shown in the top part of
Fig. 5.1 and the output that it produces after being processed by LaTeX is shown in the
bottom part of Fig. 5.1. The opening command of the thebibliography environment
requires a mandatory argument which is used just to determine the appearance of the
output produced. For example, if you are referring to less than 10 things, then use a
single numeral for this argument;[2] if you are referring to more than 9 items but less
than 100, then use two numerals for this argument; and so on.

In the thebibliography environment items are introduced by a \bibitem{*key*}
command; the argument *key* is made up out of letters, numerals and punctuation characters other than the comma. To refer to an item in the bibliography you have to use

---

[1] In Diller (1990) I used a customized version of the list environment in order to produce the bibliography
and simply "hardwired" all the references into this bibliography in the body of the book.

[2] All the numerals have the same width, namely half an em in the current font, so it does not matter which
you use.

```
\begin{thebibliography}{7}
\bibitem{hal:towards}
Michael Hallett,
''Towards a Theory of Mathematical Research Programmes (I)'',
{\it British Journal for the Philosophy of Science},
vol.~30 (1979), pp.~1--25.
%
\bibitem{lak:proofs}
Imre Lakatos,
{\it Proofs and Refutations:
The Logic of Mathematical Discovery},
[Cambridge, Cambridge University Press, 1976].
\end{thebibliography}
```

References

[1] Michael Hallett, "Towards a Theory of Mathematical Research Programmes (I)", *British Journal for the Philosophy of Science*, vol. 30
(1979), pp. 1–25.

[2] Imre Lakatos, *Proofs and Refutations: The Logic of Mathematical Discovery*, [Cambridge, Cambridge University Press, 1976].

Figure 5.1: Using the `thebibibliography` environment.

---

a `\cite{key}` command. LaTeX automatically generates numerical cross-referencing
labels. Thus—given the input shown in the top part of Fig. 5.1—`\cite{lak:proofs}`
generates [2] and `\cite{hal:towards}` generates [1]. However, you need to run LaTeX
at least twice in order to get the cross-referencing information into your output; the
first time you run LaTeX the information in the `thebibliography` environment is written to the **aux** file and the next time you run LaTeX this information is used to generate
the labels that appear in the output.

The general form of the `\cite` command is `\cite[text]{key-list}`, where *key-list*
is a sequence of one or more keys—if more than one is present, then they should
be separated by commas—and *text* is an optional annotation. For example, the input `\cite{lak:proofs,hal:towards}` generates [2, 1] and the output [2, pp. 1–8] is
generated by the input `\cite[pp.~1--8]{lak:proofs}`.

```
\begin{thebibliography}{Lakatos 76}
\bibitem[Hallett 79]{hal:towards}
Michael Hallett,
''Towards a Theory of Mathematical Research Programmes (I)'',
{\it British Journal for the Philosophy of Science},
vol.~30 (1979), pp.~1--25.
%
\bibitem[Lakatos 76]{lak:proofs}
Imre Lakatos,
{\it Proofs and Refutations:
The Logic of Mathematical Discovery},
[Cambridge, Cambridge University Press, 1976].
\end{thebibliography}
```

References

[Hallett 79] Michael Hallett, "Towards a Theory of Mathematical Research Programmes (I)", *British Journal for the Philosophy of Science*, vol. 30 (1979), pp. 1–25.

[Lakatos 76] Imre Lakatos, *Proofs and Refutations: The Logic of Mathematical Discovery*, [Cambridge, Cambridge University Press, 1976].

Figure 5.2: The optional argument to the \bibitem command.

The \bibitem command can have an optional argument as shown in the top part of Fig. 5.2. This is used as the label to the reference throughout the document. In this case the "width" argument to the thebibliography environment should be the widest optional argument to the \bibitem command used within that argument. In this case \cite{lak:proofs} generates [Lakatos 76] and \cite{hal:towards} generates [Hallett 79].

5.3   Using BIBTEX to Create a Bibliography

5.3.1   Introduction

BIBTEX is a widely available system used for producing bibliographies in conjunction with LATEX; it was implemented by Oren Patashnik.[3] In order to use it you first have to create a file with extension bib containing a sequence of entries—the structure of these is explained in the next subsection—and, then, in your LATEX input file you need to include—in addition to the standard \cite command—some additional commands peculiar to BIBTEX which tell it how to format the bibliography it produces and what the names of the bib files containing database entries are that it should use; these are explained in subsection 5.3.3.

5.3.2   The Structure of the bib File

Introduction

A bib file contains one or more entries each of which looks something like this:

```
@book{il:pr:lmd,
    address   = "Cambridge",
    author    = "Imre Lakatos",
    isbn      = "0 521 21078 X (hard covers)
                 0 521 29038 4 (paperback)",
    note      = "Edited by John Worrall and Elie Zahar",
    publisher = "Cambridge University Press",
    title     = "Proofs and Refutations:
                 The Logic of Mathematical Discovery",
    year      = 1976}
```

The general form of such an entry is *publication-type{key, field-list}*. The available possibilities for *publication-type* are given in Table 5.1 together with a brief description of what sort of material each kind of entry should be used for. Unlike LATEX much of BIBTEX is not case sensitive. Thus, @book can appear as @BOOK or even as @BooK. Instead of using curly braces to enclose the *key* and *field-list* of an entry ordinary parentheses—that is to say, (and)—can be used. If any braces occur inside these delimiters, then they must come in matching pairs and this applies even to \{ and \}.

The *key* is what will appear in any \cite commands that you use to refer to the publication in question. For example, to refer to Lakatos's *Proofs and Refutations* you would use the command \cite{il:pr:lmd}.

The *field-list* is separated from the key by a comma and it consists of a list of fields separated by commas. An example of a field is author = "Imre Lakatos" and here

---

[3] If BIBTEX is available on your computer or network, then Patashnik's documentation—called "BIBTEXing"—should be available somewhere on-line as well. It contains more information about BIBTEX than is contained here.

@article{*key,field-list*} This kind of entry in the bibliographic database is used for articles or papers that have been published in journals, periodicals or magazines.

@book{*key,field-list*} This is used for books which have a named publisher.

@booklet{*key,field-list*} This is used for a work that has been printed and bound, but which has no indication on it identifying who produced it.

@conference{*key,field-list*} This is used for an article or paper that is published in the proceedings of some conference. (This kind of entry is exactly the same as the @inproceedings type.)

@inbook{*key,field-list*} This is used for chapters—or other parts—of a book. It can even be used just for a collection of pages from a book.

@incollection{*key,field-list*} This is used for chapters—or other parts—of a book which have their own titles. The book in question may have, for example, each chapter written by a different person.

@inproceedings{*key,field-list*} This is used for an article or paper that is published in the proceedings of some conference. (This kind of entry is exactly the same as the @conference type.)

@manual{*key,field-list*} Used for manuals or other kinds of technical documentation.

@mastersthesis{*key,field-list*} This is used for a dissertation or thesis written for a Master's degree.

@misc{*key,field-list*} Used when something you want to refer to fits nowhere else.

@phdthesis{*key,field-list*} This is used for a doctoral thesis or dissertation.

@proceedings{*key,field-list*} This is used for the proceedings of a conference as distinct from a single paper in such a collection.

@techreport{*key,field-list*} This is used for a research or technical report produced by an institution such as a school or department in a university or an industrial research laboratory.

@unpublished{*key,field-list*} This is used for a document—such as a typescript—that has a title and an author but has not been published in any way. A samizdat document may belong in this category.

Table 5.1: Different kinds of *publication-type*.

author is the name of the field and "Imre Lakatos" is the text of the field. Field-names are not case-sensitive, so author could appear are AUTHOR or even as AutHOr. The field-list is either enclosed in double quotation marks or an opening and closing curly brace. If a field-text consists *entirely* of numerals, such as 1976, then there is no need to enclose it in double quotation marks. (In the *key* and *field-list* multiple spaces around commas or equals signs make no difference to the output.)

The following is a complete list of all the field-names that are currently recognized by BibTeX:

address Usually you just need to give the city or town where the publisher of the book has its main office. If the place is not well known, then it is a good idea to include more information in order to help any interested reader to locate the work.

annote Currently, this field is ignored by all standard bibliography styles, but it may be used by non-standard styles that produce an annotated bibliography. Hence, it should be used for such annotations.

author This holds the name of the author of the work or their names if there are more than one.

booktitle If only part of a book is being referred to, then its title should be included here.

chapter The number of a chapter or other sectional unit being referred to.

crossref Used for the key of the database entry whose fields will be inherited by this entry if they are not explicitly included. (Included fields are used in preference.) See the example discussed in subsection 5.3.4 below.

edition An indication of which edition is being referred to. For example, 7 or "Thirty-ninth". If a numeral is not used, then an ordinal with an initial upper-case letter should be used.

editor This holds the name of the editor of a book being referred to (or their names if there are more than one) or the name of the editor of a book—such as the proceedings of a conference—part of which is being referred to (or their names if there are more than one).

howpublished This field is optional for two kinds of publication and it indicates how the item in question was published. The text should start with an initial upper-case letter.

institution This holds the name of the institution—for example, "Programming Research Group"—under whose auspices the technical report being referred to was produced.

journal The name of the journal in which the article being referred to was published. Various abbreviations may be available on your system; check with someone who knows.

key You should not confuse this field-name with the *key* that is used in `\cite` commands. This is used for sorting the entry when no other field usually used for sorting is present.

month Use either `jan, feb, mar, apr, may, jun, jul, aug, sep, oct, nov` or `dec`.

note Any additional information that you want to appear in the bibliography that is produced, such as `note = "Edited by John Worrall and Elie Zahar"`. Note that the first word should have an initial uppercase letter.

number The number of the work being referred to.

organization The sponsors of a conference or the organization associated with a technical manual.

pages The range of page numbers or a page number or several of these. For example, `"679--703"`, `"33--45, 60--63"` or `"35, 40--43, 70"`.

publisher The name of the publishing house. For example, `"Cambridge University Press"` or `"Springer"`.

school The name of a department or school to which a thesis was submitted.

series Some books are published in series; the name of such a series appears here.

title The title of a book or article or whatever.

type There are many varieties of technical reports; here, you should state which one the work you are referring to is.

volume The volume number of a journal or the volume number of a book or conference proceedings that is one of a series.

year The year associated with a work that you are referring to. Usually, something like `1976`, but the standard BIBTEX style can handle text like `"Circa 1600"` whose last four non-punctuation characters are numerals.

Note that the field-name `isbn` that appears in the entry for Lakatos's *Proofs and Refutations* is not one that is (currently) recognized by BIBTEX. It causes no error or warning message when processed and is included just for information; it does not appear in any bibliography produced.

Depending on which *publication-type* you are using different fields are either mandatory, optional or ignored. (The status of some fields is more complicated than this threefold classification as explained below.) For example, in producing a database entry for a book, like Lakatos's *Proofs and Refutations*, only the `publisher`, `title` and `year` fields have to be present. Furthermore, either the `author` or the `editor` field must be present (but not both) and at most one of the `volume` and `number` fields can be present (but both can be absent). The `address`, `crossref`, `edition`, `key`, `month`, `note` and `series` fields are optional, that is to say, they are used if present; every other kind of field is simply ignored. In the table shown in Table 5.2 six different kinds of field are shown. These are indicated by the five letters A, E, O, R and V and also by leaving a blank. These have the following meaning:

A This is used in the `@inbook` column to indicate that you can either include a `chapter` field or a `pages` field or both in the *field-list* argument. If neither are present, then a warning is issued but the output in the bibliography produced looks okay.

E This is used in the `@book` and `@inbook` columns to indicate that either the `author` or the `editor` fields can be included. If both of these fields are present, then a warning message is issued when you run BibTeX and the `editor` field is ignored. If neither of these fields is present—nor a `key` field—then you get a warning informing you that BibTeX cannot sort this bibliographic entry. It does, however, appear in the bibliography that is produced.

O This is used to indicate that the field in question is optional. That is to say, the information will be used if it is present, but no problems will be caused by its absence.

R This is used to indicate that the field in question is mandatory or required. If the field is left out, then an error message will be produced when you run BibTeX and it is possible that the bibliography produced will not be formatted properly.

V This letter occurs in the columns for the following types of bibliographic entries: `@book`, `@conference`, `@inbook`, `@incollection`, `@inproceedings` and `@proceedings`. It is used to indicate that either the `volume` or `number` fields can be present. If both are present, then you get a warning message and the `number` field is ignored. If just the `volume` field is present or both are absent, everything goes ahead smoothly. If just the `number` is present when the `series` field is absent, then you get a warning message but the output looks okay.

␣ This indicates that the field—even if present—is simply ignored.

	@article	@book	@booklet	@conference	@inbook	@incollection	@inproceedings	@manual	@mastersthesis	@misc	@phdthesis	@proceedings	@techreport	@unpublished
address		O	O	O	O	O	O	O	O		O	O	O	
annote														
author	R	E	O	R	E	R	R	O	R	O	R		R	R
booktitle				R		R	R							
chapter					A	O								
crossref	O	O	O	O	O	O	O	O	O	O	O	O	O	O
edition		O			O	O		O						
editor		E		O	E	O	O					O		
howpublished			O							O				
institution													R	
journal	R													
key	O	O	O	O	O	O	O	O	O	O	O	O	O	O
month	O	O	O	O	O	O	O	O	O	O	O	O	O	O
note	O	O	O	O	O	O	O	O	O	O	O	O	O	R
number	O	V		V	V	V	V					V	O	
organization				O			O	O				O		
pages	O			O	A	O	O							
publisher		R		O	R	R	O					O		
school									R		R			
series		O		O	O	O	O					O		
title	R	R	R	R	R	R	R	R	R	O	R	R	R	R
type					O				O		O		O	
volume	O	V		V	V	V	V					V		
year	R	R	O	R	R	R	R	O	R	O	R	R	R	O

Table 5.2: Status of fields for different types of publication in a BIBTEX database entry.

The author, editor *and* title *Fields*

The name of the author of a work goes into the author field. It is a good idea to give as much information as possible in a BIBTEX entry and this also applies to people's names. If the surname comes first, then it should be followed by a comma; thus, the following two fields are equivalent:

```
author = "Karl Raimund Popper",
author = "Popper, Karl Raimund",
```

How the name actually appears in the bibliography produced depends on several factors and often the given names will only appear as initials.

Names which contain such "auxiliary" words as 'von', 'tom' or 'le' pose no problem, but they should be entered in lowercase letters. For example:

```
editor = "T. tom Dieck",
editor = "tom Dieck, T.",
```

(Leave a space and do *not* put a tilde after initials.) Some people have surnames which consist of two words that are not hyphenated. These should be entered as follows:

```
author = "Brinch Hansen, Per",
```

that is to say, the entire surname should come before the comma.

If two or more people have written or edited a book, then their names should be separated by and and if a work has, say, more than six authors, you can terminate its text with the words and others which will appear as '*et al.*' when the bibliography is produced. The following are equivalent:

```
author = "Windy Dryden and Joseph Yankura",
author = "Windy Dryden and Yankura, Joseph",
```

If a name contains either a comma or the word 'and', then that should be enclosed in curly braces. In fact, anything enclosed in curly braces will not be processed by BIBTEX in any way; it will simply be written to the bbl file without alteration. This is also useful in ensuring that the names of countries or people, say, that appear in titles do not occur in the bibliography that is produced with initial lowercase letters. For example,

```
title = "Ponsford and {Woodfull}: A Premier Partnership",
```

Note that the special function of and to separate names of multiple authors or editors only applies inside the text of an author or editor field. People disagree about what words should be capitalized in titles; the most important rule to follow is that of being consistent.

Mathematical expressions can occur in the titles of some articles and this poses no problem for BIBTEX. For example, the following database entry is perfectly acceptable:

```
@article{nha:ur,
   author  = "N. H. Abel",
   journal = "Journal {f\"ur} Reine und Argewandte Mathematik",
   pages   = "311--339",
   title   = "Untersuchungen {\"uber} die Reihe
              $\displaystyle1 + {m \over 1}x
               + {m.(m-1) \over 2}x^2
               + {m.(m-1)(m-2) \over 2.3}x^3 \ldots$",
   volume  = 1,
   year    = 1826}
```

What this produces is shown in the bibliography to this book on p. 267; the effect of the \displaystyle command is explained in the glossary.

Abbreviations

If you are going to refer a lot to articles published in the same journal, then it would be a good idea to use an abbreviation for it as follows:

```
@string{bjps = "British Journal for the Philosophy of Science"}
```

This can occur anywhere in a bib file, but it must come before any use of it. Note that the case of letters in neither @string nor bjps is significant. Note also that abbreviations must begin with a letter and that they cannot contain any of the following symbols:

```
 "  #  %  ’  (  )  ,  {  }
```

Abbreviations can take the place of the text part of any field, for example:

```
@article{mh:ttmrp:i,
   author  = "Michael Hallett",
   journal = bjps,
   pages   = "1--25",
   title   = "Towards a Theory of Mathematical
              Research Programmes {(I)}",
   volume  = 30,
   year    = 1979}
```

5.3.3 Producing the Bibliography

In order to get BIBTEX to produce a bibliography for you it is necessary to include both a \bibliographystyle and a \bibliography command inside the document environment of your input file. The \bibliographystyle command usually comes immediately after the \begin{document} command, but it has to come before any \cite commands; and the \bibliography command usually comes close to the end

```
\documentstyle[11pt]{article}
\begin{document}
\bibliographystyle{plain}
\noindent
Hallett \cite{mh:ttmrp:i} develops Lakatos's
views on the philosophy of mathematics presented,
for example, in \cite{il:pr:lmd}.
\bibliography{pom}
\end{document}
```

Hallett [1] develops Lakatos's views on the philosophy of mathematics presented, for example, in [2].

References

[1] Michael Hallett. Towards a theory of mathematical research programmes (I). *British Journal for the Philosophy of Science*, 30:1–25, 1979.

[2] Imre Lakatos. *Proofs and Refutations: The Logic of Mathematical Discovery*. Cambridge University Press, Cambridge, 1976. Edited by John Worrall and Elie Zahar.

Figure 5.3: Using BIBTEX.

of the document environment in the place where you want the bibliography produced to occur. These things are illustrated in Fig. 5.3 where the LATEX commands at the top produce the output at the bottom. Note that information about a work with key *key* is placed into the bibliography by BIBTEX *only* if at least one \cite{*key*} command occurs in your input file. If you want a work placed in the bibliography that you do not cite—but which occurs in one of your bib files—then you have to use a \nocite{*key*} command. A \nocite{*} command in your input file causes *every* work in the BIBTEX database files mentioned in the \bibliography command to appear in the bibliography produced.

The general format of the \bibliography command is:

\bibliography{*bib-file-list*}

where *bib-file-list* is a list of the first or base names of one or more bib files; if the list contains more than one member, then they should be separated by commas. In

Fig. 5.3 the command \bibligraphy{pom} occurs. This assumes the existence of a file pom.bib which should contain—at least—the entries for Lakatos's book, shown on p. 58 above, and for Hallett's article, shown on p. 65 above.

The general format of the \bibliographystyle command is:

\bibliographystyle{*bib-style*}

where the standard possibilities for *bib-style* are plain, unsrt, abbrv and alpha. The style of bibliography produced if the plain option is chosen is shown in Fig. 5.3. The entries in the bibliography produced are sorted alphabetically by author automatically by BIBTEX; works by the same author appear sorted numerically by year; and works by the same author published in the same year are sorted alphabetically by title.

If the unsrt option is chosen instead, then the entries in the bibliography produced look exactly the same as if the plain option had been used *except* that they are not sorted; they appear in the bibliography produced in the order in which references to them occur in the input file.

If the abbrv option is chosen, then the order of the entries in the bibliography produced is exactly the same as if the plain option had been used; the only difference is that given names and certain other words are abbreviated.

If the alpha option is chosen, then the bibliography produced is sorted as if the plain option had been chosen, but it looks as shown in Fig. 5.4. The command \cite{il:pr:lmd} produces the citation [Lak76] and \cite{mh:ttmrp:i} produces [Hal79]. That is to say, the labels produced automatically by LaTeX consist of the first three letters of a single author's name followed by the last two digits of the year of publication (all enclosed in square brackets).

To actually get LaTeX and BIBTEX to generate and include a bibliography in the output corresponding to your input file you need to run both LaTeX and BIBTEX on your input file: first of all you process your input file in the usual way by running LaTeX on it, then you process it using BIBTEX—in many operrating systems this is achieved by means of the command bibtex *file* where *file* is the name of your input file—and then you run LaTeX twice on your input file. (In exceptional circumstances you may need to process your input file even more times than this.)

5.3.4 The crossref Field

The way in which the crossref field works is best explained by means of an example. Let the contents of the file ide.bib be as shown in Fig. 5.5. Then the input file shown at the top of Fig. 5.6 produces the output shown at the bottom: the reference to Kripke's paper *inherits* any fields that it is missing from the entry with key mkm:ii. Note that the booktitle field is ignored if present in a @book entry; it is only included in the entry with key mkm:ii so that it can be inherited by other entries in the database. Furthermore, the cross-referenced entry—here the one with key mkm:ii— must come *after* any entries which reference it; in this example those with keys ml:ir

References

[Hal79] Michael Hallett. Towards a theory of mathematical research pro-
         grammes (I). *British Journal for the Philosophy of Science*, 30:1–25,
         1979.

[Lak76] Imre Lakatos. *Proofs and Refutations: The Logic of Mathematical
         Discovery.* Cambridge University Press, Cambridge, 1976. Edited
         by John Worrall and Elie Zahar.

Figure 5.4: Output of the `alpha` option to the `\bibibliographystyle` command.

```
@incollection{ml:ir,
    author    = "Michael Lockwood",
    crossref  = "mkm:ii",
    pages     = "199--211",
    title     = "Identity and Reference"}

@incollection{sk:in,
    author    = "Saul Kripke",
    crossref  = "mkm:ii",
    pages     = "135--164",
    title     = "Identity and Necessity"}

@book{mkm:ii,
    address   = "New York",
    booktitle = "Identity and Individuation",
    editor    = "Milton K. Munitz",
    publisher = "New York University Press",
    title     = "Identity and Individuation",
    year      = 1971}
```

Figure 5.5: Contents of the BibTeX database file `ide.bib`.

```
\documentstyle[11pt]{article}
\begin{document}
\bibliographystyle{plain}
\noindent
Kripke \cite{sk:in} is a good paper.
\bibliography{ide}
\end{document}
```

Kripke [1] is a good paper.

References

[1] Saul Kripke. Identity and necessity. In Milton K. Munitz, editor, *Identity and Individuation*, pages 135–164. New York University Press, New York, 1971.

Figure 5.6: Illustrating the output when `crossref` is used.

and `sk:in`. If you cite two or more items containing a cross-referenced item, then that is automatically included in any bibliography produced as shown in Fig. 5.7 on p. 70.

5.3.5 The `harvard` Option

In the Harvard or author–date system references are given by mentioning the author (or authors) and year of publication of a work. It is possible to get BIBTEX to produce such references, but it is not a standard option.[4] In order to get BIBTEX to produce references in the Harvard style you need to choose the `harvard` option to the `\documentstyle` command and either the `agsm`, `dcu` or `kluwer` option to the `\bibliographystyle` command. Fig. 5.8 on p. 71 illustrates these things. The options `agsm`, `dcu` and `kluwer` produce slightly different bibliographies.

Also available is a `\citationstyle` command which has two options, namely `agsm` (the default) or `dcu`; the differences between these two are shown in Table 5.3 on p. 72. Note that the `\citasnoun` command *cannot* accept a list of keys as its argument; it only works for a single key.

---

[4] Peter Williams implemented the `harvard` family of bibliography styles and if this is available on your system, so will be his documentation and this contains further information about this non-standard option.

```
\documentstyle[11pt]{article}
\begin{document}
\bibliographystyle{plain}
\noindent
Kripke \cite{sk:in} and Lockwood
\cite{ml:ir} are good papers.
\bibliography{ide}
\end{document}
```

Kripke [1] and Lockwood [2] are good papers.

References

[1] Saul Kripke. Identity and necessity. In Munitz [3], pages 135–164.

[2] Michael Lockwood. Identity and reference. In Munitz [3], pages 199–211.

[3] Milton K. Munitz, editor. *Identity and Individuation.* New York University Press, New York, 1971.

Figure 5.7: Another example of the output using `crossref`.

5.4   Preparing an Index

5.4.1   Getting the Information

Whereas the production of a bibliography is fully automated in LaTeX, the production of an index is not. In order to produce an index you need to include a \makeindex command in the preamble of your input file and within the document environment you need to include some \index{*text*} commands. Any characters can occur in *text* (but all braces—including \{ and \} must come in matching pairs) unless the \index command occurs inside the argument of another command, when *text* can only include letters, numerals and punctuation marks. When LaTeX is run on such an input file, an idx file with the same first or base name is written;[5] the idx file contains commands of the form \indexentry{*text*}{*p*} where *p* was the value of the **page** counter when \index{*text*} was processed.

---

[5] If an idx file exists, then it is overwritten; to prevent such overwriting you need to include a \nofiles command in the preamble of your input file.

```
\documentstyle[11pt,harvard]{article}
\begin{document}
\bibliographystyle{agsm}
\noindent
Citations look like \citeasnoun{mh:ttmrp:i} or \cite{il:pr:lmd}.
\bibliography{pom}
\end{document}
```

Citations look like Hallett (1979) or (Lakatos 1976).

References

Hallett, M. (1979), 'Towards a theory of mathematical research programmes (I)', *British Journal for the Philosophy of Science*, **30**, 1–25.

Lakatos, I. (1976), *Proofs and Refutations: The Logic of Mathematical Discovery*, Cambridge University Press, Cambridge. Edited by John Worrall and Elie Zahar.

Figure 5.8: Using the `harvard` option.

5.4.2 Making the Index

To make an index in LaTeX you use the `theindex` environment. Inside this you can use the `\item`, `\subitem`, `\subsubitem` and `\indexspace` commands. The `\item` command begins an entry in the index produced, the `\subitem` command begins sub-entries which are slightly indented and what `\subsubitem` produces is indented still more than that. The `\indexspace` command is used to separate groups of entries beginning with different letters of the alphabet.

5.4.3 Bridging the Gap

The problem of using LaTeX to make an index is that of getting the information in an idx file into a `theindex` environment. One thing that exists—though it is not very useful—is that you can run LaTeX on the file `idx.tex`; when you do this you will get a prompt asking you for the name of a file. Say you input `lakatos.tex`; then a file called `idx.dvi` will be generated and if you print this off on a printer, it will tell you all the arguments to all the `\index` commands that occurred on page 1 and all the arguments of all the `\index` commands that occurred on page 2 and so on.

	output		input
agsm	dcu		
(Lakatos 1976)	(Lakatos, 1976)	\cite{il:pr:lmd}	
(Lakatos 1976, Hallett 1979)	(Lakatos, 1976; Hallett, 1979)	\cite{il:pr:lmd, mh:ttmrp:i}
Lakatos (1976)	Lakatos (1976)	\citeasnoun{il:pr:lmd}
(Lakatos 1976, pp. 23–34)	(Lakatos, 1976, pp. 23–34)	\cite[pp. 23--34]{il:pr:lmd}
Lakatos (1976, pp. 23–34)	Lakatos (1976, pp. 23–34)	\citeasnoun [pp. 23--34]{il:pr:lmd}

Table 5.3: Harvard citations in two varieties.

Some people have written programs which take an `idx` file and produce an alphabetically sorted list of items in a `theindex` environment. Investigate to see if one of these exists on your system; if it does not, then you will have to generate the entries in the `theindex` environment manually.

5.5   Preparing a "Glossary"

LaTeX contains commands called \makeglossary and \glossary that work analogously to the \makeindex and \index commands. A file with extension `glo` is written or overwritten and this contains \glossaryentry commands which are analogous to \indexentry commands. Many people are misled by the word 'glossary' in these command names; they just mirror the index-producing commands. Note that there is no `theglossary` environment analogous to the `theindex` environment. The `description` environment explained in section 4.3 is best used for producing what most people think of as a glossary.

6

Formatting Articles, Reports, Books and Letters

6.1 The article Document Style

6.1.1 Introduction

The overall structure of a LaTeX input file has already been discussed in chapter 2. In the case of articles this becomes:

```
\documentstyle[opt-list]{article}
    dec-seq
\begin{document}
    text
\end{document}
```

In this section further commands which relate to the large-scale organization of an input file for producing articles are explained.

By default one-sided "printing" is in effect, that is to say, all pages are (conceptually) right-handed and odd-numbered ones. This means, for example, that the head, body and foot regions of both odd- and even-numbered pages are positioned in the same place on the physical piece of paper relative to the left and top edges of the paper. The length parameter \evensidemargin, therefore, has no effect on the appearance of the output. To change this default choose the twoside option to the \documentstyle command. (All the length parameters that affect the appearance of the page—and what they do—are shown in Fig. C.4 on p. 258.)

The default page style is plain, that is to say, the head region is empty and the page number appears in the centre of the foot region. And—by default—the \raggedbottom declaration is in force; this means that inter-paragraph vertical space is kept constant and, so, the height of the text on each page may vary slightly. To force the height of material on each output page to be the same include the \flushbottom declaration in

```
\documentstyle[11pt,own]{article}
\title{Lakatos's Philosophy of Mathematics}
\author{Antoni Diller}
\begin{document}
\bibliographystyle{plain}
\maketitle
\begin{abstract}
\noindent
In this paper I investigate the influence of Popper's
''evolutionary'' epistemology on Lakatos's account of the
growth of mathematical knowledge by means of proofs and
refutations.
\end{abstract}
    text
\bibliography{pom}
\end{document}
```

Figure 6.1: The contents of the input file `lpm.tex`.

the preamble of your input file. (Note that if you choose the **twoside** option to the \documentstyle command, then the default becomes the \flushbottom declaration.)

6.1.2   Bibliography

It may seem strange to discuss bibliographies so early on in this chapter as they almost invariably come near the end of any work in which they occur at all, but if you are using BibTeX to produce your bibliography, then you need to include a \bibliographystyle command soon after the start of the **document** environment; and near to the end of the **document** environment you have to include a \bibliography command. Thus, your input file is going to look something like what appears in Fig. 6.1. This assumes the existence of a personal style file called **own.sty** and also the existence of a file containing BibTeX database entries called **pom.bib**. Note that the \bibliography command will automatically generate the unnumbered section heading 'References' when you process your input file.

If you are using the **thebibliography** environment to produce a bibliography, then this should come just before the \end{document} command (if you want it to be the last thing in the output document). Note that the **thebibliography** environment generates the section heading 'References' automatically (without any number being attached to it).

6.1.3 Title, Author and Date

The title is produced by the \maketitle command which—if it occurs at all in the input file—must be placed within the document environment. If the \maketitle command is used, then it has to be preceded by both \title and \author declarations. Optionally, it may also be preceded by a \date declaration; if this is omitted, then the current date is used. This appears, for example, as 'February 24, 1992'. Note that by default the title does *not* appear on a page by itself; if you do want the title, author and date information to be placed on a page all by itself, then choose the titlepage option to the \documentstyle command. (This also makes the abstract—if one is present—appear on a separate page as well.)

The title itself occurs as an argument to the \title declaration. You can use the \\ command within the argument to the \title declaration in order to force a line break. One or more \thanks commands can also appear within the argument to the \title declaration. These produce footnotes. Unlike normal footnotes, the markers produced are regarded as having zero width. This produces better looking output when the footnote marker is placed at the end of a line. If a \thanks command does not end a line, then it should be followed by a \␣ command in order to insert some inter-word space.

The author or authors of the article occur as the argument to the \author declaration. If more than one author is included, then they should be separated by an \and command. Just as in the case of the \title declaration, you can use \\ to force the end of a line and footnotes can be produced using the \thanks command.

The optional \date declaration can be used to produce a date of your choice (or, in fact, any other information). If this declaration is omitted, then the date on which you ran LaTeX on your input file is used as the date. Just as in the case of the \title declaration, you can use \\ to force the end of a line and footnotes can be produced using the \thanks command.

A maximum of nine \thanks commands can occur in the arguments of the \title, \author and \date commands. The footnotes produced are not indicated by numerical footnote marks, but by the following nine symbols *, †, ‡, §, ¶, ‖, **, †† and ‡‡.

When several people have jointly contributed to a paper, it is often difficult to decide the order in which their names should appear. The following formula may help resolve this problem:[1]

$$V_i = \frac{4c_i + 2p_i + 2g_i + 2a_i + d_i + e_i}{t_i},$$

where c_i is a measure of i's conceptual input, p_i his planning input, g_i his contribution to data acquisition, a_i his contribution to data analysis, d_i his contribution to preparing the first draft, e_i his contribution to the final editing and t_i is the time invested. The value V_i of each collaborator is calculated using this formula and the person with the largest value of V_i comes first, then the next largest, and so on.

---

[1] This is based on a formula given by Sindermann (1982), pp. 14–15, where other ways of resolving this problem are also discussed.

sectioning command	level number	in table of contents	numb-ered
\part	0	yes	yes
\section	1	yes	yes
\subsection	2	yes	yes
\subsubsection	3	yes	yes
\paragraph	4	no	no
\subparagraph	5	no	no

Table 6.1: Sectioning commands in the `article` document style.

6.1.4 Abstract

If you wish your document to have an abstract, then include this in an `abstract` environment. This should come within the `document` environment of your input file and usually the best place for it is just after the `\maketitle` command. Note that by default the first line of the abstract produced is indented. This paragraph indentation can be suppressed by using a `\noindent` command. By default the abstract produced does *not* appear on a page by itself, but by choosing the `titlepage` option to the `\documentstyle` command you can force it to appear on a page by itself. An example of the use and placement of the `abstract` environment is shown in Fig. 6.1.

6.1.5 Sectioning Commands

The sectioning commands that are available in the `article` document style are `\part`, `\section`, `\subsection`, `\subsubsection`, `\paragraph` and `\subparagraph`.   And associated with each sectioning command there is a level number—as shown in Table 6.1—and this is used to determine whether or not the *heading* associated with a sectioning command occurs in the table of contents—if there is one—and whether or not the *heading* associated with the sectioning command that appears in the final document is numbered or not.[2] There are two counters that control these things, namely `tocdepth` and `secnumdepth`. All headings of sectional units with level numbers less than or equal to the value of the counter `tocdepth` will appear in the table of contents (if there is one) and all sectional units with level numbers less than or equal to the value of the `secnumdepth` counter are numbered. By default the value of both `tocdepth` and `secnumdepth` is 3 and the information in Table 6.1 relating to which sectioning commands are numbered and which headings appear in a table of contents applies to these default values.

You should not use a sectioning command with level number i (for $2 \le i \le 5$) if it

---

[2] Articles do not usually have a table of contents, but one can be produced by using the `\tableofcontents` command. This is explained below in the context of a discussion of the `report` document style.

is not preceded by a sectioning command with level number $i - 1$; though, of course, other sectioning commands with level number $i - 1$ may intervene as may arbitrary textual material and other LaTeX commands. Thus, the \section command can be used even if no \part commands are used.

Associated with each sectioning command there is a counter whose name is the same as the name of its corresponding sectioning command except that it does not have an initial backslash character. For example, the counter associated with the \section command is called section. At the start of an article all counters associated with sectioning commands are initialized to zero; they are incremented by their corresponding sectioning commands *before* the number of the section unit is produced. Sectioning commands with level number i (for $1 \le i \le 4$) reset all counters associated with sectioning commands with level numbers greater than i to zero when they are incremented. Note that this does not apply to \part; so, if the section before a \part command was numbered 8, then the first section following that occurrence of the \part command will be numbered 9.

The general form of the \section command is:

\section[*entry*]{*heading*}

(All sectioning commands behave in a similar fashion; so, although what I say here will be said about the \section command, it applies to all the sectioning commands.) If the optional argument *entry* is absent, then by default *heading* will appear in the table of contents if one is produced. If *entry* is present, then it will appear in the table of contents, but *heading* will appear in the document produced. If *entry* is present, then it is a moving argument; but if it is absent, *heading* is the moving argument.[3]

There is also a *-form of the \section command and it is often used in conjunction with an \addcontentsline command as follows:

\section*{*heading*}
\addcontentsline{toc}{section}{*heading*}

The effect of the \section* command is that the heading produced in the output document is neither numbered nor does it appear in the table of contents (even if one is produced). The effect of the \addcontentsline command is to get the *heading* into the table of contents. (Note that it is section without an initial backslash that occurs as the second argument to the \addcontentsline command.) This combination of commands is used if you are producing a document with a table of contents in which sections are numbered but you want to include an unnumbered section—such as a glossary or a single appendix.

The effect of an \appendix declaration is to alter the way in which sections are labelled. The first \section command following the \appendix declaration is labelled 'A', the next 'B', and so on. Note that the \appendix declaration does not take any arguments.

---

[3] For an explanation of what a moving argument is see section B.4.

6.1.6   Labelling of Formulas, Figures and Tables

If you use the `equation` and `eqnarray` environments to generate equation numbers, then they are numbered consecutively throughout the output document starting at 1. If any figures occur in your document, they are numbered consecutively throughout the output document starting at 1. If any tables occur in your document, they are numbered consecutively throughout the output document starting at 1. Note that there can be an equation, a figure and a table all numbered 1, etc.

6.1.7   Running Heads

One-sided "Printing"

As already mentioned the default page style for articles is `plain`, that is to say, it is as if the following command `\pagestyle{plain}` had been included in the preamble of your input file.[4] The effect of this is that the head region is empty and the foot region only contains the page number and that is centred.

If you want the head and foot regions to be empty throughout the output document, then you need to include the command `\pagestyle{empty}` in the preamble of your input file and *also* you need to include the command `\thispagestyle{empty}` in your input file inside the `document` environment and near to the beginning of that environment so that it is in force when LaTeX outputs the first page of your document.

If you choose the `headings` page style, that is to say, if you include the command `\pagestyle{headings}` in the preamble of your input file, then running heads are produced in the head region of the page. Normally, a running head will consist of a section number and heading—in that order and all in uppercase slanted type—starting at the left-hand edge of the head region and the page number in Roman type flush right in the head region. For example, if the command:

```
\section{Referential Transparency and Opacity}
```

occurs in your input file and the value of the `section` counter is 2 and that of the `page` counter is 6, then the running head will look something like this:

2 REFERENTIAL TRANSPARENCY AND OPACITY	6

(The frame will not appear in the running head; it is just added here for clarity.) If you have altered the value of the counter `secnumdepth` so that sections are not numbered, then neither will the section number appear in the running head; and if you have used the *-form of the `\section` command, then the *heading* argument will not appear in the head region.

---

[4] To begin with in this subsection I am assuming that the `twoside` option to the `\documentstyle` command has not been chosen as it complicates matters still further.

If you want to put your own words into the running head, then you need to choose the **myheadings** option to the **\pagestyle** command and then you can use the **\markright**{*text*} command in the preamble to place *text* into the running head on all pages (except the first).

Two-sided "Printing"

If you choose the **twoside** option to the **\documentstyle** command and include the command **\pagestyle{headings}** in the preamble of your input file, then the running head on odd-numbered (right-handed) pages—except the first—will consist of the section and subsection numbers separated by a full stop and the subsection heading flush left in slanted type and the page number flush right in Roman type; and on even-numbered (left-handed) pages the running head will consist of the page number flush left in Roman type and flush right will appear the section number and heading in uppercase slanted type. For example, if the value of the **page** counter is 5, that of the **section** counter 2 and that of the **subsection** counter 2 as well and the last **\subsection** command was the following:

\subsection{Opaque Features of Imperative Languages}

then the left running head will look like this (apart from the frame):

2.2 Opaque Features of Imperative Languages	5

Under the same conditions and if the last **\section** command was:

\section{Referential Transparency and Opacity}

then the right running head will look like this (apart from the frame):

6	*2 REFERENTIAL TRANSPARENCY AND OPACITY*

If you have altered the value of the counter **secnumdepth** so that either sections or subsections are not numbered, then neither will the suppressed number or numbers appear in the running head; and if you have used the *-form of either the **\section** or the **\subsection** command, then the corresponding *heading* will not appear in the running head.

If you want to put your own words into the running heads, then you need to choose the **myheadings** option to the **\pagestyle** command and then you can use the **\markboth**{*text*$_1$}{*text*$_2$} command to place *text*$_1$ into the running head on even-numbered pages and *text*$_2$ into the running head on odd-numbered pages.

6.2   The report Document Style

6.2.1   Introduction

The report document style is similar to the article one in that most of the defaults are the same; one of the main differences is that the \chapter sectioning command is available. By default the output is formatted in the one-sided manner, but this can be altered by means of the twoside option to the \documentstyle command. The default page style is plain, that is to say, the head is empty and the page number appears in the centre of the foot. If the headings page style is used, then the head contains the chapter name and page number—unless the twoside document style option has been used, when the head contains the chapter name and page number on even pages and the section name and page number on odd pages. This can be altered by using the myheadings option and associated commands.

If the \flushbottom declaration is included, then the height of the text on each output page will be the same—vertical blank space being added where necessary—but the default is as if the \raggedbottom declaration had been included. This allows the height of the text in the output to vary slightly from page to page. (If the twoside option is included, then the default becomes the \flushbottom declaration.) If the \maketitle command is present—usually just after the beginning of the document environment—then a separate title page is generated. As in the case of articles it has to be preceded by both \author and \title declarations and may be preceded by a \date declaration; \thanks commands can occur in the arguments of these as explained in subsection 6.1.3 above. If you wish to include an abstract, then the abstract environment should follow soon after the \maketitle command. The abstract will appear on a separate page.

Parts have a level number of −1 and chapters one of 0. The default value of the counter secnumdepth is 2. This means that all sectional units with level numbers greater than or equal to 2 are numbered, that is to say, subsections and larger units. The default value of the counter tocdepth is 2. This means that all sectional units with level numbers greater than or equal to 2 appear in the table of contents if there is one, that is to say, subsections and larger units. This information is also presented in Table 6.2. If the chapter before the \part command was 8, then the chapter number following it will be 9.

If you use the equation and eqnarray environments to generate equation numbers, then they are numbered consecutively throughout each chapter beginning with X.1—where X is the number of the chapter—and continuing with X.2, and so on. If any figures occur in your document, they are numbered consecutively throughout each chapter beginning with X.1—where X is the number of the chapter—and continuing with X.2, and so on. If any tables occur in your document, they are numbered consecutively throughout each chapter beginning with X.1—where X is the number of the chapter—and continuing with X.2, and so on. Note that there can be an equation, a figure and a table all numbered X.1, etc. Note also that if an equation or eqnarray

sectioning command	level number	in table of contents	numb-ered
\part	−1	yes	yes
\chapter	0	yes	yes
\section	1	yes	yes
\subsection	2	yes	yes
\subsubsection	3	no	no
\paragraph	4	no	no
\subparagraph	5	no	no

Table 6.2: Sectioning commands in the book and report document styles.

environment, figure or table occurs before any \chapter command, then X will be 0.

The effect of an \appendix declaration is to alter the way in which chapters are labelled. The first \chapter command following the \appendix declaration is labelled 'A', the next 'B', and so on. If your input file contains a thebibliography environment, then the chapter heading 'Bibliography' is generated (without any number being attached to it).

6.2.2 Root and Data Files

The Basic Idea

The report document style is usually used for quite lengthy documents and when working on a large piece of writing it is a good idea to split the input file into a number of separate input files. There are, no doubt, several ways in which this can be done but I will present a method of doing this that I have arrived at after several years of experimentation.

Imagine that you are toying with the idea of writing a book on logic and initially think that this will consist of six chapters; for each chapter you need a *root* and a *data* file. For example, in the case of chapter 1 the root file could be called root01a.tex and the data file data01a.tex.[5] The possible contents of six root and six data files are shown in Fig. 6.2; be careful not to include an \end{document} in any data file. The commands \input, \include and \includeonly are LATEX's mechanism for allowing the input of a document to be split across several files. They are fully explained on p. 83 below and a concise description of what they do appears in the glossary contained in appendix C.

---

[5] The reason for using 01 as part of the base name rather than just simply 1 is that if you decide to have more than nine chapters and use an operating system that lists your files alphabetically, then using 01, etc., will result in, for example, root09a.tex being followed by root10a.tex; the reason for including the letter a as part of the base name is that sometimes you may want to split a large chapter into several input files and the root files for these could be called, for example, root01a.tex, root01b.tex, and so on, and the corresponding data files would then be data01a.tex, data01b.tex, and so on.

```
%
% Your own definitions
% go here, where
% they are safe.
%
%
```

own.sty

```
\include{data01a}
\include{data02a}
\include{data03a}
\include{data04a}
\include{data05a}
\include{data06a}
```

common.tex

```
\documentstyle
[11pt,own]{report}
\includeonly{data01a}
\begin{document}
\input{common}
\end{document}
```

root01a.tex

```
\chapter{Introduction}
\typeout{Introduction}
%
To be written.
```

data01a.tex

⋮   ⋮

```
\documentstyle
[11pt,own]{report}
\includeonly{data06a}
\begin{document}
\input{common}
\end{document}
```

root06a.tex

```
\chapter{Graph Proofs}
\typeout{Graph Proofs}
%
To be written.
```

data06a.tex

Figure 6.2: Root, data, common and style files.

\include{*file*} This command is used in conjunction with \includeonly{*file-list*} for producing only part of a large document whose content has been split into several input files. Note that the result of processing *file* will—if it appears at all—always start on a new page and it will terminate as if a \clearpage command had been included at the end of *file*.tex.

\includeonly{*file-list*} This command can only occur in the preamble of your input file. The argument *file-list* is a list of zero or more extensionless filenames. If two or more are present, then they are separated by commas. (An item *file* in *file-list* refers to *file*.tex.) If *file* occurs in *file-list*, then the command \include{*file*} does not have to occur in the body of the input file. Only the text contained in a *file* that appears in *file-list* occurs in the output produced by LaTeX, but that input is processed as if all the files had been processed as well and so, for example, cross-references between files work correctly.

\input{*file*} This has the same effect as if the contents of the file *file* were present in this part of the input file. If *file* has no extension, then the file *file*.tex is included. The braces are optional.

If you do decide to use this method for splitting a large document into several input files, then it is almost essential to have your own style file as at least one command *has* to go there if it is used at all, namely the \newcounter command. In any case, it is a very good idea to put all your global definitions and declarations in the style file, such as, things like declarations that alter the size of the body region and definitions of your own commands and environments.

In order to get dvi files from this set-up you need to run LaTeX on each of the root files. It is most sensible to process the root files in chapter order beginning with root01a.tex. One of the minor drawbacks of this way of splitting your input is that you will need to process each root file at least *three* times in order to get any cross-referencing information correct.

When the work you are writing is nearing completion, you will need to produce a title page, a table of contents and other similar things for it. The easiest way to do this would be to create a root00a.tex and data00a.tex files as shown in Fig. 6.3. You would then process the file root00a.tex at least twice in order to produce the additional material. The meanings of the commands in root00a.tex that have not been explained already are as follows:

\nofiles When LaTeX is run a number of additional files are or may be created, namely the aux, glo, idx, lof, lot and toc files. (For example, if your original file is called *file*.tex, then the auxilary file is called *file*.aux.) If you include the \nofiles declaration in the preamble of your input file—the only place it can occur—then none of these additional files are written to. In particular, if any of them already exist, then they are not overwritten.

```
\documentstyle
[11pt,own]{report}
\title{Logic}
\author{Antoni Diller}
\includeonly{data00a}
% \nofiles
\makeindex
\makeglossary
\begin{document}
\pagenumbering{roman}
\maketitle
\tableofcontents
\listoffigures
\listoftables
\include{data00a}
\pagenumbering{arabic}
\input{common}
\end{document}
```

```
\chapter*{Preface}
\typeout{Preface}
\addcontentsline{toc}
{chapter}{Preface}
%
To be written.
%
\chapter*
{Acknowledgements}
\typeout
{Acknowledgements}
\addcontentsline{toc}
{chapter}
{Acknowledgements}
%
To be written.
%
%
```

root00a.tex   data00a.tex

Figure 6.3: The `root00a.tex` and `data00a.tex` files.

\makeindex This command can only occur in the preamble of an input file. It causes an `idx` file to be written or overwritten which contains the `\indexentry` commands generated by any `\index` commands that appear in your input file. A `\nofiles` declaration in the preamble suppresses the writing (or overwriting) of the `idx` file.

\makeglossary This command can only occur in the preamble of your input file. It causes a `glo` file to be written or overwritten which contains the `\glossaryentry` commands generated by any `\glossary` commands that appear in your input file. A `\nofiles` declaration in the preamble suppresses the writing (or overwriting) of the `glo` file.

\pagenumbering{*num-style*} This global declaration specifies how page numbers will appear. The parameter *num-style* can be either `arabic` (for Arabic numerals), `roman` (for lowercase Roman numerals), `Roman` (for uppercase Roman numerals), `alph` (for lowercase letters) and `Alph` (for uppercase letters). The default value is `arabic`. (Note that the `\pagenumbering` global declaration redefines `\thepage` to be `\`*num-style*`{page}`.)

`\tableofcontents` This command produces a table of contents at the place in the input file where it occurs. You need to run LaTeX at least twice to get a correct table of contents. It causes a `toc` file to be written or overwritten except if you have included a `\nofiles` command.

`\listoffigures` This command produces a list of figures at the place in the input file where it occurs. You need to run LaTeX at least twice to get a correct list of figures. It causes a `lof` file to be written or overwritten except if you have included a `\nofiles` command.

`\listoftables` This command produces a list of tables at the place in the input file where it occurs. You need to run LaTeX at least twice to get a correct list of tables. A new `lot` file is produced unless you include a `\nofiles` command.

Including a Bibliography

There are no problems involved in combining this way of splitting your input file into several files with using either the `thebibliography` environment or BibTeX to produce a bibliography. If you want to use the `thebibliography` environment, then you just put it at the end of the data files—usually a bibliography comes just before the index—and that is all you have to do; `\cite` commands can occur in any data file. As usual, you will have to process all the root files at least twice—and maybe more times—in order to get the references correct.

Say you want to use BibTeX to produce a bibliography and you have decided to make `data06a.tex` into the bibliography. You need to put a `\bibliographystyle` command in *every* root file; this goes inside the `document` environment before the `\input{common}` command. And in `data06a.tex` you need to put a `\bibliography` command; if you are going to use `data06a.tex` as the bibliography, then you should make sure that it contains no `\chapter` or other sectioning commands.[6] Note that you only need to run BibTeX on the root file corresponding to the data file that contains the `\bibliography` command; after you have done that you still need to run LaTeX on all the root files at least two more times, that is to say, including the root file corresponding to the data file that contains the `\bibliography` command.

6.3   The book Document Style

The book document style is almost the same as the report one, except that several of the defaults are different. The twoside option to the `\documentstyle` command is the default and this formats the output in a form suitable for printing on both sides of a page. This cannot be altered. The default page style is headings, that is to say, the head contains the chapter name and page number on even pages and the section name and page number on odd pages. This can be altered by using the myheadings option

---

[6] I usually put my bibliography in a file called `data88a.tex` and the index in `data99a.tex`.

and associated commands or by using the `plain` or `empty` options to the `\pagestyle` command.

If the `\raggedbottom` declaration is used, then the height of the text on each output page may vary slightly from page to page. The default, however, is the `\flushbottom` declaration which means that the height of the text on all pages is the same. If the `\maketitle` command is present—usually just after the beginning of the `document` environment—then a separate title page is generated. As in the case of articles it has to be preceded by both `\author` and `\title` declarations and may be preceded by a `\date` declaration; `\thanks` commands can occur in the arguments of these as explained in subsection 6.1.3 above. The `abstract` environment cannot be used in a book.

Level numbers of sectional units are the same as for the `report` option and are shown in Table 6.2 on p. 81; in particular parts have a level number of −1 and chapters one of 0. If the chapter before the `\part` command was 8, then the chapter number following it will be 9. Because two-sided printing is the default each chapter will start on an odd-numbered page; this may result in a blank page being placed before new chapters. Furthermore, if you use the `\part{`*heading*`}` command, then the argument *heading* will always appear on an odd-numbered page; this may result in additional blank pages being placed immediately before and immediately after that page. The default value of the counter `secnumdepth` is 2. This means that all sectional units with level numbers greater than or equal to 2 are numbered, that is to say, subsections and larger units. The default value of the counter `tocdepth` is 2. This means that all sectional units with level numbers greater than or equal to 2 appear in the table of contents if there is one, that is to say, subsections and larger units. This information is summarized in Table 6.2.

If you use the `equation` and `eqnarray` environments to generate equation numbers, then they are numbered consecutively throughout each chapter beginning with X.1—where X is the number of the chapter—and continuing with X.2, and so on. If any figures occur in your document, they are numbered consecutively throughout each chapter beginning with X.1—where X is the number of the chapter—and continuing with X.2, and so on. If any tables occur in your document, they are numbered consecutively throughout each chapter beginning with X.1—where X is the number of the chapter—and continuing with X.2, and so on. Note that there can be an equation, a figure and a table all numbered X.1, etc. Note also that if an `equation` or `eqnarray` environment, figure or table occurs before any `\chapter` command, then X will be 0.

The effect of an `\appendix` declaration is to alter the way in which chapters are labelled. The first `\chapter` command following the `\appendix` declaration is labelled 'A', the next 'B', and so on.

6.4   The `letter` Document Style

The letter displayed in Fig. 6.4 was produced by means of the commands shown in

27 Hudson Street,
Athens,
Wessex,
A26 7YY.

July 10, 1992

Dr Albert Grovenor,
"Appleblossom",
Whittington Green,
Hemlock.

Dear Albert,

Thank you very much for your letter of 30 June 1992 and the enclosed specimen. I carried out a full analysis—as you requested—but the results were so extraordinary that I can only give them to you in person.

Yours sincerely,

James Holmes

PS: I will be away on holiday until the 22nd.
cc: Mrs Dickens
    Prof. Cooper

Figure 6.4: Example of a letter formatted by LaTeX.

```
\documentstyle[11pt]{letter}
\address{27 Hudson Street,\\
         Athens,\\
         Wessex,\\
         A26 7YY.}
\signature{James Holmes}
\begin{document}
%
\begin{letter}{Dr Albert Grovenor,\\
              ''Appleblossom'',\\
              Whittington Green,\\
              Hemlock.}
\opening{Dear Albert,}
Thank you very much for your letter of 30 June 1992 and the
enclosed specimen.  I carried out a full analysis---as you
requested---but the results were so extraordinary that I can
only give them to you in person.
\closing{Yours sincerely,}
\ps{PS: I will be away on holiday until the 22nd.}
\cc{Mrs Dickens \\ Prof.~Cooper}
\end{letter}
%
\end{document}
```

Figure 6.5: Example of a use of the `letter` environment.

Fig. 6.5. Note that the sample output shown in Fig. 6.4 only gives a rough idea of what letters produced by LaTeX look like as it is not "drawn" to scale; the positioning of the various units of the letter on the page is only an approximation of what appears on the actual LaTeX output.

In order to get LaTeX to format letters you have to choose the `letter` document style. The address of the letter's sender is declared in the preamble by means of the `\address` command and the sender's name is declared there by means of the `\signature` command; end-of-line commands can occur in the arguments of both of these declarations. These letters can all be to different people, but LaTeX assumes that they all come from the same person writing from a single address. You can—but do not have to—use a `\date` command in the preamble to declare a date; if you do not do so, then LaTeX automatically inserts into the output the date on which you processed your input file. One reason for this is that you can include several `letter` environments within the document environment of a single LaTeX input file.

Inside the document environment each letter is produced by means of one letter environment. The name and address of the recipient of the letter is added as an argument to the command which opens the letter environment. The greeting is produced by the \opening command and the salutation by the closing command. A postscript is produced by the \ps command and carbon copies are indicated by \cc. Enclosures can be indicated by the \encl command. Note that the \cc and \encl commands produce 'cc:' and 'encl:' in the final document, but the \ps command does not produce 'PS'.

Inside the letter environment most commands are available; though some—like the sectioning commands—which make no sense in a letter cannot be used. Note that paragraphs are not indented, but rather extra space is inserted between them.

The only other command which is specific to the letter document style is the \makelabels command. This is a command that takes no arguments and which has to be placed in the preamble of the input file (if it is used at all). It causes a list of all the recipient addresses to be produced on a new page following all the letters generated. These can be photocopied onto sticky labels, if so desired, or cut up and glued or sellotaped on to envelopes.

7

Basic Mathematical Formatting

7.1 Introduction

As already mentioned, TeX was commissioned by the American Mathematical Society and one of its great strengths is its ability to correctly typeset mathematical formulas—even very complicated ones. When using TeX or LaTeX to produce mathematical formulas you must never forget that the mathematics you write should be correctly punctuated. This is well expressed in Hart (1983), pp. 56–57, as follows:

> A mathematical formula or equation, whether occurring in the text or displayed, should be regarded as in every way an integral part of the sentence in which it occurs, and be punctuated accordingly. Thus, individual formulae may be separated by commas, groups by semicolons, and where a formula occurs at the end of a sentence it should be followed by a full point.

Most people naturally punctuate in-text mathematical formulas correctly; but many people when they first start using TeX or LaTeX fail to correctly punctuate displayed formulas. These should be followed by a comma, semicolon or full stop as appropriate. For example, if you want to include the following formula in a document that you are writing:

$$\frac{d}{dx} \sinh^{-1} u = \frac{1}{\sqrt{u^2 + 1}}\frac{du}{dx},$$

then you must not forget the comma (or other appropriate punctuation mark) at the end. This displayed formula was produced by the following commands:

```
\[
\frac{d}{dx} \sinh^{-1} u =
\frac{1}{\sqrt{u^2 + 1}}\frac{du}{dx},
\]
```

(The meaning of the commands \frac, \sinh and \sqrt will be explained in due course.) You should notice two things particularly about these commands. The first is that the comma that comes at the end of the mathematical formula is followed by the command \] that ends the displayed math environment. It would be wrong to put the comma *after* that command, because the comma would not appear in the correct place. When typing in-text formulas, however, punctuation marks should come *after* the closing single dollar sign in order to ensure that the output looks correct.

The second thing that you should notice is that I did *not* punctuate the displayed LATEX commands. This is because the rule about punctuating *mathematical* formulas correctly does not apply to displayed computer programs or program fragments—nor does it apply to displayed chemical formulas—where there might be confusion between those punctuation marks that occur as part of the formula or program fragment being displayed and those punctuation marks that are part of the sentence in whose scope the formula or program fragment occurs. If I followed the LATEX commands above with a full stop, then you might think that that full stop was part of the input that you had to type in order to get LATEX to produce the mathematical formula displayed above.

Most primitive and plain TEX commands are available in LATEX and one consequence of this is that there are usually several different ways of producing the same formula. For example, the formula displayed above could also have been produced by means of the following TEX commands:[1]

```
$$
{d \over dx} \sinh^{-1} u =
{1 \over \sqrt{u^2 + 1}}{du \over dx},
$$
```

Note that the comma terminating this formula comes *before* the closing double dollar signs; it would be incorrect to put this comma *after* the closing double dollar signs. The only difference between using the constructs \[*form*\] and $$*form*$$ in order to produce a single displayed mathematical formula occurs if you choose the **fleqn** option to the \documentstyle command; in that case displayed formulas produced by the $$*form*$$ construct continue to be centred *but* displayed formulas produced by the \[*form*\] construct are no longer centred; they are instead indented from the left edge of the body region on the output page by the value of the rigid length parameter \mathindent.

7.2   Decorating Expressions

7.2.1   Introduction

People who use mathematical notation a lot like to decorate the symbols that they use in a variety of ways; in this section I explain how to get TEX to produce various

---

[1] The meaning of the command \over is explained in section 7.5 below.

kinds of accents, how to get it to underline and overline expressions and how to get
it to produce subscripts, superscripts and limits. The simplest kind of decoration is
the prime and to produce the primed version of a symbol you simply follow it with a
closing single quotation mark; thus x' produces x'. This can be iterated; thus to
get the doubly primed expression x'' you need the input $\text{\$x''\$}$.

7.2.2 Accents

It is common in mathematical writing to decorate symbols—especially variables—
with various sorts of accents. If you want TeX to produce, for example, the decorated
symbol $\ddot{z}$, then you need to include in your input file the commands $\text{\$\textbackslash ddot z\$}$. The
command \ddot places a dieresis over the next single character that follows it. Instead
of leaving a space between \ddot and the character it decorates you could use braces
around that character, thus $\text{\$\textbackslash ddot\{z\}\$}$ also produces $\ddot{z}$. TeX provides the following
accents in math mode:

output	input	output	input
$\acute{a}$	\acute a	$\dot{f}$	\dot f
$\bar{b}$	\bar b	$\grave{g}$	\grave g
$\breve{c}$	\breve c	$\hat{h}$	\hat h
$\check{d}$	\check d	$\tilde{\imath}$	\tilde \imath
$\ddot{e}$	\ddot e	$\vec{\jmath}$	\vec \jmath

This table also illustrates the use of the commands \imath and \jmath to produce a
dotless i and a dotless j in math mode. You should use these if you want to decorate
either letter with an accent.

All the above accents come in a single size and if you put any of them around
an expression consisting of more than a single symbol, then TeX just centres the
accent over the whole expression. Thus, the input $\text{\$\textbackslash tilde\{x + y\} = \textbackslash hat\{y + x\}\$}$
produces $\tilde{x + y} = \hat{y + x}$. However, TeX has two commands that produce accents that
grow depending on the size of the expression that they decorate. These commands are
\widehat and \widetilde and they each produce accents in three sizes:

output	input	output	input
$\widehat{k}$	\widehat{k}	$\widetilde{q}$	\widetilde{q}
$\widehat{lm}$	\widehat{lm}	$\widetilde{rs}$	\widetilde{rs}
$\widehat{nop}$	\widehat{nop}	$\widetilde{tuv}$	\widetilde{tuv}

Note that the commands \widehat and \widetilde do not produce accents of arbitrary size; they only produce the three sizes shown.

There are different TeX commands which are used for producing accents over letters
outside math mode and these are explained on p. 23 above.

7.2.3   Underlining, Overlining and Related Decorations

TeX has a variety of methods of decorating expressions of any size. They are illustrated in the following table:

output	input
$\overline{\phi \land \psi}$	\overline{\phi \land \psi}
$\underline{\phi \land \psi}$	\underline{\phi \land \psi}
$\overrightarrow{\phi \land \psi}$	\overrightarrow{\phi \land \psi}
$\overleftarrow{\phi \land \psi}$	\overleftarrow{\phi \land \psi}
$\overbrace{\phi \land \psi}$	\overbrace{\phi \land \psi}
$\underbrace{\phi \land \psi}$	\underbrace{\phi \land \psi}

7.2.4   Subscripts and Superscripts

To produce a subscripted expression like x_i you include in your input file x_i. Instead of using the underline character to produce subscripts it is also possible to use the command \sb. Thus, the subscripted formula x_i can also be produced by including $x\sb i$ in your input file. Braces (that is to say, curly brackets) are used to enclose an expression made up of several symbols that is to appear as a subscript. If no opening brace immediately follows the underline character, then only the next symbol is made into the subscript. Thus, x_γ,δ produces x_γ, δ whereas $x_{\gamma,\delta}$ produces $x_{\gamma,\delta}$. Superscripts are produced either by the caret symbol ^ or by the command \sp. Thus, both x^3 and $x\sp3$ produce x^3. With suitable changes, what was said above concerning subscripts also holds for superscripts.

Formulas sometimes have both subscripts and superscripts. To get x_i^3 you need to put in your input file either x_i^3 or x^3_i. When TeX produces a symbol which has both a subscript and a superscript the superscript is usually vertically above the subscript as in Γ_j^2 but this does not always happen. For example, in Γ_j^2 the subscript and superscript are not aligned vertically. In order to get such vertical alignment you need to type ${\mit\Gamma}{}_j^2$ which produces Γ_j^2. (The declaration \mit is a type-changing declaration that produces the *math italic* font.)

The subscripts and superscripts that you attach to symbols can themselves have subscripts and superscripts. Thus, 7^{x_i} produces 7^{x_i} and $\Delta_{x^\ast}$ produces $\Delta_{x^\ast}$. Note that the symbols used for subscripts and superscripts are smaller that those used for in-text and displayed formulas. This holds for most symbols and not just for letters and numerals. Note, for example, the size of the two plus signs and the parentheses in the expression $(x + y)^{(x+y)}$. (Note also that the amount of space either side of the two plus signs is also different.) If a subscript or superscript itself has a subscript or superscript, then that appears even smaller in the output; but additional subscripts or superscripts do not get smaller: TEX has just three different sizes of type available for typesetting mathematical formulas. To force TEX to use a different type size than it would by default you can use the commands \textstyle, \scriptstyle and \scriptscriptstyle. Thus, $(x+y)^{\textstyle(x+y)}$ produces $(x + y)^{(x + y)}$. Note that as well as using the same size of type for both the formula and superscript in this example the spacing around the plus signs is the same as well. In \scriptstyle and \scriptscriptstyle TEX has different rules to follow about spacing than in \textstyle and \displaystyle (which is the default for formulas displayed on a line by themselves). Spacing in mathematical formulas is fully discussed in the next chapter.

7.2.5 Combining Underlining and Overlining with Subscripts

Sometimes mathematical formulas combine underlining and overlining with subscripts as the following example from Munkres (1991), p. 100, illustrates:

$$\int_Q f = \int_{\mathbf{x} \in A} \underline{\int_{\mathbf{y} \in B}} f(\mathbf{x}, \mathbf{y}) = \int_{\mathbf{x} \in A} \overline{\int_{\mathbf{y} \in B}} f(\mathbf{x}, \mathbf{y}).$$

This is slightly tricky to produce, but the following commands do the job:

```
$$
\int_Q f = \int_{{\bf x} \in A}
\underline{\int_{\bf y}}_{\raise.75ex\hbox{$\scriptstyle{}\in B$}}
f ({\bf x}, {\bf y}) =
\int_{{\bf x} \in A}
\overline{\int_{\bf y}}_{\raise.5ex\hbox{$\scriptstyle{}\in B$}}
f ({\bf x}, {\bf y}).
$$
```

The primitive TEX command \raise*len box*—with no space separating the arguments *len* and *box*—raises *box* vertically by the distance *len*, which can be negative, and the \hbox command makes a horizontal box. The lengths .75ex and .5ex used here were found, by the way, by a process of trial-and-error.

7.2.6 Combining Subscripts with \underbrace and \overbrace

A subscripted expression attached to the \underbrace command produces a label underneath it and a superscripted expression attached to the \overbrace command produces a label on top of it. For example, the following expression (based on one that appears in Diller (1990), p. 28):

$$
\underbrace{\{ \overbrace{n \colon \mathbf{N}}^{\rm signature} \mid \overbrace{n \neq 0 \wedge n \bmod 2 = 0}^{\rm predicate} \bullet \overbrace{n}^{\rm term} \}}_{\rm set\ comprehension},
$$

was produced by the following commands:

```
$$
\underbrace{\{
\overbrace{\mathstrut n \colon {\bf N}}^{\rm signature}
\mid \overbrace{\mathstrut n \not= 0 \land
                n \bmod 2 = 0}^{\rm predicate}
\bullet \overbrace{\mathstrut n}^{\rm term}
\}}_{\rm set\ comprehension},
$$
```

The plain TEX command \mathstrut produces an empty box in math mode whose height is that of a parenthesis, that is to say, either (or), in the current type size; it is used here to ensure that the overbraces produced appear at the same height above the formulas over which they occur. Note also the need for the command \␣ in {\rm set\ comprehension}; this is needed because TEX is still in math mode inside these curly braces and so spacing is done as it is usually done in math mode.

7.2.7   Limits

Something that is quite common in some parts of mathematics is to place variables and more complicated expressions above and/or below other symbols. This happens, for example, in the following displayed formula:

$$
\sum_{i=1}^{i=n} i^2 = \frac{n(n+1)(2n+1)}{6}.
$$

Formulas like the $i=1$ and $i=n$ in this example I shall call *limits* for convenience. Limits are obtained using the same commands that produce subscripts and superscripts. Thus, the above formula was obtained using the following commands:

```
$$\sum_{i = 1}^{i = n} i^2 = {n (n + 1) (2n + 1) \over 6}.$$
```

If I want to include the above formula as an in-text one, then I need to use these commands:

```
$\sum_{i = 1}^{i = n} i^2 = {n (n + 1) (2n + 1) \over 6}$.
```

The only things that have changed are that I have replaced the double dollar signs of the previous example with single dollar signs and I have moved the full stop outside the closing single dollar sign whereas it was just before the closing double dollar signs in the previous case. In-text the formula to find the sum of the first n positive whole numbers looks like this: $\sum_{i=1}^{i=n} i^2 = \frac{n(n+1)(2n+1)}{6}$. Note that the expression that was the limit above the summation sign in the displayed formula has become a superscript in the in-text formula and the expression that was the limit below the summation sign in the displayed formula has become a subscript in the in-text formula. A further difference is that the summation sign itself is smaller in the in-text formula than in the displayed formula. (Yet another difference is that the fraction has changed size as well.) There are a number of mathematical symbols that behave like this and a complete list can be found in section A.3.

In order to produce the following example of the differentiation of an integral:

$$\frac{d}{dx} \int_{\sin x}^{\cos x} e^t dt = \cos x e^{\sin x} + \sin x e^{\cos x},$$

you need to include the following commands in your input file:

```
$$
{d \over dx} \int_{\sin x}^{\cos x} e^t dt
= \cos x e^{\sin x} + \sin x e^{\cos x},
$$
```

Some people may think that this formula looks better if the subscript and superscript to the integral sign appear as limits below and above it like this:

$$\frac{d}{dx} \int\limits_{\sin x}^{\cos x} e^t dt = \cos x e^{\sin x} + \sin x e^{\cos x}.$$

To obtain this the only change you need to make to the TEX commands displayed above is to replace `\int_{\sin x}^{\cos x}` with `\int\limits_{\sin x}^{\cos x}`. The command `\limits`—which comes *after* the command for the symbol that it is to act on—forces subscripted and superscripted expressions to appear as limits. It is most useful in display style but can also be used to force limits in text style. The related command `\nolimits` forces those expressions that would otherwise appear as upper limits to appear instead as subscripts and those expressions that would otherwise appear as lower limits to appear instead as superscripts. For example, the commands:

```
$$\sum\nolimits_{i = 1}^{i = n} i^3.$$
```

produce the following displayed formula:

$$\sum\nolimits_{i=1}^{i=n} i^3.$$

There is also a `\displaylimits` command which is similar to `\limits` except that if it occurs in text style, then the subscripted and superscripted expressions occur as subscripts and superscripts.

7.3   Definition by Cases

In order to produce the following definition by cases from Ore (1988), p. 293:

$$\lambda(2^\alpha) = 2^{\beta-2} \begin{cases} \beta = \alpha, & \text{when } \alpha \geq 3 \\ \beta = 3, & \text{when } \alpha = 2 \\ \beta = 2, & \text{when } \alpha = 1 \end{cases}$$

you need the following LaTeX commands:

```
\[
\lambda (2^\alpha) = 2^{\beta-2}
\left\{
\begin{array}{cl}
\beta = \alpha, & \mbox{when $\alpha \geq 3$} \\
\beta = 3, & \mbox{when $\alpha = 2$} \\
\beta = 2, & \mbox{when $\alpha = 1$}
\end{array}
\right.
\]
```

but in my opinion the plain TEX \cases command is both simpler and produces a better looking result:

$$\lambda(2^\alpha) = 2^{\beta-2} \begin{cases} \beta = \alpha, & \text{when } \alpha \geq 3 \\ \beta = 3, & \text{when } \alpha = 2 \\ \beta = 2, & \text{when } \alpha = 1 \end{cases}$$

This was produced by these commands:

```
$$
\lambda (2^\alpha) = 2^{\beta-2}
\cases{\beta = \alpha, & when $\alpha \ge 3$\cr
\beta = 3, & when $\alpha = 2$\cr
\beta = 2, & when $\alpha = 1$\cr}
$$
```

In the case of the plain TEX \cases command there is no need for an \mbox or \hbox command because what follows the ampersand is *not* processed in math mode.

7.4   Delimiters

7.4.1   Standard Expanding Bracket-like Symbols

TEX has a large variety of delimiters. The following table shows the six basic types of delimiters that come in pairs:

output	input	name
(x, y)	`$(x, y)$`	parentheses
$\{x, y\}$	`$\{x, y\}$`	braces or
	`$\lbrace x, y\rbrace$`	curly brackets
$[x, y]$	`$[x, y]$`	square brackets or
	`$\lbrack x, y\rbrack$`	(just) brackets
$\langle x, y \rangle$	`$\langle x, y\rangle$`	angle brackets
$\lceil x, y \rceil$	`$\lceil x, y\rceil$`	"ceiling" brackets
$\lfloor x, y \rfloor$	`$\lfloor x, y\rfloor$`	"floor" brackets

Angle brackets are *not* produced by the signs `<` and `>`. These produce the less-than and greater-than relation symbols. Curly braces are often used to represent sets when these are introduced either by enumeration or by abstraction as the following examples show:

$\{2, 3, 5, 7, 11\}$	`$\{2, 3, 5, 7, 11 \}$`
$\{\, x \mid x \le 100 \,\}$	`$\{\, x \mid x \le 100 \, \}$`
$\{\, x : x \le 100 \,\}$	`$\{\, x : x \le 100 \, \}$`

Note the command `\,` (which adds a thin amount of space) in the cases where sets are introduced by abstraction; this is the correct way of producing such expressions.

All the delimiters mentioned so far have a *natural size*; for example, typing `\{` without qualification in math mode—in text or display style—will always produce an opening or left curly brace of the same size. (Although the slash and backslash symbols are rarely if ever used as opening or closing delimiters, this is also true of them, that is to say, they too have a natural size.) Often in displayed mathematical formulas larger-sized delimiters are required. Not surprisingly, therefore, there is a mechanism in TeX for getting variable-sized delimiters in displayed formulas and its general format is:

`\left`*delim*$_1$ *form* `\right`*delim*$_2$

First, the formula *form* is processed and then delimiters of the correct size to fit around it are chosen automatically by TeX. For example, the commands:

`$$\sum_{i = 1}^n i^3 = \left( \sum_{i = 1}^n i \right)^2.$$`

produce the following displayed equation:

$$\sum_{i=1}^n i^3 = \left(\sum_{i=1}^n i \right)^2 .$$

Note that both `\left` and `\right` have to be present, but a full stop can take the place of either *delim*$_1$ or *delim*$_2$ and that results in no output.

$$\left(\begin{matrix}2&7&6\\9&5&1\\4&3&8\end{matrix}\right) \qquad \left\{\begin{matrix}2&7&6\\9&5&1\\4&3&8\end{matrix}\right\} \qquad \left[\begin{matrix}2&7&6\\9&5&1\\4&3&8\end{matrix}\right]$$

$$\left(\begin{matrix}2&7&6\\9&5&1\\4&3&8\end{matrix}\right\} \qquad \left\lceil\begin{matrix}2&7&6\\9&5&1\\4&3&8\end{matrix}\right\rceil \qquad \left\lfloor\begin{matrix}2&7&6\\9&5&1\\4&3&8\end{matrix}\right\rfloor$$

$$\left\uparrow\begin{matrix}2&7&6\\9&5&1\\4&3&8\end{matrix}\right\Uparrow \qquad \left\updownarrow\begin{matrix}2&7&6\\9&5&1\\4&3&8\end{matrix}\right\Updownarrow \qquad \left\downarrow\begin{matrix}2&7&6\\9&5&1\\4&3&8\end{matrix}\right\Downarrow$$

$$\left\rbrace\begin{matrix}2&7&6\\9&5&1\\4&3&8\end{matrix}\right\lbrace \qquad \left\vert\begin{matrix}2&7&6\\9&5&1\\4&3&8\end{matrix}\right\Vert \qquad \left\Vert\begin{matrix}2&7&6\\9&5&1\\4&3&8\end{matrix}\right\vert$$

$$\left\langle\begin{matrix}2&7&6\\9&5&1\\4&3&8\end{matrix}\right\rangle \qquad \left\vert\begin{matrix}2&7&6\\9&5&1\\4&3&8\end{matrix}\right\Vert \qquad \left\backslash\begin{matrix}2&7&6\\9&5&1\\4&3&8\end{matrix}\right/$$

Table 7.1: Delimiters in TeX (output).

As already mentioned, all the delimiters introduced so far have a natural size; there are, however, additional delimiters in TeX which do not have a natural size but which can occur in formulas if they are preceded—or qualified—by either a \left or \right command. All delimiters known to TeX—including those with a natural size and those without—are shown in Table 7.1 (and the commands that produce them are shown in Table 7.2; the **array** environment that occurs in the definition of \tempest is explained in section 7.6 below). The slash and backslash are included only for completeness; they rarely appear as opening or closing symbols—usually they appear in the middle of formulas representing binary operations. All the delimiters in Table 7.1—*except* the two angle brackets, the slash and the backslash—can grow to any size depending just on the size of the expression they enclose.

Note that the commands \uparrow, \Uparrow, \updownarrow, \Updownarrow, \downarrow, \Downarrow, \vert and \Vert do *not* produce delimiters unless they are preceded by either \left or \right. Note also that following either \left or \right the less-than sign < can take the place of \langle, the greater-than sign > can take the place of \rangle, the vertical line | can take the place of \vert and the command \| can take the place of \Vert.

```
\left(                \left\{               \left[
\tempest              \tempest              \tempest
\right)               \right\}              \right]


\left\lgroup          \left\lceil           \left\lfloor
\tempest              \tempest              \tempest
\right\rgroup         \right\rceil          \right\rfloor


\left\uparrow         \left\updownarrow     \left\downarrow
\tempest              \tempest              \tempest
\right\Uparrow        \right\Updownarrow    \right\Downarrow


\left\lmoustache      \left\arrowvert       \left\bracevert
\tempest              \tempest              \tempest
\right\rmoustache     \right\Arrowvert      \right\bracevert


\left\langle          \left\vert            \left\backslash
\tempest              \tempest              \tempest
\right\rangle         \right\Vert           \right/


                      \def\tempest%
                      {\begin{array}{ccc}
                      2 & 7 & 6 \\
                      9 & 5 & 1 \\
                      4 & 3 & 8
                      \end{array}}
```

Table 7.2: Delimiters in TEX (input).

7.5   Fractions and Fraction-like Structures

There are several ways in which you can produce a fraction in LATEX. It is possible to use the slash symbol /. Whereas the symbols for addition (+), multiplication (×) and division (÷) are binary operations, TEX treats / as an ordinary symbol because when used to represent division it is normal typesetting practice *not* to put any extra space either side of it. Fractions involving a horizontal line can be produced either by the

LATEX \frac command or by using the primitive TEX command \over as this example illustrates:

output   TEX   LATEX

$$\frac{n!}{i!(n-i)!}$$ {n!\over i!(n-i)!}   \frac{n!}{i!(n-i)!}

In my opinion the primitive TEX command is preferable because it fits into a family of commands for producing closely related spatial arrangements of symbols, as this table shows:

$$x \atop y$$ $$\frac{x}{y}$$ $$x \above y$$

{x \atop y}   {x \over y}   {x \above 2pt y}

$$\binom{x}{y}$$ $$\left[x \atop y\right]$$ $$\left\{x \atop y\right\}$$

{x \choose y}   {x \brack y}   {x \brace y}

Furthermore, if you wanted to produce this:

$$\left\langle x \atop y \right\rangle,$$

then you would need the commands:

    $${x \atopwithdelims\langle\rangle y},$$

In fact, the plain TEX commands \choose, \brack and \brace are defined in terms of the primitive TEX command \atopwithdelims.

As a further example of the \over command, the formula from Ramanujan displayed in chapter 1 and reproduced here:[2]

$$\cfrac{1}{1+\cfrac{e^{-2\pi\sqrt{5}}}{1+\cfrac{e^{-4\pi\sqrt{5}}}{1+\cfrac{e^{-6\pi\sqrt{5}}}{1+\ddots}}}} = \left(\frac{\sqrt{5}}{1+\sqrt[5]{5^{3/4}\left(\frac{\sqrt{5}-1}{2}\right)^{5/2}-1}} - \frac{\sqrt{5}+1}{2}\right) e^{2\pi/\sqrt{5}},$$

was produced by the following commands:

---

[2] An alternative way of producing this in TEX is given in Borde (1992), p. 63, where it is equation (11).

```
$$
{1 \over\displaystyle 1 +
   {\strut e^{-2\pi\sqrt{5}} \over\displaystyle 1 +
     {\strut e^{-4\pi\sqrt{5}} \over\displaystyle 1 +
       {\strut e^{-6\pi\sqrt{5}} \over\displaystyle 1 +
{\rule{0mm}{2mm} \makebox[5mm]{} \atop \ddots}}}}}
=
\left( {\sqrt{5} \over 1 + \sqrt[5]{5^{3/4}}
\left( {\sqrt{5} - 1 \over 2} \right)^{5/2} - 1}} -
{\sqrt{5} + 1 \over 2} \right) e^{2\pi / \sqrt{5}}.
$$
```

The command \strut used here is similar to the \mathstrut command mentioned
above; it generates an invisible box with no width whose height is the normal distance
between baselines.

7.6   The array Environment

7.6.1   Introduction

The array environment that is available in LaTeX is a very flexible way of producing
regular two-dimensional arrangements of mathematical symbols such as tables and
matrices. (The use of the word 'regular' is meant to suggest that the arrangement of
symbols is made up out of rows and/or columns of symbols—or other arrays—in a
fairly obvious way. When this is not the case you are probably better off using the
picture environment.) In my opinion the flexibility of the array environment is both
its main strength and also its major weakness. It is its main strength because it is
very good for producing fairly complicated or unusual one-off spatial arrangements
of symbols and it is its main weakness because when used to typeset such common
patterns of symbols as occur, for example, in matrices and definition by cases, then
the results are not always typeset correctly. (See section 7.7 for an alternative way of
producing matrices and section 7.3 for an alternative way of producing definition by
cases.) And although the array environment is very flexible it is unable to produce
some standard arrangements of symbols such as labelled matrices. (See p. 109 below
for how to get these.)

Note that the array environment is very similar to the tabular environment described in section 4.8 and all the features of that environment also work with the array
environment, so not all of them will be described again here; the main difference is
that the array environment can only be used in math mode and the entries in the
array are themselves (usually) processed in math mode.

7.6.2   Simple Matrix Equations

Although—as I shall show below in section 7.7—there are better ways of producing matrices than by using the `array` environment, it can be used to typeset them. For example, the following matrix equation (based on equation (23.2) in Patterson and Rutherford (1965), p. 62):

$$
\begin{bmatrix} y_1 \\ y_2 \\ \vdots \\ y_p \end{bmatrix}
=
\begin{bmatrix}
a_{11} & a_{12} & \cdots & a_{1q} \\
a_{21} & a_{22} & \cdots & a_{2q} \\
\vdots & \vdots & \ddots & \vdots \\
a_{p1} & a_{p2} & \cdots & a_{pq}
\end{bmatrix}
\begin{bmatrix} x_1 \\ x_2 \\ \vdots \\ x_q \end{bmatrix},
$$

is produced by means of these commands:

```
$$
\left[\begin{array}{c}
     y_1 \\ y_2 \\ \vdots \\ y_p
     \end{array}\right] =
\left[\begin{array}{cccc}
     a_{11} & a_{12} & \cdots & a_{1q} \\
     a_{21} & a_{22} & \cdots & a_{2q} \\
     \vdots & \vdots & \ddots & \vdots \\
     a_{p1} & a_{p2} & \cdots & a_{pq}
     \end{array}\right]
\left[\begin{array}{c}
     x_1 \\ x_2 \\ \vdots \\ x_q
     \end{array}\right],
$$
```

The commands `\vdots`, `\cdots` and `\ddots` are only available in math mode and there they produce ellipses consisting of three vertical dots, three centred dots and three diagonal dots, respectively.

In the opening of the `array` environment there must always be a *preamble*.[3] For example, `\begin{array}{c}` contains the single letter c as its preamble and in the command `\begin{array}{cccc}` the preamble is cccc. The single letter c in the preamble means that the array produced contains just a single column of entries and all the entries on all the rows are centred. In the case when the preamble is cccc this means that the array produced will consist of four columns of entries and entries in each column will be centred. In addition to c you can also use either l or r. The argument l means that the entries in that column will be typeset flush left and r means that they will be typeset flush right.

The actual rows of the array are separated by double backslashes \\, but it is a mistake to end the final row of the array with a double backslash (unless it is followed

---

[3] Note that any valid `tabular` environment *preamble* is also a valid `array` environment *preamble* with the same meaning. So, everything I said about `tabular` preambles in section 4.8 is also correct for `array` preambles.

by a \hline or \cline command). Entries within rows are separated by ampersands
&. So, if your array has n columns, you will need $n - 1$ ampersands and it would be a
mistake to use more or less than this number of ampersands. Note that the use of one
or more \multicolumn commands may decrease the number of ampersands required.

You can use declarations within the entries of the array but their scope—unless they
are global—is restricted to the entry in which they occur. In other words, their scope
is terminated by the next &, \\ or \end{array} command or symbol. For example:

$$
\begin{array}{ccc}
$\Phi \quad \Psi \quad B$

$\Gamma \quad \Gamma \quad S$

$T \quad A \quad Z$
$$

```
$$
\begin{array}{ccc}
\bf \Phi     & \Psi    & B \\
\mit\Gamma & \Gamma & \cal S \\
T            & \rm A  & Z
\end{array}
$$
```

7.6.3   Tables of Values

The following table of the values of the function x^x:

x	0.1	0.2	0.3	0.4	0.5	0.6	0.7	0.8	0.9	1.0
x^x	0.794	0.725	0.697	0.693	0.707	0.736	0.779	0.837	0.910	1.0

was produced by the following commands:

```
$$
\arraycolsep=4pt
\begin{array}{|l||*{10}{r@{.}l|}} \hline
x & 0 & 1 & 0 & 2 & 0 & 3 & 0 & 4 & 0 & 5 &
    0 & 6 & 0 & 7 & 0 & 8 & 0 & 9 & 1 & 0 \\ \hline
%
x^x & 0 & 794 & 0 & 725 & 0 & 697 & 0 & 693 & 0 & 707 &
    0 & 736 & 0 & 779 & 0 & 837 & 0 & 910 & 1 & 0 \\ \hline
\end{array}
$$
```

The value of the rigid length parameter \arraycolsep is half the amount of horizontal
space placed between the columns produced by the **array** environment. The presence
of a vertical bar in the preamble produces a vertical line in the array produced and the
expression *{i}{*pre*} is equivalent to i copies of *pre* where this is any legitimate combination of preamble commands. The @-expression @{.} that occurs in the preamble
of the array above has the effect of inserting a full stop in every row; a further effect of
@-expressions in general is that their presence removes space normally inserted between
columns.

The following proof is from Diller (1990), p. 112:

$$
\begin{array}{lrll}
1 & (1) & P & ass \\
2 & (2) & P \Rightarrow Q & ass \\
1,2 & (3) & Q & 1,2 \; \Rightarrow\text{-}elim \\
4 & (4) & Q \Rightarrow R & ass \\
1,2,4 & (5) & R & 3,4 \; \Rightarrow\text{-}elim \\
2,4 & (6) & P \Rightarrow R & 5 \; \Rightarrow\text{-}int
\end{array}
$$

It was produced by means of the following commands:

```
$$
\begin{array}{lrll}
1        & (1) & P         & \ass \\
2        & (2) & P \imp Q & \ass \\
1, 2     & (3) & Q         & 1, 2\ \impelim \\
4        & (4) & Q \imp R & \ass \\
1, 2, 4 & (5) & R         & 3, 4\ \impelim \\
2, 4     & (6) & P \imp R & 5\ \impint
\end{array}
$$
```

The commands \ass, \imp, \impelim and \impint are to be understood as having been defined like this:

```
\def\ass{{\it ass}}
\def\imp{\mathbin\Rightarrow}
\def\impelim{\hbox{$\imp$-\it elim}}
\def\impint{\hbox{$\imp$-\it int}}
```

The meaning and significance of the command \mathbin is explained in the next chapter.

7.6.4   General Format

The general format of the command that opens the **array** environment is:

```
\begin{array}[pos]{preamble}
```

Here, *pos* is an optional parameter which can be either **t** or **b**. Associated with every mathematical expression and formula is an imaginary line—known as the *axis*—at the height at which a minus sign would go. This is also true of the box produced by an **array** environment. The imaginary line is roughly half way between the top and bottom of the resulting spatial arrangement of symbols, but it can be altered by including a *pos* parameter. The actual parameter **t** makes the imaginary line associated with the first row of the array into the imaginary line of the whole array; whereas **b** makes the imaginary line associated with the last row of the array into the imaginary line of the whole array. Sensible examples of this are difficult to think of, so here is a silly one:

$$
\begin{array}{cc}
 & u & v \\
1 \; 2 \; = & w & x \\
3 \; 4
\end{array}
$$

```
$$
\begin{array}[t]{cc}
1 & 2 \\ 3 & 4
\end{array} =
\begin{array}[b]{cc}
u & v \\ w & x
\end{array}
$$
```

7.6.5   The \multicolumn Command

The \multicolumn command was explained in connection with the tabular environment in subsection 4.8.2 below; it is very useful in putting lines inside a matrix and I present two examples of that here. The following array comes from Munkres (1991), p. 8:

$$
C = \left[\begin{array}{cccccc}
1 & 0 & * & 0 & * & * \\
0 & 1 & * & 0 & * & * \\
0 & 0 & 0 & 1 & * & * \\
0 & 0 & 0 & 0 & 0 & 0
\end{array} \right].
$$

It was produced in the book you are reading now by these commands:

```
$$
\def\temp{\multicolumn{1}{c|}{0}}
C = \left[
\begin{array}{cccccc}
1      & 0 & \ast  & 0 & \ast & \ast \\ \cline{1-1}
\temp & 1 & \ast  & 0 & \ast & \ast \\ \cline{2-3}
0      & 0 & \temp & 1 & \ast & \ast \\ \cline{4-6}
0      & 0 & 0     & 0 & 0    & 0
\end{array}
\right].
$$
```

This is from p. 20 of Munkres (1991):

$$
\det \left[\begin{array}{c|c}
\begin{array}{cccc} b & 0 & \ldots & 0 \end{array} & \\
\begin{array}{c} a_2 \\ \vdots \\ a_n \end{array} & D
\end{array} \right] = b(\det D).
$$

It was produced in the book you are now reading by the following commands:

```
$$
\def\tempa{\multicolumn{1}{|c}{}}
\def\tempb{\multicolumn{1}{c|}{}}
%
\det \left[\begin{array}{cccc}
b       & 0        & \ldots & 0        \\ \cline{2-4}
a_2     & \tempa &         & \tempb \\
\vdots & \tempa & D       & \tempb \\
a_n     & \tempa &         & \tempb \\ \cline{2-4}
\end{array}\;\right] = b (\det D).
$$
```

7.7   Matrices in TEX

In my opinion the plain TEX \matrix and related commands are much more convenient
for producing matrices that LATEX's array environment.[4] Compare, for example, the
following ways of producing a 3-by-3 matrix:

TEX   LATEX

$$
\begin{bmatrix} 2 & 7 & 6 \\ 9 & 5 & 1 \\ 4 & 3 & 8 \end{bmatrix}
\qquad
\begin{bmatrix} 2 & 7 & 6 \\ 9 & 5 & 1 \\ 4 & 3 & 8 \end{bmatrix}
$$


```
$$
\left[
\matrix{2 & 7 & 6\cr
        9 & 5 & 1\cr
        4 & 3 & 8\cr}
\right]
$$
```

```
\[
\left[
\begin{array}{ccc}
2 & 7 & 6\\
9 & 5 & 1\\
4 & 3 & 8
\end{array}
\right]
\]
```

Because matrices with large parentheses surrounding them are so common plain TEX
contains a \pmatrix command for producing them. Compare, for example, the following two ways of producing such a matrix:

---

[4] You can use the plain TEX commands mentioned in this section in any LATEX input file and they will be
correctly processed.

TEX   LATEX

$$
\begin{pmatrix} 2 & 7 & 6 \\ 9 & 5 & 1 \\ 4 & 3 & 8 \end{pmatrix}
\qquad\qquad
\begin{pmatrix} 2 & 7 & 6 \\ 9 & 5 & 1 \\ 4 & 3 & 8 \end{pmatrix}
$$

```
$$
\pmatrix{2 & 7 & 6\cr
         9 & 5 & 1\cr
         4 & 3 & 8\cr}
$$
```

```
\[
\left(
\begin{array}{ccc}
2 & 7 & 6\\
9 & 5 & 1\\
4 & 3 & 8
\end{array}
\right)
\]
```

Plain TEX also has a \bordermatrix command for producing labelled matrices. There probably is a way of producing this in LATEX:

$$
\bordermatrix{ & c_1 & c_2 & c_3 \cr
r_1 & 2 & 7 & 6 \cr
r_2 & 9 & 5 & 1 \cr
r_3 & 4 & 3 & 8 }
$$

but the following plain TEX commands suffice:

```
$$
\bordermatrix{& c_1 & c_2 & c_3 \cr
        r_1 & 2 & 7 & 6 \cr
        r_2 & 9 & 5 & 1 \cr
        r_3 & 4 & 3 & 8 \cr}
$$
```

Note the use of the primitive TEX command \cr inside the arguments of the \matrix, \pmatrix and \bordermatrix commands in order to end the current line; do not use this command with any LATEX commands or environments. Note also that unlike \\ the command \cr has to come at the end of the final line of the array.

7.8   Equation Arrays and Labelling Formulas

The following bracket abstraction algorithm comes from Diller (1988), p. 96:

$$
\begin{aligned}
[x]E   &= \mathbf{K}E, \\
[x]x   &= \mathbf{I}, \\
[x]Ex &= E, \\
[x]EX &= \mathbf{B}E([x]X), \\
[x]XE &= \mathbf{C}([x]X)E, \\
[x]XY &= \mathbf{S}([x]X)([x]Y).
\end{aligned}
$$

You should notice that it is correctly punctuated. Just because you are writing mathematics does not mean that you should forget everything you have ever learnt about punctuation. In LaTeX this sort of equation array is produced by the following commands:

```
\begin{eqnarray*}
{[x]} E    & = &  {\bf K} E, \\
{[x]} x    & = &  {\bf I}, \\
{[x]} E x  & = &  E, \\
{[x]} E X  & = &  {\bf B} E ([x] X), \\
{[x]} X E  & = &  {\bf C} ([x] X) E, \\
{[x]} X Y  & = &  {\bf S} ([x] X) ([x] Y).
\end{eqnarray*}
```

The `eqnarray*` environment produces an equation array in which no line is labelled. The result is rather like using an **array** environment with preamble `rcl`; except that the expressions in the first and third columns are typeset in display style, whereas the expression in the second column is typeset in text style; and the `\multicolumn` command cannot be used inside the `eqnarray*` environment. The end of a row is indicated by the control symbol `\\` and the items in each of the three columns are separated by ampersands `&`. There is no need for an end-of-line control symbol at the end of the final line. If added, then an extra blank line will be produced. The `\lefteqn` command can be used inside an `eqnarray*` (or `eqnarray`) environment in order to produce a formula that LaTeX thinks is zero inches wide.

Note that the characters `[x]` have been enclosed in curly brackets. This is because the end-of-line control symbol can take an optional parameter which is interpreted as indicating the amount of vertical space to be left between this line and the previous one.

To produce a single displayed mathematical formula with a numerical label you need to use the **equation** environment. Thus, the labelled formula:

$$(x + y)(x - y) = x^2 - y^2. \tag{7.1}$$

was produced by the following commands:

```
\begin{equation}
(x + y)(x - y) = x^2 - y^2.
\label{AA}
\end{equation}
```

Note that the label is generated automatically. It would still have been produced even if the \label command were not present. The function of the \label command is to enable you to refer to this formula from other parts of the piece that you are writing. The general format of the \label command is \label{*key*}, where *key* is any sequence of letters, numerals and punctuation marks, that is to say, the 16 characters that LATEX regards as punctuation marks. Lowercase and uppercase letters are treated as being distinct, thus **aa** and **AA** are different keys. To refer to a labelled formula containing a \label{*key*} command you use a \ref{*key*} command. Thus, (\ref{AA}) produces (7.1). Note that in referring to formulas labelled with a \label command using \ref you have to add the parentheses yourself; they are not produced automatically by LATEX. If you want to refer to the page on which this formula occurs, then use the \pageref command; for example, p.~\pageref{AA} produces 'p. 110'. The tilde just inserts the normal amount of inter-word space, but it inhibits line-breaking.

By default the labels generated automatically by LATEX are placed on the extreme right-hand side of the output page. If you want the numerical labels to be placed on the extreme left-hand side of the output page instead, then you must use the leqno option to the \documentstyle command.

In order to produce a number of displayed and numbered equations you can use the eqnarray environment. For example, the commands:

```
\begin{eqnarray}
(x + y + z)^2 & = & (x + y + z) (x + y + z), \label{BB} \\
& = & x^2 + 2xy + y^2 \nonumber \\
&   & \qquad \mbox{} + 2yz + z^2 + 2zx. \label{CC}
\end{eqnarray}
```

produce the following labelled series of displayed equations:

$$
\begin{aligned}
(x + y + z)^2 &= (x + y + z)(x + y + z), &\quad (7.2)\\
&= x^2 + 2xy + y^2 \\
&\quad + 2yz + z^2 + 2zx. &\quad (7.3)
\end{aligned}
$$

The \nonumber command inhibits the automatic production of a label on the line where it occurs.

7.9 Axioms, Postulates, Definitions, Lemmas, Propositions, Theorems and Corollaries

Ever since Euclid wrote the *Elements* around 300 BC the axiomatic presentation of results has been very popular; not only with mathematicians, but also with logicians, scientists and philosophers.[5] The \newtheorem declaration allows you to carry on writing in this tradition. For example, the declaration:

```
\newtheorem{definition}{Definition}
```

defines two things, namely a new environment called definition and also a counter with the same name. This declaration can go anywhere in your input file, but it makes most sense to either put it in the preamble or in your own style file. The definition environment created by the above declaration is used like any other built-in environment. Thus the commands:

```
\begin{definition}
A {\bf point} is that which has no part.
\end{definition}
```

which the reader will recognize to be Euclid's first definition in the *Elements*—Euclid (1956), p. 153—produce:

Definition 1 *A **point** is that which has no part.*

If we wanted to include Euclid's 5th definition out of sequence, we would need the commands:

```
\setcounter{definition}{4}
\begin{definition}
A {\bf surface} is that which has length and breadth only.
\end{definition}
```

These produce the following, from Euclid (1956), p. 153:

---

[5] The *Elements*—Euclid (1956)—still make interesting reading today; which of our writings will continue to be read in 4286? The way in which mathematical results are arrived at is very different from the way in which they are conventionally reported in academic papers and books; Lakatos, especially, has stressed this. For more information see Lakatos (1976) and Lakatos (1978); Hallett (1979a) and Hallett (1979b) are also useful. Gjertsen (1989), pp. 117–129, traces some of the deleterious effects of Euclid's work on philosophy and science; though, surprisingly, he does not mention Lakatos.

Definition 5 *A* **surface** *is that which has length and breadth only.*

It is possible to define several new environments in the same input file with the \newtheorem declaration. In addition to the definition environment already mentioned we could create a common environment for common notions and a prop environment for propositions:

```
\newtheorem{common}{\sc Common notion}
\newtheorem{post}{Postulate}
\newtheorem{prop}{Proposition}
```

If we did this, then the first time we used the common environment the common notion produced would be labelled 1 and the second time we used it the common notion produced would be labelled 2 and so on. Similarly, with the prop environment. For example, the commands:

```
\setcounter{common}{4}
\begin{common}
The whole is greater than the part.
\end{common}
```

produce the following common notion, from Euclid (1956), p. 155:

COMMON NOTION 5 *The whole is greater than the part.*

And the commands:

```
\setcounter{post}{4}
\begin{post}
\rm
That, if a straight line falling on two straight lines
make the interior angles on the same side less than two
right angles, the two straight lines, if produced indefinitely,
meet on that side on which are the angles less than the two
right angles.
\end{post}
```

produce, also from Euclid (1956), p. 155:

Postulate 5 That, if a straight line falling on two straight lines make the interior angles on the same side less than two right angles, the two straight lines, if produced indefinitely, meet on that side on which are the angles less than the two right angles.

And the commands:

```
\setcounter{prop}{4}
\begin{prop}
\rm
In isosceles triangles the angles at the base are equal to one
another, and, if the equal straight lines be produced further,
the angles under the base will be equal to one another.
\end{prop}
```

produce the following proposition, from Euclid (1956), p. 251:

Proposition 5 In isosceles triangles the angles at the base are equal to one another, and, if the equal straight lines be produced further, the angles under the base will be equal to one another.

The numbering of definitions, common notions and propositions would normally be entirely independent of one another. Sometimes, however, we might like to have our definitions, common notions and propositions all numbered consecutively in the same sequence. This would be achieved by means of the following declarations:

```
\newtheorem{definition}{Definition}
\newtheorem{common}[definition]{\sc Common notion}
\newtheorem{prop}[definition]{Proposition}
```

By default when environments created by the **\newtheorem** declaration are used then the numbering is continuous throughout the entire document that is produced. Thus, if you are using the **\newtheorem** declaration in a book to define a **definition** environment, then if the last use of this environment in the first chapter generated the number 15, then the first use of this environment in the second chapter will generate the number 16. You can, however, have your definitions numbered consecutively within chapters. This is achieved by giving the **\newtheorem** declaration an additional parameter which is the name of the sectional unit within which you want definitions, for example, to be numbered. For example, the declaration:

```
\newtheorem{definition}{Definition}[chapter]
```

would—in the situation described earlier—result in the first definition of chapter 2 being numbered 2.1. The two optional arguments can be combined like this:

```
\newtheorem{definition}{Definition}[chapter]
\newtheorem{common}[definition]{\sc Common notions}
```

but both optional arguments *cannot* be present together.

The environments created by the \newtheorem declaration can take an optional argument as the following example—from Euclid (1956), p. 349—shows:

Proposition 47 (Pythagoras) *In right-angled triangles the square on the side subtending the right angle is equal to the squares on the sides containing the right angle.*

This was produced by means of these commands:

```
\setcounter{prop}{46}
\begin{prop}[Pythagoras]
In right-angled triangles the square on the side subtending
the right angle is equal to the squares on the sides containing
the right angle.
\end{prop}
```

8

Further Ideas in Mathematical Formatting

8.1 Introduction

There are a large number of built-in mathematical symbols available in TeX and complete lists of them are provided in appendix A. Many people who use TeX and LaTeX find, however, that sometimes they want to make use of symbols in addition to those that are provided by default; in section 8.3 I explain some of the ways in which it is possible to define your own idiosyncratic symbols. In order to do this correctly, however, you need to know something about the "classes" or "categories" to which TeX assigns different mathematical symbols; for example, the plus sign and the set union symbol ∪ belong to the category of binary operation symbols, whereas the equals sign and the subset symbol ⊆ belong to the category of binary relation symbols. Without this information you are likely to mess things up when you try to introduce your own symbols; therefore, most of the categories of symbol known to TeX are explained in section 8.2. In subsection 8.2.3 I list many pairs of symbols which look the same and yet belong to different categories; if you use the wrong one, your output is likely going to look wrong.

In section 8.4 I turn my attention to a different topic and that is the reinstatement and use of the plain TeX commands `\eqalign`, `\eqalignno` and `\leqalignno`. Lamport says that these commands are made obsolete by the `eqnarray` and `eqnarray*` environments that are available in LaTeX; however, there are a number of things that cannot be done by those LaTeX environments that can be done by the more "primitive" TeX commands. I state what those things are and then explain how to use these TeX commands.

kind of atom	name	example	command
ordinary	Ord	`\lambda`	`\mathord`
large operator	Op	`\bigsqcup`	`\mathop`
binary operation	Bin	`\oslash`	`\mathbin`
relation	Rel	`\succ`	`\mathrel`
opening	Open	`\lceil`	`\mathopen`
closing	Close	`\rceil`	`\mathclose`
punctuation	Punct	`,`	`\mathpunct`
inner	Inner	`{1 \over 2}`	`\mathinner`

Table 8.1: Kinds of math atoms.

	Ord	Op	Bin	Rel	Open	Close	Punct	Inner
Ord	0	1	(2)	(3)	0	0	0	(1)
Op	1	1	*	(3)	0	0	0	(1)
Bin	(2)	(2)	*	*	(2)	*	*	(2)
Rel	(3)	(3)	*	0	(3)	0	0	(3)
Open	0	0	*	0	0	0	0	0
Close	0	1	(2)	(3)	0	0	0	(1)
Punct	(1)	(1)	*	(1)	(1)	(1)	(1)	(1)
Inner	(1)	1	(2)	(3)	(1)	0	(1)	(1)

Table 8.2: Spacing between different math atoms.

8.2 Spacing in Mathematical Formulas

8.2.1 Introduction

If you look carefully at a mathematical formula like the following:[1]

$$x = 12 - 2y + t = 14 - 3t,$$

you will notice that the amount of space between a symbol for a binary relation (like the equals sign) and its operands is slightly larger than the amount of space for a binary operation (like the plus sign) and its operands. In fact, TEX puts a thick amount of space between a symbol for a binary relation and its operands—if these are numerals or variables—and a medium amount of space between a symbol for a binary operation and its operands—again, if these are numerals or variables. A thick amount of space is normally five eighteenths of a quad and a medium amount of space is normally two ninths of a quad, where a quad is a horizontal amount of space one em wide. In the following formula:

$$\sin \theta = \sin(\theta + 2\pi),$$

TEX puts a thin amount of space—normally one sixth of a quad—between the function name 'sin' and its argument θ, but it puts no space between the function name and a following opening symbol.

In order to decide how much space to put between different sorts of symbol TEX partitions symbols—or atoms, as they are also known—into *kinds*; the most important of these are shown in Table 8.1.[2] (Complete lists of mathematical symbols—grouped according to their kind—are included in appendix A.) In Table 8.2—reproduced from Knuth (1986), p. 170—the numbers 0, 1, 2 and 3 indicate how much space is inserted between atoms of different types.[3] Thus, if you look in the table for the entry corresponding to an atom of type Close followed by one of type Ord (that is to say, you pick the entry where the row labelled Close intersects the column labelled Ord), you will find the number 0. This means that no space is inserted between atoms of these types when they occur in that order in a math formula. The number 1 indicates that a thin amount of space is inserted, 2 means that a medium amount of space is inserted and 3 means that a thick amount of space is inserted. Some of the entries in the table are parenthesized: an entry (i) means that space corresponding to the number i is inserted between these atoms in display and text style, but no space is inserted between them

---

[1] This is taken from Ore (1988), p. 127.

[2] There are actually thirteen different kinds of atom in TEX; for a detailed discussion of them—and also a precise definition of what constitutes an atom—see Knuth (1986), pp. 157–159.

[3] Note that the entries in Table 8.2 are exactly the same as those that occur in Knuth (1986), p. 170; many writers on TEX reproduce this table, but some with differences from Knuth's version. Thus, in the version of Eijkhout (1992), p. 196, the entries corresponding to a Rel atom followed by either an Open, Close, Punct or Inner atom are different from those shown in Table 8.2 and in the version of Krieger and Schwarz (1989), p. 135, the authors have the value (3) in six entries corresponding to a Close, Punct and Inner atom being followed by either a Bin or Rel atom.

style	normal	cramped
display	D	D'
text	T	T'
script	S	S'
scriptscript	SS	SS'

Table 8.3: Notation for styles of mathematical formulas.

superscript	S	S'	S	S'	SS	SS'	SS	SS'
formula	D	D'	T	T'	S	S'	SS	SS'
subscript	S'	S'	S'	S'	SS'	SS'	SS'	SS'

Table 8.4: Relative styles of subscripts and superscripts.

in script or scriptscript style. For example, if you look at this formula:

$$\sum_{i=1}^{i=n} i = \frac{n(n+1)}{2},$$

you will notice that in the limits of the summation sign—which TeX treats like a subscript and a superscript—no space has been inserted between the equals sign and its operands. A star $*$ occurs in some of the entries in Table 8.2. Concerning these Knuth (1986), p. 170, writes that 'such cases never arise, because Bin atoms must be preceded and followed by atoms compatible with the nature of binary operations.' And Eijkhout (1992), p. 196, explains that the reason why the $*$ cases cannot arise is because in those cases the Bin atom is converted to an Ord atom. Thus, in the expression $(2+)$ TeX regards the $+$ as being an Ord atom.

8.2.2   Styles of Mathematical Formulas

TeX uses three different sizes of type for producing mathematical formulas; they are text size, script size and scriptscript size. And it can typeset formulas in eight different styles, namely the normal and cramped versions of display, text, script and scriptscript

numerator α	T	T'	S	S'	SS	SS'	SS	SS'
α \over β	D	D'	T	T'	S	S'	SS	SS'
denominator β	T'	T'	S'	S'	SS'	SS'	SS'	SS'

Table 8.5: Relative styles of numerators and denominators.

style. The abbreviations for these that Knuth (1986), p. 140, uses are shown in Table 8.3. The cramped versions are very similar to the normal versions except that superscripts are not raised so high.

Tables 8.4 and 8.5 tell you in which style TEX typesets subscripts, superscripts, numerators and denominators. For example, if a formula containing a subscript and superscript is being typeset in cramped text style, that is to say, T', we look at Table 8.4 and find the occurrence of T' in the middle row; this tells us that both the subscript and superscript are typeset in cramped script style S'. TEX also contains the declarations `\displaystyle`, `\textstyle`, `\scriptstyle` and `\scriptscriptstyle` which force what follows them to be typeset in the style that the name of the command suggests.

8.2.3   Confusables

In books on English usage you will often find a section listing pairs of words that are often confused. For example, the differences between the following pairs of words might be explained: complementary/complimentary, principal/principle, shall/will, stationary/stationery, and so on. Here I do something similar for certain pairs of TEX's commands for mathematical symbols.

`\colon` and :

The colon : in math mode is not treated as a punctuation symbol. It is regarded as being a symbol for a binary relation. One consequence of this is that the following patterns of symbols are easy to generate:

$p:q::r:s$ `$p:q::r:s$`
$X := X + 7$ `$X := X + 7$`

If you want to use the colon as a punctuation symbol in math mode, then you must call it `\colon`. Note the difference in the following two formulas:

$f:X \to Y$ `$f \colon X \to Y$`
$f : X \to Y$ `$f : X \to Y$`

I used to think that the second of these was incorrect—as suggested by Knuth (1986), pp. 134 and 438—but now I am not so sure as in some contexts 'is of type' and 'is an element of' are virtually synonymous.

`\setminus` and `\backslash`

The command `\setminus` produces a symbol for a binary relation which is used to represent set difference; whereas `\backslash` produces an ordinary symbol used, for example, to represent the double cosets of G by H or the fact that p divides n.

$\Gamma \setminus \Delta$ `$\Gamma \setminus \Delta$`
$G\backslash H$ `$G \backslash H$`
$p\backslash n$ `$p \backslash n$`

\mid and | or \vert

The command \mid produces the binary relation symbol |; whereas the command \vert (or the symbol |) produces an ordinary symbol. Following \left or \right, however, \vert and | produce a delimiter that can grow to any size.

\parallel and \| or \Vert

The command \parallel produces the binary relation symbol ||; whereas the command \Vert (or the command \|) produces an ordinary symbol. Following \left or \right, however, \Vert and \| produce a delimiter that can grow to any size.

\langle and <

The command \langle produces an opening symbol (or left delimiter) that looks like ⟨; whereas < produces a symbol for a binary relation and should not be used for an opening angle bracket. After \left or \right, however, \langle and < can be used interchangeably and the result is a left angle bracket that is usually larger than that produced by \langle.

\rangle and >

The command \rangle produces a closing symbol (or right delimiter) that looks like ⟩; whereas > produces a symbol for a binary relation and should not be used for a closing angle bracket. After \left or \right, however, \rangle and > can be used interchangeably and the result is a right angle bracket that is usually larger than that produced by \rangle.

\perp and \bot

Both these commands produce a symbol that looks like ⊥, but \perp produces a binary relation symbol and \bot produces an ordinary symbol used, for example, to represent the least element of a partial order or lattice.

\dag and \dagger

The commands \dag and \dagger both produce the symbol †, but \dagger produces a binary operator symbol whereas \dag produces an ordinary symbol.

\ddag and \ddagger

The commands \ddag and \ddagger both produce the symbol ‡, but \ddagger produces a binary operator symbol whereas \ddag produces an ordinary symbol.

8.3 Inventing Notations

8.3.1 Introduction

It was said of Jordan's writings that if he had 4 things on the same footing (as a, b, c, d) they would appear as a, M_3', ϵ_2 and $\Pi_{1,2}''$.

Littlewood (1986), p. 60.

Many people using LaTeX find that some of the symbols they want to use are either unavailable or—by default—belong to the wrong kind of symbol. In this section I look at a number of ways of defining your own symbols. If you do try to define your own symbols in TeX, then one of the most important things to get correct is the kind of symbol that you are defining, that is to say, whether it is an ordinary symbol or a large operator symbol or whatever. On the right of Table 8.1 are listed the TeX commands for producing the basic eight kinds of symbol. The command \mathord, for example, is used to produce an ordinary symbol like a variable; there is, however, an easier way to get TeX to treat a symbol as an ordinary one and that is to enclose it in curly braces—see Knuth (1986), p. 134—and this is illustrated in the equation:

$$radius * 2 = diameter,$$

produced by means of the commands:

```
$${\it radius} * 2 = {\it diameter},$$
```

There is no need, for example, to input \mathord{\it radius}.

This example illustrates a further point about TeX: in mathematics it is rare to use multi-letter identifiers and the juxtaposition of variables usually represents multiplication; the defaults of TeX capture these mathematical conventions precisely. Thus, if you include $radius$ in your input, it will be typeset in such a way as to represent the multiplication of six quantities, namely r, a, d, i, u and s. To get multi-letter identifiers in math mode you need to include something like ${\it radius}$ though any other type-changing declaration can also be used.

In defining a large operator you need to tell TeX how to treat subscripts and superscripts. For example, Roscoe and Hoare (1988) contains on p. 181 the formula:

$$\mathop{\rm IF}_{i=1}^n b_i P_i = \mathop{\rm IF}_{i=1}^n b_i^* P_i.$$

To get this in LaTeX you input

```
$$\IF_{i=1}^n b_i P_i = \IF_{i=1}^n b_i^* P_i.$$
```

where \IF is defined as \def\IF{\mathop{\rm IF}\limits}. The command \limits makes subscripts and superscripts appear as limits under and over, respectively, the symbol being defined both in text and display style. Other possibilities are the

`\nolimits` command—when subscripts and superscripts always appear as such—and `\displaylimits`—when subscripts and superscripts appear as such in text style but appear as limits in display style.

In Diller (1990) occurs the symbol ◁ produced by `\domcores` defined as:

`\def\domcores{\mathbin{\lhd{\mkern-16.2mu}-}}`

The command `\mkern`*len* produces *len* amount of space, but it can only be used in math mode and *len* has to be expressed in terms of `mu`, that is to say, mathematical units: there are 18 mus to the em. Note that `\mkern` generates either vertical or horizontal space depending on the context in which it occurs.

Some people try to use < and > as bracket-like symbols, but the spacing does not work out correctly. If you do want to use these as delimiters, then you have to define them like `\def\lacute{\mathopen{<}}` and `\def\racute{\mathclose{>}}`. Notice the difference in spacing in the following example:

$$<x, y> \Longleftrightarrow \; < x, y > .$$

This was produced by means of the following:

`$$\lacute x, y \racute \iff < x, y>.$$`

Compare this with:

$$<x, y> \Longleftrightarrow \langle x, y \rangle,$$

produced by means of the following:

`$$\lacute x, y \racute \iff \langle x, y \rangle,$$`

8.3.2   Logical Symbols

To produce the formula $\neg(P \lor Q) \vdash \neg Q$ you need to use this sequence of LaTeX commands `$\lnot (P \lor Q) \vdash \lnot Q$`. Because the symbols ∨, ∧ and ¬ are often used in logical formulas they have additional names which reflect this. Thus, the symbol ∨, as well as being produced by the command `\vee`, is also produced by `\lor` (for 'logical or') and the symbol ∧, as well as being produced by the command `\wedge`, is also produced by `\land` (for 'logical and'). The symbol ¬ can be produced either by `\neg` or by `\lnot`. Also available is the command `\iff` which produces the symbol ⟺. Although biimplication is a binary operation and not a relation symbol it is customary to place slightly more space around it than the other logical connectives and Knuth's definition of `\iff` reflects this. Thus, the formula:

$$h \equiv k \pmod{n} \Longleftrightarrow h - k \in n\mathbf{Z},$$

from MacLane and Birkhoff (1967), p. 51, can be produced by these commands:

`$$h \equiv k\pmod{n} \iff h - k \in n {\bf Z},$$`

symbol	command	alternative
¬	\neg	\lnot
∧	\wedge	\land
∨	\vee	\lor
⇒	\Rightarrow	
⟹	\Longrightarrow	
⟺	\Longleftrightarrow	\iff
∀	\forall	
∃	\exists	
⊢	\vdash	
⊨	\models	

Table 8.6: Basic logical symbols in TEX.

Table 8.6 summarizes the commands available in TEX for producing basic logical symbols. The symbols ⇒ and ⟹ are just called \Rightarrow and \Longrightarrow, respectively. If you are going to use a lot of logical formulas in your document, then it would be a good idea to give a more appropriate name to the symbol that you decide to use for implication. Calling it \implies seems a good idea. This can be achieved thus:

    \let\implies=\Rightarrow

The TEX command \let just copies the definition of the command on the right of the equals sign—which is optional—and associates it with the command on the left of the equals sign; thus, the effect of the above \let command is to make \implies and \Rightarrow exact equivalents. (See Knuth (1986), pp. 206–207, for more information.) The following formula, from MacLane and Birkhoff (1967), p. 76:

$$ab = ac \Rightarrow b = c,$$

was produced by these commands:

    $$a b = a c \implies b = c,$$

What has been said so far about logical symbols is really only appropriate for their use in mathematical articles and books which are not specifically about logic. This is because in such books you rarely come across a formula involving several implication or biimplication signs. When writing primarily about logic it makes more sense to define both implication and biimplication to be binary operation symbols rather than anything else and the following commands achieve this:

    \def\imp{\mathbin\Rightarrow}
    \def\biimp{\mathbin\Longleftrightarrow}

Peirce's law $((P \Rightarrow Q) \Rightarrow P) \Rightarrow P$ can then be obtained by means of the commands
`$((P \imp Q) \imp P) \imp P$`.

Some people prefer to use alternative symbols for the common propositional connectives. For example, say you want to use $\supset$ for material implication, $\equiv$ for biimplication, & for conjunction, v for disjunction and $\sim$ for negation. This can be achieved by means of the following commands:

```
\def\myimplies{\mathbin\supset}
\def\mybiimp{\mathbin\equiv}
\def\myand{\mathbin\&}
\def\myor{\mathbin{\rm v}}
\def\mynot{\mathop\sim}
```

The formula $\sim(P \& Q) \supset (\sim P \, v \sim Q)$ can then be obtained by means of the commands
`$\mynot (P \myand Q) \myimplies (\mynot P \myor \mynot Q)$`. Compare this with $\sim (P \& Q) \supset (\sim Pv \sim Q)$, which was obtained by means of the commands `$\sim (P \& Q) \supset (\sim P {\rm v} \sim Q)$`. That is to say, the same symbols are used in both cases, but in the second formula their default "categories" are unaltered. Note that the names `\myimplies`, etc., are only used for illustrative purposes; you should use whatever names you feel are most appropriate. You could also redefine the commands `\land`, etc. If you consistently use `\land` in a document and then decide to change the symbol that you have been using for conjunction, all you have to do is to redefine it (using `\def` or `\renewcommand`).

8.4   Reinstating `\eqalign`, `\eqalignno` and `\leqalignno`

8.4.1   Reasons for Reinstatement

Lamport (1986), p. 205, says that the plain TEX commands `\eqalign`, `\eqalignno` and `\leqalignno` 'are made obsolete by LATEX's eqnarray and eqnarray* environments.' (He actually comments them out in `lplain.tex`.) I think that he is wrong in thinking that these TEX commands are obsolete and here I will explain how you can reinstate them, but before doing that I will try to say why I think they should be reinstated. There are three main reasons:

(1) The spacing around the symbol that occurs in the central column of an **eqnarray** or **eqnarray*** environment is greater than the usual spacing around that symbol (whatever it may be). This makes for very strange-looking displays when that symbol occurs elsewhere on the same line.

(2) The labels produced by the **equation** and **eqnarray** environments are *numerical* labels and—while it is possible to produce labelled formulas with *numerical* labels out of sequence—it is not possible to use these environments to produce labels consisting of entire words or Greek letters; using `\eqalign` (and sometimes `\displaylines`) it is possible to get non-numerical labels attached to formulas.

(3) Sometimes in a series of equations aligned on, say, the equals sign you want to insert one or more explanatory lines of text and then carry on the series of equations *still* aligned on the equals sign. This is not possible using the LaTeX environments, but is possible using the more "primitive" TeX commands.

Before going through some examples which illustrate these three points I will show you how to reinstate the TeX commands being discussed. If you are unable to alter the file `lplain.tex`, then you need to copy the definitions of \eqalign, \eqalignno and \leqalignno into your own style file. Alternatively, they appear in Knuth (1986), p. 362, and are reproduced here for your convenience:

```
\def\eqalign#1{\null\,\vcenter{\openup\jot \m@th
    \ialign{\strut\hfil$\displaystyle{##}$&$
        \displaystyle{{}##}$\hfil \crcr#1\crcr}}\,}

\def\eqalignno#1{\displ@y \tabskip=\centering
    \halign to\displaywidth{\hfil$\@lign\displaystyle{##}$
        \tabskip=0pt &$\@lign\displaystyle{{}##}$
        \hfil\tabskip=\centering
        &\llap{$\@lign##$}\tabskip=0pt\crcr #1\crcr}}

\def\leqalignno#1{\displ@y \tabskip=\centering
    \halign to\displaywidth{\hfil$\@lign\displaystyle{##}$
        \tabskip=0pt &$\@lign\displaystyle{{}##}$
        \hfil\tabskip=\centering &\kern-\displaywidth\rlap{$\@lign##$}
        \tabskip=\displaywidth\crcr #1\crcr}}
```

Note that if you do decide to reinstate these commands, then you will need to alter \centering to \@centering in their definitions, because Lamport has usurped the TeX \@centering command for his own purposes.

8.4.2   Repetition of Aligned Symbols

In Whitehead (1978), p. 535, there occurs the following series of equations:

$$h_1(\alpha) = h_2(\alpha) = 0 \qquad \textit{if } r \textit{ is odd;}$$
$$2h_0(\alpha) = 0, \qquad 3h_1(\alpha) = 0, \qquad h_2(\alpha) = -h_1(\alpha) \qquad \textit{if } r \textit{ is even.}$$

In the book you are now reading this was produced by the following TeX commands:

```
{\it
$$
\eqalign{
h_1(\alpha)     & = h_2 (\alpha) = 0 \qquad \hbox{if $r$ is odd};\cr
2h_0 (\alpha) & = 0, \qquad 3h_1 (\alpha)   = 0, \qquad
h_2 (\alpha)   = - h_1 (\alpha) \qquad \hbox{if $r$ is even}.\cr}
$$}
```

Using LaTeX's `eqnarray*` environment the appearance of this series of equations would be:

$$
\begin{aligned}
h_1(\alpha) &= h_2(\alpha) = 0 \qquad \textit{if r is odd;} \\
2h_0(\alpha) &= 0, \qquad 3h_1(\alpha) = 0, \qquad h_2(\alpha) = -h_1(\alpha) \qquad \textit{if r is even.}
\end{aligned}
$$

In the same book this series of equations appears on p. 558:

$$
\begin{aligned}
\text{Ker } \beta' = \rho_2^*(\text{Ker } \beta) = \rho_2^*(\text{Im } \alpha) &= \text{Im}(\rho_2^* \circ \alpha) = \text{Im}(i_2' \circ \gamma) \\
&= i_2'(\text{Im } \gamma).
\end{aligned}
$$

In the book you are now reading this was produced by these TeX commands:

```
$$
\def\Ker{\mathop{\rm Ker}\nolimits}
\def\Hom{\mathop{\rm Hom}\nolimits}
\def\IM{\mathop{\rm Im}\nolimits}
\eqalign{\Ker \beta' = \rho^\ast_2 ( \Ker \beta)
= \rho^\ast_2 ( \IM \alpha)
& = \IM ( \rho^\ast_2 \circ \alpha) = \IM (i'_2 \circ \gamma)\cr
& = i'_2 (\IM \gamma).\cr}
$$
```

Using LaTeX the following would be the appearance of the result by default:

$$
\begin{aligned}
\text{Ker } \beta' = \rho_2^*(\text{Ker } \beta) = \rho_2^*(\text{Im } \alpha) &= \text{Im}(\rho_2^* \circ \alpha) = \text{Im}(i_2' \circ \gamma) \\
&= i_2'(\text{Im } \gamma).
\end{aligned}
$$

It is possible to alter the default spacing around the central symbol in the `eqnarray` and `eqnarray*` environments, but if you decide to do this, then you have the further problem of having to decide what to alter it to. If you alter it to a thick amount of space, then it will look okay when the central column is occupied by binary *relations* but sometimes you will want binary *operations* to appear in the central column and then the spacing will look decidedly strange.

If you think that the issue of spacing is not very important, then you should look through a book produced using LaTeX—such as Benson (1991), for example—and you will almost certainly be distracted by the variable amount of space surrounding the same symbols. To give just one example, on p. 2 there occurs:

$$0 = M_0 \leq \cdots \leq M_r \quad = \quad M$$
$$0 = M'_0 \leq \cdots \leq M'_s \quad = \quad M$$

The use of the `eqnarray*` environment here draws your eyes to the equals sign on the right of the multiple equations; it gives them prominence. Yet, the surrounding text tells us that what is at issue is the *length* of the two series of submodules; the fact that the last term in both of them is the same is of lesser significance. Using \eqalign these two series would appear as:

$$0 = M_0 \leq \cdots \leq M_r = M$$
$$0 = M'_0 \leq \cdots \leq M'_s = M$$

This was produced using these commands:

```
$$
\eqalign{0 = M_0   \leq \cdots \leq M_r  & = M \cr
         0 = M'_0 \leq \cdots \leq M'_s & = M \cr}
$$
```

In the equation produced using \eqalign undue prominence is not given to the equals signs that appear on the right-hand sides of the equations.

8.4.3   Labels out of Sequence

Sometimes you will want to give a label to a formula which is different from the numerical sequence that LaTeX generates automatically. For example, you may want to label the reduction rule for the combinator **S** by (**S**) like this:

$$\mathbf{S}fgx \rightarrow fx(gx), \tag{S}$$

In order to produce this you need the following TeX commands:

```
$${\bf S} f g x \rightarrow f x (g x),\eqno({\bf S})$$
```

And in order to get several aligned and labelled formulas like this:

$$\mathbf{B}fgx \rightarrow f(gx), \tag{B}$$
$$\mathbf{C}fxy \rightarrow fyx, \tag{C}$$

you need the following commands:

```
$$
\eqalignno{{\bf B} f g x & \rightarrow f (g x),&({\bf B})\cr
           {\bf C} f x y & \rightarrow f y x,   &({\bf C})\cr}
$$
```

It is also possible to get the label to appear on the extreme left-hand of the page. For example, a commonly used rule such as that of β-reduction might appear like this:

$$(\beta) \qquad\qquad (\lambda x.M)N \rightarrow M[x := N].$$

This was obtained by means of the following commands:

```
$$(\lambda x.M)N \rightarrow M[x:=N].\leqno(\beta)$$
```

Note that what follows the \leqno command is still in math mode. And in order to get several aligned and labelled formulas like this:

$$(\alpha) \qquad\qquad \lambda x.X[y := x] \rightarrow \lambda y.X,$$
$$(\eta) \qquad\qquad \lambda x.X x \rightarrow X,$$

you need the following TEX commands:

```
$$
\leqalignno{\lambda x.X  [y := x] & \rightarrow \lambda y.X,
                         &(\alpha)\cr
           \lambda x.X x       & \rightarrow X,
                         &(\eta)  \cr}
$$
```

In the examples of \eqalign and \leqalign presented above to produce non-numerical labels there has been a symbol on which the equations have been aligned, namely $\rightarrow$, but sometimes people want to label formulas or equations in which there is no convenient symbol to be used for alignment purposes. TEX has a \displaylines command that can be used to achieve this. For example, the following:

$$\Delta \vdash x{:}\sigma, \qquad \text{if } x{:}\sigma \in \Delta, \qquad\qquad\qquad TAUT$$

$$\frac{\Delta \vdash M{:}\sigma \rightarrow \tau \quad \Delta \vdash N{:}\sigma}{\Delta \vdash MN{:}\tau}, \qquad\qquad\qquad COMB$$

$$\frac{\Delta_x \cup \{x{:}\sigma\} \vdash M{:}\tau}{\Delta \vdash \lambda x.M{:}\sigma \rightarrow \tau}, \qquad\qquad\qquad ABS$$

was produced by these commands:

```
$$
\displaylines{
\hfill
{\Delta \vdash x \colon \sigma, \qquad
\hbox{if}\ x \colon \sigma \in \Delta},\hfill
\llap{\it TAUT}
\cr\cr
```

```
\hfill
{{\Delta \vdash M \colon \sigma \fun \tau \qquad
{\Delta \vdash N \colon \sigma}}
\over {\Delta \vdash MN \colon \tau}},\hfill
\llap{\it COMB}
\cr\cr
\hfill
{{\Delta_x \cup \{ x \colon \sigma \} \vdash M \colon \tau}
\over {\Delta \vdash \lambda x.M \colon \sigma \fun \tau}},\hfill
\llap{\it ABS}\cr}
$$
```

It is also possible to get the labels on the left as in the following example based on Curry and Feys (1974), p. 59:[4]

(ρ) $a \mathrel{\rm R} a;$

(σ) if $a \mathrel{\rm R} b,$ then $b \mathrel{\rm R} a;$

(τ) if $a \mathrel{\rm R} b,$ and $b \mathrel{\rm R} c,$ then $a \mathrel{\rm R} c;$

(μ) if $a \mathrel{\rm R} b,$ then $(ca) \mathrel{\rm R} (cb);$

(ν) if $a \mathrel{\rm R} b,$ then $(ac) \mathrel{\rm R} (bc).$

These were produced by means of the following commands:

```
$$
\displaylines{\def\R{\mathrel{\rm R}}
\rlap{($\rho$)} \hfill a \R a; \hfill\cr
\rlap{($\sigma$)} \hfill \hbox{if} \quad a \R b, \quad
\hbox{then} \quad b \R a; \hfill\cr
\rlap{($\tau$)} \hfill \hbox{if} \quad a \R b, \quad
\hbox{and} \quad b \R c, \quad
\hbox{then} \quad a \R c; \hfill\cr
\rlap{($\mu$)} \hfill \hbox{if} \quad a \R b, \quad
\hbox{then} \quad (ca) \R (cb); \hfill\cr
\rlap{($\nu$)} \hfill \hbox{if} \quad a \R b, \quad
\hbox{then} \quad (ac) \R (bc). \hfill\cr}
$$
```

8.4.4   Explanatory Notes in Aligned Equations

Consider this tautology:

$$(P \vee Q) \wedge R \Longleftrightarrow (P \wedge R) \vee (Q \wedge R). \tag{8.1}$$

It was produced by means of the following commands:

---

[4] They call (ρ) *reflexiveness*, (σ) *symmetry*, (τ) *transitivity*, (μ) *right monotony* and (ν) *left monotony*.

```
\begin{equation}
( P \lor Q ) \land R \iff ( P \land R ) \lor ( Q \land R ).
\label{DD}
\end{equation}
```

The following sequence of formulas:

$$
\begin{aligned}
x \in (U \cup V) \cap W &\Longleftrightarrow (x \in U \cup V) \land x \in W, \\
&\Longleftrightarrow (x \in U \lor x \in V) \land x \in W, \\
&\Longleftrightarrow (x \in U \land x \in W) \lor (x \in V \land x \in W),
\end{aligned}
$$

which follows by using the tautology (8.1),

$$
\begin{aligned}
&\Longleftrightarrow (x \in U \cap W) \lor (x \in V \cap W), \\
&\Longleftrightarrow x \in (U \cap W) \cup (V \cap W),
\end{aligned}
$$

was produced by means of the following commands:

```
$$\eqalignno{
x \in ( U \cup V ) \cap W
& \iff ( x \in U \cup V ) \land x \in W, \cr
& \iff ( x \in U \lor x \in V ) \land x \in W, \cr
& \iff ( x \in U \land x \in W ) \lor
        ( x \in V \land x \in W ), \cr
\noalign{\hbox{which follows by using the tautology \(ref{DD}),}}
& \iff ( x \in U \cap W ) \lor ( x \in V \cap W ), \cr
& \iff x \in ( U \cap W ) \cup ( V \cap W ), \cr
}$$
```

The `\noalign{`*text*`}` command is a primitive TEX command that is used to put *text* between two rows of an arrangement of information produced by TEX commands; do *not* use it with LATEX's array environment, for example. It is commonly used in the form `\noalign{\smallskip}` to put extra vertical space between the rows of, say, a `\cases` construct.

8.4.5   General Format of \eqalign, \eqalignno and \leqalignno

The general form of the `\eqalign` command is:

```
\eqalign{lhs₁&rhs₁\cr
         lhs₂&rhs₂\cr
              ⋮
         lhsₙ&rhsₙ\cr}
```

This plain TEX command can only be used in math mode and display style to produce several displayed formulas aligned on the symbols that follow the ampersands.

The formulas *lhs*_i and *rhs*_i are typeset in display style. This command needs to be reinstated—as described in subsection 8.4.1—before it can be used.

The general form of the \eqalignno command is:

$$\eqalignno\{lhs_1 \& rhs_1 \& en_1\backslash cr$$
$$lhs_2 \& rhs_2 \& en_2\backslash cr$$
$$\vdots$$
$$lhs_n \& rhs_n \& en_n\backslash cr\}$$

This plain TEX command can only be used in math mode and display style to produce several displayed formulas aligned on the symbols that follow the ampersands. The formulas *lhs*_i and *rhs*_i are typeset in display style. The expressions *en*_i—which usually are numerical labels—are placed on the extreme right-hand side of the body region of the page; if any such expressions are omitted, then so should the preceding ampersand. This command needs to be reinstated—as described in subsection 8.4.1—before it can be used.

The general form of the \leqalignno command is:

$$\leqalignno\{lhs_1 \& rhs_1 \& en_1\backslash cr$$
$$lhs_2 \& rhs_2 \& en_2\backslash cr$$
$$\vdots$$
$$lhs_n \& rhs_n \& en_n\backslash cr\}$$

This plain TEX command can only be used in math mode and display style to produce several displayed formulas aligned on the symbols that follow the ampersands. The formulas *lhs*_i and *rhs*_i are typeset in display style. The expressions *en*_i—which usually are numerical labels—are placed on the extreme left-hand side of the body region of the page; if any such expressions are omitted, then so should the preceding ampersand. This command needs to be reinstated—as described in subsection 8.4.1—before it can be used.

The general form of the \displaylines command is:

$$\displaylines\{form_1\backslash cr$$
$$form_2\backslash cr$$
$$\vdots$$
$$form_n\backslash cr\}$$

This typesets each of the *form*_i on a line by itself and each of them is centred.

8.4.6   Using \eqalign, \eqalignno and \leqalignno with \label

If you do reinstate \eqalign, \eqalignno and \leqalignno, then you may find that you want some of the labels associated with formulas involving these commands to be produced automatically by LATEX and, furthermore, you may wish to use LATEX's cross-referencing facilities, namely \label and \ref, to be able to refer to such formulas. Here, I explain how to do these things.

If you use \eqalign to produce a single formula spanning several lines and which you want to refer to, then it is easiest to put the formula inside an equation environment as follows:

```
\begin{equation}
\label{EE}
\eqalign{\{& P \in 1 \upto 10 \land T = t \}\cr
        & \Gamma_1\cr
     \{&  P \in 1 \upto 10 \land
           T = t \oplus \{ P \mapsto V \} \land
           {\it REP} = {\it okay} \}.\cr}
\end{equation}
```

These commands produce the following partial correctness specification:

$$\{P \in 1 \mathinner{\ldotp\ldotp} 10 \land T = t\}$$
$$\Gamma_1 \tag{8.2}$$
$$\{P \in 1 \mathinner{\ldotp\ldotp} 10 \land T = t \oplus \{P \mapsto V\} \land REP = okay\}.$$

Note that the \label command has to come before the \eqalign command.

If you use double dollar signs to produce a single displayed equation that you wish to be numbered automatically by LATEX, then you need to use the following commands:

```
\refstepcounter{equation}
$$
{\bf B} f g x \rightarrow f (g x).\eqno{(\theequation)}
\label{FF}
$$
```

These produce, as you would expect, the following:

$$\mathbf{B} fgx \rightarrow f(gx). \tag{8.3}$$

Associated with each counter *ctr* there is a command \the*ctr* which is the text that actually appears in your document and usually the contents of \the*ctr* are used for cross-referencing purposes; thus the command \theequation holds the textual output associated with the counter equation and in the book and report document styles \theequation is defined to be \arabic{chapter}.\arabic{equation} with a full stop separating the two numerals. The command \refstepcounter{*ctr*} increments the counter *ctr* and makes \the*ctr* into the *current* \ref *value*, that is to say, what is picked up by an appropriately placed \label command.[5]

---

[5] See section B.3 for more information about counters and current \ref values.

To combine \eqalign with \label when you want to produce several labelled formulas is slightly more complicated. First, you need to include these commands in your style file:

\def\ardlabel#1{\let\@currentlabel=\theequation\label{#1}}

The command \@currentlabel actually contains the current \ref value and because the sign @ forms part of its name it has to go into a style file. I have suggested that you call your style file own.sty and that you include own as as one of the options to the \documentstyle command that is present in your input file. With that done the following commands are necessary:

```
\refstepcounter{equation}
$$
\def\S{{\bf S}}
\def\K{{\bf K}}
\def\red{\rightarrow}
\eqalignno{
\S (\K \S) \K f g x & \red \K \S f (\K f) g x,
& (\theequation)\ardlabel{GG}\cr
%
\refstepcounter{equation}
& \red \S (\K f) g x,
& (\theequation)\ardlabel{HH}\cr
%
& \red \K f x (g x),\cr
%
\refstepcounter{equation}
& \red f (g x).
& (\theequation)\ardlabel{II}\cr
}$$
```

These produce the following:

$$
\begin{aligned}
S(KS)Kfgx &\rightarrow KSf(Kf)gx, & (8.4)\\
&\rightarrow S(Kf)gx, & (8.5)\\
&\rightarrow Kfx(gx),\\
&\rightarrow f(gx). & (8.6)
\end{aligned}
$$

9

Examples of Mathematical Formatting

9.1 The Fibonacci Numbers

The Fibonacci numbers—$fib(n)$ for $n \geq 0$—can be defined like this:

$$
\begin{aligned}
fib(0) &= 0, \\
fib(1) &= 1, \\
fib(n) &= fib(n-1) + fib(n-2), \qquad \text{if } n > 1.
\end{aligned}
$$

This was produced by means of these commands:

```
$$
\eqalign{
\fib(0) & = 0,\cr
\fib(1) & = 1,\cr
\fib(n) & = \fib(n-1) + \fib(n-2),\qquad
\hbox{if $n > 1$}.}
$$
```

where the command \fib was defined like this:

```
\def\fib{\mathop{\it fib}\nolimits}
```

The command \qquad produces horizontal space which is two ems wide and is the correct amount of space to use in cases like this.

The following program—using an Algol-like syntax—calculates Fibonacci numbers. On termination the variable a contains the value of $fib(n)$:

$$
\begin{aligned}
a &:= 0; \\
b &:= 1;
\end{aligned}
$$

137

$$i := 0;$$
$$\textbf{while } n \neq i \textbf{ do}$$
$$(b := a + b;$$
$$a := b - a;$$
$$i := i + 1)$$

This was obtained by using the `tabbing` environment; in fact, it was produced using the following commands:

```
\begin{tabbing}
$a\:$\=$:= 0$; \kill
$a$\>$:= 0$; \\
$b$\>$:= 1$; \\
$i$\>$:= 0$; \\
${\bf while}\ n \not= i\ {\bf do}$ \\
\pushtabs
\hspace*{1em}\=$($\=$b\:$\=$:= a + b$; \kill
\>$($\>$b$\>$:= a + b$; \\
\>\>$a$\>$:= b - a$; \\
\>\>$i$\>$:= i + 1)$
\poptabs
\end{tabbing}
```

The first line here—the one terminated by `\kill`—sets the tab positions. The `\kill` command tells LATEX that the characters occurring on that line are not to occur in the final output; but do *not* use an end-of-line command `\\` before the `\kill` command. The control symbol `\=` actually sets the tabs. In order to actually use the n-th tab position you need n occurrences of the control symbol `\>`. The `\pushtabs` command stores the current tab settings and they are restored by the `\poptabs` command; here, the `\pushtabs` command is just used to "lose" one set of tab settings so that another set can be created. (Further information about the `tabbing` environment can be found in section 4.12 above.)

9.2   Fancy Arrays

The following program fragment:

$$
\Delta \begin{cases}
\begin{aligned}
&\textbf{begin new } I; \\
&\left. \begin{aligned} OUT &:= T\,[1]; \\ I &:= 1; \end{aligned} \right\} \Delta_1 \\
&\left. \begin{aligned} \textbf{while } &I \neq 10 \textbf{ do} \\ &\Delta_3 \left\{ \begin{aligned} I &:= I + 1; \\ OUT &:= OUT + T\,[I] \end{aligned} \right. \end{aligned} \right\} \Delta_2 \\
&\textbf{end}
\end{aligned}
\end{cases}
$$

was produced by the following commands:

```
$$
\begin{array}{l}
{\bf begin}\ {\bf new}\ I; \\
   \Delta \left\{
   \begin{array}{l}
      \left.
      \begin{array}{l}
      {\it OUT} := {\it T} \, [1]; \\
      I := 1;
      \end{array}
      \right\} \Delta_1 \\
      %
      \left.
      \begin{array}{l}
      {\bf while}\ I \not= 10\ {\bf do} \\
         \Delta_3 \left\{
         \begin{array}{l}
         I := I+1; \\
         {\it OUT} := {\it OUT} + T \, [I]
         \end{array}
         \right.
      \end{array}
      \right\} \Delta_2
      \end{array}
      \right. \\
   {\bf end}
\end{array}
$$
```

The idea behind the construction of this can easily be illustrated by considering the innermost pair of labelled assignments, namely:

$$
\Delta_3 \begin{cases} I := I + 1; \\ OUT := OUT + T[I] \end{cases}
$$

which was produced by the following commands:

```
$$\Delta_3 \left\{
\begin{array}{l}
I := I+1; \\
{\it OUT} := {\it OUT} + T \, [I]
\end{array}
\right.$$
```

The idea here is very similar to the use of the **array** environment in order to produce matrices as explained in subsection 7.6.2 above. This **array** then becomes a single element in another instance of the **array** environment and so on till the program fragment is built up.

9.3   Some Standard Derivatives

Some elementary calculus books contain lists of integrals and derivatives; here, some straightforward derivatives are presented:

$$\frac{d}{dx}\sin^{-1}u = \frac{1}{\sqrt{1-u^2}}\frac{du}{dx}, \qquad \text{if } -\tfrac{\pi}{2} < \sin^{-1}u < \tfrac{\pi}{2},$$

$$\frac{d}{dx}\cos^{-1}u = \frac{-1}{\sqrt{1-u^2}}\frac{du}{dx}, \qquad \text{if } 0 < \cos^{-1}u < \pi,$$

$$\frac{d}{dx}\tan^{-1}u = \frac{1}{1+u^2}\frac{du}{dx}, \qquad \text{if } -\tfrac{\pi}{2} < \tan^{-1}u < \tfrac{\pi}{2},$$

$$\frac{d}{dx}\cot^{-1}u = \frac{-1}{1+u^2}\frac{du}{dx}, \qquad \text{if } 0 < \cot^{-1}u < \pi,$$

$$\frac{d}{dx}\sec^{-1}u = \frac{1}{u\sqrt{u^2-1}}\frac{du}{dx}, \qquad \text{if } 0 < \sec^{-1}u < \tfrac{\pi}{2},$$

$$= \frac{-1}{u\sqrt{u^2-1}}\frac{du}{dx}, \qquad \text{if } \tfrac{\pi}{2} < \sec^{-1}u < \pi,$$

$$\frac{d}{dx}\csc^{-1}u = \frac{1}{u\sqrt{u^2-1}}\frac{du}{dx}, \qquad \text{if } -\tfrac{\pi}{2} < \csc^{-1}u < 0,$$

$$= \frac{-1}{u\sqrt{u^2-1}}\frac{du}{dx}, \qquad \text{if } 0 < \csc^{-1}u < \tfrac{\pi}{2}.$$

They were produced by means of the following commands:

```
$$
\begin{array}{r@{\:=\:}l@{\qquad}l}
\displaystyle {d \over dx} \sin^{-1} u
& \displaystyle
{1 \over \sqrt{1 - u^2}} {du \over dx},
& \mbox{if $- {\pi \over 2} < \sin^{-1}u < {\pi \over 2}$},
\\[4ex]
\displaystyle
{d \over dx} \cos^{-1} u
& \displaystyle
```

```
{-1 \over \sqrt{1 - u^2}} {du \over dx},
& \mbox{if $0 < \cos^{-1}u < \pi$},
\\[4ex]
\displaystyle
{d \over dx} \tan^{-1} u
& \displaystyle
{1 \over 1 + u^2} {du \over dx},
& \mbox{if $- {\pi \over 2} < \tan^{-1}u < {\pi \over 2}$},
\\[4ex]
\displaystyle
{d \over dx} \cot^{-1} u
&\ \displaystyle
{-1 \over 1 + u^2} {du \over dx},
& \mbox{if $0 < \cot^{-1}u < \pi$},
\\[4ex]
\displaystyle
{d \over dx} \sec^{-1} u
& \displaystyle
{1 \over u \sqrt{u^2 - 1}} {du \over dx},
& \mbox{if $0 < \sec^{-1}u < {\pi \over 2}$},
\\[4ex]
& \displaystyle
{-1 \over u \sqrt{u^2 - 1}} {du \over dx},
& \mbox{if ${\pi \over 2} < \sec^{-1}u < \pi$},
\\[4ex]
\displaystyle
{d \over dx} \csc^{-1} u
& \displaystyle
{1 \over u \sqrt{u^2 - 1}} {du \over dx},
& \mbox{if $-{\pi \over 2} < \csc^{-1}u < 0$},
\\[4ex]
& \displaystyle
{-1 \over u \sqrt{u^2 - 1}} {du \over dx},
& \mbox{if $0 < \csc^{-1}u < {\pi \over 2}$}.
\end{array}
$$
```

The **array** environment was used here rather than the **eqnarray*** environment because such a table of deriveatives looks better if the side conditions are aligned as well as the equals signs. Note the use of the @-expression in the preamble to the **array** environment in order to insert space in every row produced.

```
{ % open scope for temporary definitions
\arraycolsep=14.5pt  % default = 5pt
\def\arraystretch{2} % default = 1

\def\tempa{\begin{array}{|c|c|c|c|} \hline
          & & & \\ \hline \end{array}}

\def\tempb{\begin{array}{|c|c|} \hline
          & \\ \hline & \\ \hline \end{array}}

\def\tempc{\begin{array}{c|c|c} \cline{2-3}
          & & \multicolumn{1}{|c|}{} \\ \hline
          \multicolumn{1}{|c|}{} & & \\ \cline{1-2}
          \end{array}}

\def\tempd{\begin{array}{c|c|} \hline
          \multicolumn{1}{|c|}{} & \\ \hline
          & \\ \cline{2-2} & \\ \cline{2-2} \end{array}}

\def\tempe{\begin{array}{|c|c} \hline
          & \multicolumn{1}{|c|}{} \\ \hline
          & \\ \cline{1-1} & \\ \cline{1-1} \end{array}}

\def\tempf{\begin{array}{c|c|c} \cline{2-2} & & \\ \hline
          \multicolumn{1}{|c|}{} & & \multicolumn{1}{|c|}{}
          \\ \hline \end{array}}

\def\tempg{\begin{array}{c|c|c} \cline{1-2}
          \multicolumn{1}{|c|}{} & & \\ \hline
          & & \multicolumn{1}{|c|}{} \\ \cline{2-3}
          \end{array}}

$$\begin{array}{cccc}
\multicolumn{2}{c}{\tempa} & \tempb & \tempc \\
\tempd     & \tempe        & \tempf & \tempg
\end{array}$$
} % close scope for temporary definitions
```

Figure 9.1: Commands that produce the seven tetrominoes.

9.4   The Seven Tetrominoes

The following are the seven tetrominoes:[1]

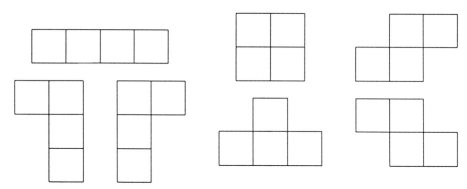

The commands which produced them are those in Fig. 9.1. A more sensible way to produce these tetrominoes would be to use the **picture** environment explained in chapter 10, but I have included this way of getting them here just to make the reader aware of the capabilities of the **array** environment. Making sure that the squares that actually make up the tetrominoes really are squares was achieved by a process of trial-and-error.

9.5   Binomial Theorem

The binomial theorem—for $n \geq 0$—is the following equation:

$$(u + v)^n = \sum_{i=0}^{n} \binom{n}{i} u^{n-i} v^i,$$

where

$$\binom{n}{i} = {}_nC_i = \frac{n!}{i!(n - i)!}.$$

These two equations were produced by the following commands:

```
$$
(u + v)^n = \sum^n_{i=0} {n \choose i} u^{n-i} v^i,
$$
where
$$
{n \choose i} = {}_n C_i = {n! \over i! (n-i)!}.
$$
```

---

[1] Gardner (1988a), p. 124, says that there are only five tetrominoes as he only mentions one l-tetromino and one skew tetromino; but there is only one of each of these if your criterion of identity for tetrominoes allows flips as well as rotations. (A flip would involve taking a tetromino out of the two-dimensional plane, turning it over and putting it back.)

When $n = 3$ the binomial theorem gives:

$$(u+v)^3 = \sum_{i=0}^{3} \binom{3}{i} u^{3-i} v^i,$$

$$= \binom{3}{0} u^3 + \binom{3}{1} u^2 v + \binom{3}{2} uv^2 + \binom{3}{3} v^3,$$

$$= u^3 + 3u^2 v + 3uv^2 + v^3.$$

These last three equations were produced by the following commands:

```
$$\eqalign{
(u + v)^3 & = \sum^3_{i=0} {3 \choose i} u^{3-i} v^i,\cr
& = {3 \choose 0} u^3
+ {3 \choose 1} u^2 v
+ {3 \choose 2} u v^2
+ {3 \choose 3} v^3,\cr
& = u^3 + 3u^2v + 3uv^2 + v^3.\cr}$$
```

9.6   Framing Formulas

Some people when writing a book or article like to put formulas or other sorts of information inside a frame. The following example of this is taken from Butkovskiy (1982), p. 51:

$$-\frac{d}{dx}\left[\tan x \cdot \frac{dQ(x)}{dx}\right] = f(x),$$

$$|Q(0)| < \infty, \qquad Q\left(\frac{\pi}{4}\right) = g_1, \qquad 0 \le x \le \frac{\pi}{4}.$$

This was produced by the following commands:

```
\newlength{\lll}
\setlength{\lll}{\textwidth}
\addtolength{\lll}{-2\fboxsep}
\addtolength{\lll}{-2\fboxrule}
\noindent
\fbox{%
\begin{minipage}{\lll}
\vspace{-\abovedisplayskip}
\[
- {d \over dx}
\left[ \tan x \cdot
```

```
{dQ(x) \over dx} \right]
= f(x),
\]
\[
\mathopen| Q(0) \mathclose| < \infty,\qquad
Q \left( {\pi \over 4} \right) = g_1,\qquad
0 \le x \le {\pi \over 4}.
\]
\end{minipage}}
```

The purpose of the `\newlength`, `\setlength` and the two `\addtolength` commands is to ensure that the box produced with a frame around it is exactly as wide as the page, that is to say, the body region of the page. The length parameter `\textwidth` contains the width of the body region and the length parameters `\fboxsep` and `\fboxrule` contain, respectively, the amount of space surrounding the box produced by processing the *text* argument of the `\fbox` command and the width of the line which makes up the frame. Note the presence of the `\noindent` command which ensures that the framed formulas are not indented and the comment character % following `\fbox{` which ensures that no unnecessary space is inserted inside the framed box. The command `\vspace{-\abovedisplayskip}` was included because Lamport (1986), p. 195, says that this is the place where it has to be included; if it were omitted, then there would be more space above the first formula in the box than there was below the last one.

9.7 Text in Arrays

The following is based on the rules ∀-*elim* and ∀-*int* given on p. 118 of Diller (1990):[2]

$$\forall\text{-}elim \quad \frac{\Gamma \vdash \forall x \colon X \bullet A}{\Gamma \vdash A[t/x]}$$

Side condition: t is any term of the same type as x.

$$\forall\text{-}int \quad \frac{\Gamma \vdash A}{\Gamma \vdash \forall x \colon X \bullet A[x/a]}$$

Side condition: x is a variable of type X and a a constant of the same type which does not occur in Γ.

This arrangement of information was obtained by means of these commands:

```
{\def\tempa{\begin{array}[t]{c}
\Gamma \vdash \forall x \colon X \bullet A \\ \hline
\Gamma \vdash A[t/x]
\end{array}}
%
\def\tempb{\underline{Side condition}:
```

---

[2] The idea of presenting inference rules in this way comes from Hindley and Seldin (1986); for example, this style of presentation occurs on p. 209.

```
$t$ is any term of the same type as $x$.}
%
\def\tempc{\begin{array}[t]{c}
\Gamma \vdash A \\ \hline
\Gamma \vdash \forall x \colon X \bullet A[x/a]
\end{array}}
%
\def\tempd{\underline{Side condition}:
$x$ is a variable of type $X$ and $a$ a constant of the same type
which does not occur in $\Gamma$.}
%
$$
\begin{array}{lcp{2.5in}}
\allelim  & \tempa & \tempb \\
& & \\
\allint   & \tempc & \tempd
\end{array}
$$}
```

The commands \allelim and \allint are defined like this:

```
\def\allelim{\hbox{$\forall$-\it elim}}
\def\allint{\hbox{$\forall$-\it int}}
```

9.8   Commutative Diagrams

On p. 182 of Knuth (1986) there is a very elaborate commutative diagram which is set as an exercise for the reader to reproduce and on p. 325 in the answer to this exercise—numbered 18.46—he presents his solution. I do not reproduce all the TEX commands here; only the definitions of \normalbaselines, \mapright and \mapdown are copied from Knuth (1986).[3] Using these the following commutative diagram—which is from MacLane and Birkhoff (1967), p. 65:

$$
\begin{array}{ccc}
P & \xrightarrow{f} & Q \\
\Big\downarrow{f'} & & \Big\downarrow{g} \\
S & \xrightarrow{g'} & R
\end{array}
$$

is produced by the following commands:

---

[3] Note that the command \normalbaselines is being *redefined* here.

```
$$
\def\normalbaselines{\baselineskip20pt
    \lineskip3pt   \lineskiplimit3pt}
\def\mapright#1{\smash{
    \mathop{\longrightarrow}\limits^{#1}}}
\def\mapdown#1{\Big\downarrow\rlap
    {$\vcenter{\hbox{$\scriptstyle#1$}}$}}
%
\matrix{P     & \mapright{f}  & Q\cr
\mapdown{f'} &                & \mapdown{g}\cr
S            & \mapright{g'} & R\cr}
$$
```

These ideas can be used in the production of Frege's schema which was displayed in chapter 1 as Fig. 1.2. (Frege's schema could actually be turned into a sort of commutative diagram properly understood; but to do that here would be too much of a digression.) The following commands suffice:

```
$$\def\normalbaselines{\baselineskip1pt
  \lineskip3pt \lineskiplimit3pt }
\def\mapright#1{\smash{
  \mathop{\longrightarrow}\limits^{#1}}}
\def\mapdown#1{\Big\downarrow
  \rlap{$\vcenter{\hbox{$\scriptstyle#1$}}$}}
%
\matrix{
\matrix{\hbox{Proposition}} &
\matrix{\hbox{proper name}} &
\matrix{\hbox{concept word}} &&\cr
\mapdown{} &
\mapdown{} &
\mapdown{} &&\cr
\matrix{\vbox{\hbox{sense of the}\hbox{proposition\strut}}} &
\matrix{\vbox{\hbox{sense of the}\hbox{proper name\strut}}} &
\matrix{\vbox{\hbox{sense of the}\hbox{concept word\strut}}} &&\cr
\mapdown{} &
\mapdown{} &
\mapdown{} &&\cr
\matrix{\vbox{\hbox{meaning of the}
             \hbox{proposition\strut}
             \hbox{(truth value)\strut}}} &
\matrix{\vbox{\hbox{meaning of the}
             \hbox{proper name\strut}
             \hbox{(object)\strut}}} &
```

```
\pmatrix{\vbox{\hbox{meaning of the}
                \hbox{concept word\strut}
                \hbox{(concept)\strut}}} & \mapright{} &
\matrix{\vbox{\hbox{object falling}
             \hbox{under the\strut}
             \hbox{concept\strut}}} &\cr}$$
```

10

Pictures

10.1 Introduction

In this chapter I describe the `picture` environment in LATEX; this is useful for producing
fairly simple line drawings. If you need to produce a fairly complicated diagram and a
utility like `xfig` and the `epsf` non-standard option to the `\documentstyle` command—
described in section 4.10 above—are available on your computer system, then I would
strongly advise you to use them. Knowing about the `picture` environment is still
useful, however, as it is a very flexible mechanism for producing line drawings; and the
boxes it produces can be very small as illustrated in section 10.8 below.

10.2 Basic Principles and Ideas

10.2.1 Getting Started

In producing line diagrams using LATEX you need to give the lengths of lines and also to
specify positions in a Cartesian plane. Rather than using absolute units of length for
this purpose—such as inches or centimetres—you use a relative unit of length within
the `picture` environment and the magnitude of this is given by the `\unitlength`
rigid length parameter. Thus, the assignment `\unitlength=1mm` makes the unit of
length in `picture` environments from that point on to be one millimetre. You do
not, however, have to use the same unit of length in all your picture environments
in a single document. You can have a new assignment to the `\unitlength` length
parameter before each `picture` environment. You do not have to give the length in
millimetres. Any LATEX unit of length is acceptable. The default value for the unit of
length is 1 point. That is to say, if you do not assign any value to the `\unitlength`
length parameter, then the size of the unit that LATEX uses is 1 point (where 1 inch =
72.27 points).[1]

---

[1] See subsection B.1.1 for a complete list of length units available in TEX.

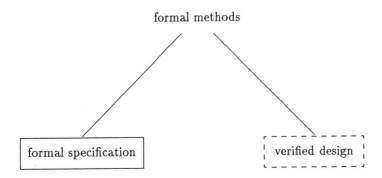

Figure 10.1: The branches of formal methods.

In order to produce the diagram which appears in Fig. 10.1 you need the following LaTeX commands:[2]

```
\begin{center}
%
\unitlength=1mm
\begin{picture}(110,50)(0,5)
%
\put(55,45){\makebox(0,0){formal methods}}
\put(20,5){\makebox(0,0){\framebox(37,9){formal specification}}}
\put(90,5){\makebox(0,0){\dashbox{1.5}(30,9){verified design}}}
%
\put(50,40){\line(-1,-1){30}}
\put(60,40){\line(1,-1){30}}
%
\end{picture}
%
\end{center}
```

The `picture` environment that produced the diagram in Fig. 10.1 starts with the command:

```
\begin{picture}(110,50)(0,5)
```

The first argument to this opening command is mandatory and it represents the size of the box that LaTeX produces. Thus, (110,50) indicates that the size of the box produced will be 110 units horizontally (that is to say, in the x direction) and 50 units

---

[2] This diagram is based on one which occurs on p. 5 of Diller (1990).

vertically (that is to say, in the y direction). It is possible to draw lines outside of this area, but LaTeX manipulates the box as if it were the size stipulated.

The second argument to the opening command, namely (0,5), is optional and it indicates an offset. Normally, that is to say, when this second argument is omitted, the origin of the Cartesian plane on which pictures are to be drawn is at the bottom left-hand corner of the box that LaTeX produces. However, if this second optional argument—say, (i,j)—is present, then that bottom left-hand corner has coordinates (i,j). Thus, in this case the coordinates of the bottom left-hand corner of the box are (0,5); the coordinates of the bottom right-hand corner of the box are (100,5); the coordinates of the top left-hand corner of the box are (0,55); and the coordinates of the top right-hand corner of the box are (110,55). When devising the LaTeX commands that you need to draw a picture, it is a good idea to either leave out the second (optional) argument or give it the value (0,0)—both of these alternatives have the same effect—and only to change it after you have completed your picture and want to position it precisely in relation to the context in which it occurs. This is often a trial-and-error process.

Within the `picture` environment only a very limited selection of commands is available. These are `\put` and `\multiput` and certain declarations such as `\thicklines` and `\thinlines`. The `\put` and `\multiput` commands are the only ones that draw lines and other shapes inside the `picture` environment. The general format of the `\put` command is:

$\put (i,j) \{picture\text{-}object\}$

This places the *picture-object* at the location in the picture whose x-coordinate is i and whose y-coordinate is j. Each picture object has a reference point associated with it and the coordinates (i,j) indicate the exact location of this reference point. (Almost anything can be considered as being a picture object, but certain things are used more frequently than others.) In the case of the commands that produced the picture in Fig. 10.1, the first three `\put` commands place text in the picture. The command:

`\put(55,45){\makebox(0,0){formal methods}}`

contains as its picture object the component:

`\makebox(0,0){formal methods}`

This is a LaTeX command that makes a box which contains the text or symbols enclosed in curly braces.[3] In this case the words 'formal methods'. The argument (0,0) indicates the size of the box produced. In this case the box has zero width and zero height. This has the consequence that the reference point is in the centre of the box that is produced when it has finished processing the text 'formal methods'. If the

---

[3] Note that the `\makebox`, `\framebox` and `\savebox` commands have a different form inside the `picture` environment from that which they have outside it; indeed, all three of them take different arguments inside the `picture` environment. For the use of these commands outside the `picture` environment see section 4.5.

argument was (i, j), then a box of width i and height j would be produced with the reference point at the bottom left-hand corner of the box. The unit of length that is used is that specified by the last assignment to the \unitlength length parameter. Thus, the effect of the command:

\put(55,45){\makebox(0,0){formal methods}}

is to place the text 'formal methods' in the picture at the position with coordinates $(55, 45)$ in such a way that the centre of the box containing the text is placed at exactly this point.

The general format of the \makebox command is:

\makebox$(i, j)$ [*pos*] {*picture-object*}

The function of the optional argument *pos* is to position the *picture-object* within the box produced by the \makebox command. If the argument *pos* is omitted, then the *picture-object* is centred within the box produced. This can be altered by using a one- or two-letter *pos* argument. The letters that can be used have to be taken from the following four possibilities: l, r, t and b. If only a single one of these is present, then its effect is as follows:

l The *picture-object* is placed flush left inside the box produced. It is mid way between the top and bottom of the box.

r The *picture-object* is placed flush right inside the box produced. It is mid way between the top and bottom of the box.

t The *picture-object* is placed near the top of the box. It is mid way between the left and right edges of the box.

b The *picture-object* is placed near the bottom of the box. It is mid way between the left and right edges of the box.

There are only four possible distinct two-letter combinations for the *pos* argument that are meaningful. (Clearly, lt is the same as tl and lr is meaningless.) Their effect is as follows:

tl The *picture-object* is positioned in the top left-hand corner of the box produced.

tr The *picture-object* is positioned in the top right-hand corner of the box produced.

br The *picture-object* is positioned in the bottom right-hand corner of the box produced.

bl The *picture-object* is positioned in the bottom left-hand corner of the box produced.

There are two commands that are closely related to the \makebox command, namely the \framebox and the \dashbox commands. The \framebox command has exactly the same arguments as the \makebox command. The only difference between them is that the \framebox command produces text with a rectangular box drawn around it.[4] The \dashbox command is similar except that it takes an extra argument. Its general format is:

\dashbox{*h*}(*i, j*)[*pos*]{*picture-object*}

The arguments (*i, j*), *pos* and *picture-object* are as for \makebox and \framebox. The command \dashbox produces text with a broken rectangular box drawn around it. The lengths of the dashes and spaces that make up the box are given by the argument *h*. When using \dashbox it is a good idea for the arguments *i* and *j* to be whole multiples of *h*. This makes the dashed box that is produced look better than it would otherwise do.

In the case of the picture in Fig. 10.1 the \framebox and \dashbox commands are themselves made into arguments for the \makebox command, which is then taken as the *picture-object* argument of a \put command, thus:

\put(20,5){\makebox(0,0){\framebox(37,9){formal specification}}}
\put(90,5){\makebox(0,0){\dashbox{1.5}(30,9){verified design}}}

The reason for this is that in both the \framebox and \dashbox command if the argument (*i, j*) has the value (0, 0), then *no* line whatsoever is drawn around the box produced. Thus, in order to get a line you need non-zero values for both *i* and *j* in the argument (*i, j*). This, however, makes the box produced difficult to position precisely in the picture that is being drawn. Putting the \framebox and \dashbox commands inside a \makebox command—which is given (0, 0) as one of *its* arguments—makes the resulting box easy to position because its reference point is in the centre of the box that is produced.

10.2.2 Straight Lines

The two sloping straight lines in Fig. 10.1 were produced by means of the commands:

\put(50,40){\line(-1,-1){30}}
\put(60,40){\line(1,-1){30}}

In order to produce a line in a picture you need a command with the following general form:

\put(*i, j*){\line(*p, q*){*l*}}

---

[4] Note that the length parameter \fboxsep has no effect inside the picture environment; no gap is always left between the box produced and the frame.

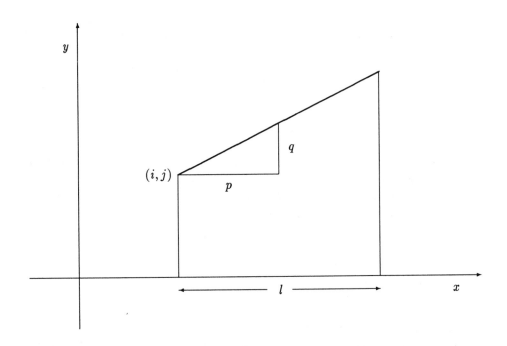

Figure 10.2: The arguments of the \put$(i,j)$\{\line$(p,q)$\{l\}\} command.

This draws a line one end of which starts at the point on the picture whose coordinates are given by the arguments (i,j). The coordinates (p,q) determine the slope of the line and the argument l determines its length. If we imagine the line that we want to draw being projected onto the x-axis, then the length of that projected line is l. (The picture in Fig. 10.2 should make this clearer.) The only exception to this occurs when we want to draw vertical lines when l gives the actual length of the line produced. This is because in this case the length of the projection of the line onto the x-axis is zero.

To produce a line with a particular slope you imagine how you would get back onto the line if you were only allowed to move horizontally and vertically. Thus, if you wanted to produce a line that was at 45° to the x-axis, you would have to move 1 unit horizontally and 1 unit vertically. The arguments p and q can be negative but they must be non-zero whole numbers without any common divisors (except -1 or $+1$) that lie between -6 and $+6$ (and the values -6 and $+6$ are allowed). Assuming that p and q are both positive numbers, this is illustrated in the diagram in Fig. 10.2.

LaTeX can produce lines in two thicknesses, namely thin and thick, and the default thickness of lines is the thin option. The lines in Fig. 10.1 are both thin. To get the thicker lines you need to include the declaration \thicklines. The scope of this can be made explicit by the use of curly braces. Alternatively, the use of the declaration

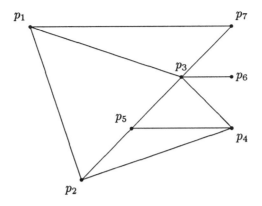

Figure 10.3: An example of a bill of materials.

\thinlines makes all lines from that point on to be thin.

Having explained all the commands relevant to the picture environment that produced the picture in Fig. 10.1 I just need to explain the remaining commands. The center environment has the effect of centring the picture that it encloses on the page.

10.3   Disks and Circles

The diagram contained in Fig. 10.3 was produced by the following LaTeX commands:[5]

```
\begin{center}
%
\unitlength=.3mm
\begin{picture}(240,180)(0,0)
%
\put(70,20){\line(-1,3){50}}
\put(70,20){\line(1,1){150}}
\put(70,20){\line(3,1){150}}
\put(20,170){\line(1,0){200}}
\put(20,170){\line(3,-1){150}}
\put(120,70){\line(1,0){100}}
\put(170,120){\line(1,0){50}}
\put(170,120){\line(1,-1){50}}
%
\put(70,20){\circle*{3.7}}
\put(20,170){\circle*{3.7}}
```

[5] This comes from p. 164 of Diller (1990).

```
\put(120,70){\circle*{3.7}}
\put(170,120){\circle*{3.7}}
\put(220,70){\circle*{3.7}}
\put(220,120){\circle*{3.7}}
\put(220,170){\circle*{3.7}}
%
\put(10,180){\makebox(0,0){$p_1$}}
\put(60,10){\makebox(0,0){$p_2$}}
\put(170,130){\makebox(0,0){$p_3$}}
\put(230,60){\makebox(0,0){$p_4$}}
\put(110,80){\makebox(0,0){$p_5$}}
\put(230,120){\makebox(0,0){$p_6$}}
\put(230,180){\makebox(0,0){$p_7$}}
%
\end{picture}
%
\end{center}
```

Most of these have been explained already. The filled in circles were produced by the
\circle* command. Thus, the filled in circle closest to the label p_1 was produced by
the command:

```
\put(20,170){\circle*{3.7}}
```

This draws a solid circular disk with diameter 3.7 (times the value of the rigid length
parameter \unitlength) whose centre is at the point whose coordinates are $(20, 170)$.
These is also a LaTeX command for drawing circles that are not filled in. The general
format of such a command is:

```
\put(i,j){\circle{d}}
```

This places a circle of diameter d on the picture in such a way that its centre is at the
point whose coordinates are (i, j). Note that LaTeX can only produce a very restricted
class of circles and disks. The largest circle it can draw is 40 points (which is about
half an inch) and the largest disk has a diameter of 15 points (which is about a fifth
of an inch). Also, there are only a finite number of diameters available. If there is not
one exactly the size you specify, then LaTeX will use the one in its repertoire that is
closest to the one you specify.

The label p_1 in Fig. 10.3 was produced by means of the command:

```
\put(10,180){\makebox(0,0){$p_1$}}
```

This illustrates how mathematical formulas can be positioned on a picture drawn by
LaTeX.

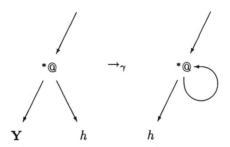

Figure 10.4: Graph-reduction of **Y**h.

10.4 Arrows and Ovals

The diagram that occurs in Fig. 10.4, which is Fig. 5.6 on p. 77 of Diller (1988), was
produced by means of the commands:

```
\begin{center}
\unitlength=1mm
\begin{picture}(60,40)(0,0)
%
\put(8,16){\vector(-1,-2){6}}
\put(12,16){\vector(1,-2){6}}
\put(18,36){\vector(-1,-2){6}}
\put(0,0){\makebox(0,0){\bf Y}}
\put(20,0){\makebox(0,0){$h$}}
\put(10,20){\makebox(0,0){$^*@$}}
%
\put(30,20){\makebox(0,0){$\rightarrow_\gamma$}}
%
\put(48,16){\vector(-1,-2){6}}
\put(58,36){\vector(-1,-2){6}}
\put(55,15){\oval(10,10)[b]}
\put(55,15){\oval(10,10)[tr]}
\put(55,20){\vector(-1,0){2}}
\put(50,15){\line(0,1){2}}
\put(50,20){\makebox(0,0){$^*@$}}
\put(40,0){\makebox(0,0){$h$}}
%
\end{picture}
\end{center}
```

The two new features of LaTeX's `picture` environment introduced here are the `\vector` and `\oval` commands. The first group of `\put` commands produce the graph to the left of the arrow $\rightarrow_\gamma$ in Fig. 10.4. For example, the command:

  `\put(18,36){\vector(-1,-2){6}}`

draws an arrow which starts at the point with coordinates $(18, 36)$ and whose projection on the x-axis is 6 units long and whose slope is given by the argument $(-1, 2)$, that is to say, it goes one unit in the left direction for every two units it goes downwards. The arrowhead of an arrow drawn by the `\vector` command is always at the end of the arrow whose coordinates are *not* given by the first argument to the `\put` command. The only exception to this is for arrows of length 0, in which case just the arrowhead itself is drawn and it occurs at the position given by the first argument to the `\put` command. The slopes with which LaTeX can draw arrows is more restrictive than the slopes that lines can have. The numbers in the slope argument must be non-zero whole numbers between -4 and $+4$.

The graph on the right of the arrow $\rightarrow_\gamma$ in Fig. 10.4 is produced by the third group of `\put` commands in the `picture` environment. The `\oval` commands produce the circular part of the middle arrow. The `\oval` command in LaTeX produces oblongs with rounded corners. Its general format is:

  `\put(`i, j`){\oval(`p, q`)[`*part*`]}`

This draws an oblong with smooth corners such that its centre is located at the point (i, j) and the oblong fits into a rectangle whose width is p units and whose height is q units. The optional *part* argument consists of a one- or two-letter code which indicates which part of the oblong is to be drawn. (If it is absent, the whole oblong is drawn.) A one-letter code draws half an oblong. Thus:

l   The left half of the oblong is drawn.

t   The top half of the oblong is drawn.

r   The right half of the oblong is drawn.

b   The bottom half of the oblong is drawn.

A two-letter code draws quarter of an oblong. Only the following four combinations are meaningful:

tl   The top left-hand quarter of the oval is drawn.

tr   The top right-hand quarter of the oval is drawn.

br   The bottom right-hand quarter of the oval is drawn.

bl   The bottom left-hand quarter of the oval is drawn.

10.5   Saving and Reusing Boxes

The following arrangement of circles:

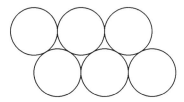

was produced by means of these commands:

```
\begin{center}
\begin{picture}(100,103.92)
\multiput(20,34.64)(40,0){3}{\circle{40}}
\multiput(0,69.28)(40,0){3}{\circle{40}}
\end{picture}
\end{center}
```

This illustrates the use of the **\multiput** command; the general format of which is:

$$\text{\textbackslash multiput}\,(i, j)\,(m, n)\,\{t\}\{picture\text{-}object\}$$

This is equivalent to the following t commands:

$$\text{\textbackslash put}\,(i, j)\,\{picture\text{-}object\}$$
$$\text{\textbackslash put}\,(i + m, j + n)\,\{picture\text{-}object\}$$
$$\text{\textbackslash put}\,(i + 2m, j + 2n)\,\{picture\text{-}object\}$$
$$\vdots$$
$$\text{\textbackslash put}\,(i + (t - 1)m, j + (t - 1)n)\,\{picture\text{-}object\}$$

LaTeX does not have a very large memory, so there is a maximum number of repetitions allowed and it is about 100.

One way of producing the arrangement of circles shown in Fig. 10.5 is by means of the following commands:

```
\newsavebox{\balls}
\savebox{\balls}(120,69.28){%
\begin{picture}(120,69.28)
\multiput(20,34.64)(40,0){3}{\circle{40}}
\multiput(0,69.28)(40,0){3}{\circle{40}}
\end{picture}}
```

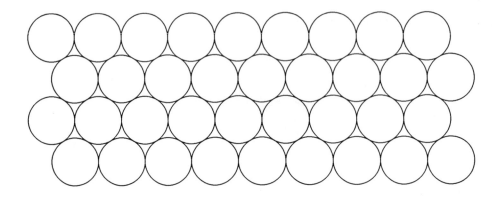

Figure 10.5: A pretty arrangement of circles.

```
\begin{picture}(340,173.2)
\multiput(0,0)(0,69.28){2}
        {\multiput(0,0)(120,0){3}{\usebox{\balls}}}
\end{picture}
```

The **\newsavebox** command here creates a *storage bin* called **\balls**. A storage bin is a region of memory that stores a box. It is a good idea to store boxes which require a lot of processing to produce and which you use several times in a document. If you use a macro rather than a stored box, then TEX will process it afresh each time it comes across it. The **\savebox** command here is similar to the **\makebox** command discussed earlier; it is processed in exactly the same way. Unlike the **\makebox** command, however, it does not produce anything that appears in the document that you are working on. Although it processes what is given to it as its argument, it puts the result into a storage bin. The general format of a **\savebox** command is:

\savebox{*cmd*}(*i, j*)[*pos*]{*picture-object*}

Here, the arguments (*i, j*), *pos* and *picture-object* have exactly the same meaning as in the case of the **\makebox** command. The argument *cmd* is the name of the storage bin that must have been introduced previously by means of a **\newsavebox** command and *cmd* must begin with an initial backslash. In order to get what is stored in a storage bin to actually appear in your document you use the **\usebox** command. LATEX has only a small amount of space at its disposal for storing boxes. If you need to store several boxes in a document, you can reclaim the space needed by, say, the **\balls** storage bin by means of the command **\sbox{\balls}{}**. The **\sbox** command is a variant of the **\savebox** command with no optional arguments.

10.6   Contract Bridge Diagrams

The contract bridge diagram shown in Fig. 1.3 in chapter 1—and reproduced here as
Fig. 10.6—is fairly easy to produce. First, the individual hands are defined in local
"commands" \north, \east, \south and \west as follows:

```
\def\north{%
\begin{tabular}{cl}
$\spadesuit$   & Q\,\,8\,\,7\,\,4 \\
$\heartsuit$   & Q\,\,10\,\,5\,\,4\,\,2 \\
$\diamondsuit$ & K\,\,7 \\
$\clubsuit$    & 7\,\,3
\end{tabular}}

\def\east{%
\begin{tabular}{cl}
$\spadesuit$   & A\,\,K\,\,J\,\,2 \\
$\heartsuit$   & A\,\,K\,\,J\,\,7 \\
$\diamondsuit$ & A\,\,6\,\,3 \\
$\clubsuit$    & K\,\,2
\end{tabular}}

\def\south{%
\begin{tabular}{cl}
$\spadesuit$   & 10\,\,3 \\
$\heartsuit$   & 3 \\
$\diamondsuit$ & J\,\,9\,\,5\,\,4 \\
$\clubsuit$    & Q\,\,J\,\,9\,\,8\,\,5\,\,4
\end{tabular}}

\def\west{%
\begin{tabular}{cl}
$\spadesuit$   & 9\,\,6\,\,5 \\
$\heartsuit$   & 9\,\,8\,\,6 \\
$\diamondsuit$ & Q\,\,10\,\,8\,\,2 \\
$\clubsuit$    & A\,\,10\,\,6
\end{tabular}}
```

Then the diagram is produced like this:

```
\begin{center}
\addtolength{\tabcolsep}{-1mm}
\unitlength=1mm
\begin{picture}(90,90)
%
```

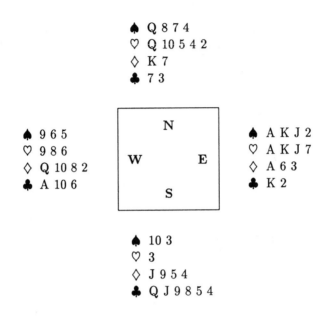

Figure 10.6: A contract bridge diagram.

```
\put(30,30){\line(1,0){30}}
\put(30,30){\line(0,1){30}}
\put(60,60){\line(-1,0){30}}
\put(60,60){\line(0,-1){30}}
%
\put(45,55){\makebox(0,0){\bf N}}
\put(55,45){\makebox(0,0){\bf E}}
\put(45,35){\makebox(0,0){\bf S}}
\put(35,45){\makebox(0,0){\bf W}}
%
\put(32.5,75){\north}
\put(67.5,44){\east}
\put(32.5,12.5){\south}
\put(0,44){\west}
%
\addtolength{\tabcolsep}{1mm}
%
\end{picture}
\end{center}
```

10.7   Small Pictures

So far all the examples of pictures that I have discussed have been fairly large. It is possible, however, to use LaTeX's picture environment to draw quite small line drawings. For example, the combination of symbols:

$$\underline{\quad}\smallsmile\!f\!\smallsmile\underline{\quad}\ \mu_\beta(f(\beta)),$$

was obtained by means of the LaTeX commands:

```
$$\fgen{\gotf} \mu_\beta(\gotf(\beta)),$$
```

where the macros \fgen and \gotf are defined as follows:

```
\def\fgen#1{\mathop{%
\unitlength=1mm
\begin{picture}(19,3.5)(0,2.4)
\put(0,3.5){\line(1,0){7}}
\put(12,3.5){\line(1,0){7}}
\put(9.5,3.5){\oval(5,5)[b]}
\put(9.5,3.5){\makebox(0,0){$#1$}}
\end{picture}}}
```

```
\def\gotf{{\sf f}} % should be Gothic ef.
```

The symbol produced by the macro \fgen is Frege's sign for the universal quantifier. Here it is being used as a second-level quantifier. The macro \fgen takes a single argument which is the binding variable. Frege used Gothic letters as binding and bound variables. Although Gothic letters are available with many LaTeX systems, I did not have access to them when writing this book. Hence, I use a sans serif letter.

In the definition of \gotf there have to be two sets of curly braces. The outermost are part of the syntax of the TeX \def macro facility, whereas the innermost pair delimit the scope of the \sf declaration. If they were absent, then when the \gotf macro was used not only the f would be in sans serif but also everything else from that point on till the next type-changing declaration.

10.8   Boxes and Very Small Pictures

Some philosophers and theoretical computer scientists use "corners" to signify quasi-quotation. These are illustrated in the expression $\ulcorner X^2 + X \urcorner$, which was produced by means of the command \qq{$X^2 + X$} where the macro \qq was defined in several stages as follows:

```
\newsavebox{\@lqq}
\savebox{\@lqq}[1mm]
{
  \unitlength=1mm
  \begin{picture}(1,2)(0,0)
  \put(0,3.5){\line(1,0){1}}
  \put(0,3.5){\line(0,-1){1}}
  \end{picture}
}

\newsavebox{\@rqq}
\savebox{\@rqq}[1mm]
{
  \unitlength=1mm
  \begin{picture}(1,2)(0,0)
  \put(1,3.5){\line(-1,0){1}}
  \put(1,3.5){\line(0,-1){1}}
  \end{picture}
}

\newcommand{\qq}[1]{\mbox{\usebox{\@lqq}#1\usebox{\@rqq}}}
```

The two \newsavebox commands here create two *storage bins* called, respectively, \@lqq and \@rqq. The use of the commercial at sign here indicates that these commands have to be placed in a style file. In LATEX a storage bin is a region of memory which stores a box that may require a lot of processing to create and which you are likely to require several times in a document. If you use a macro rather than a stored box, then TEX will process it afresh each time it comes across it. It is, therefore, best to use storage bins for frequently used complicated arrangements of symbols. The storage of corner quotation marks is used here for illustrative purposes; with such a simple example not much is saved by using storage bins. This example should be compared—and contrasted—with what was said earlier in this chapter about the production of the pretty arrangement of cicles in Fig. 10.5. Note in particular that the \savebox commands are different in the two cases.

11

Two-column Output

11.1 Introduction

In order to produce a document that has two columns of text on every page you need to choose the twocolumn option to the \documentstyle command. Most LaTeX commands have the same effect in two-column output as they do in one-column output; one of the consequences, however, of choosing the twocolumn option is that various length parameters are initialized to values that are different from what they would have been initialized to otherwise. For example, paragraph indentation is different and the indentation of list-like environments is also different.

If you just want part of your document to be typeset in the two-column format, then you can use the \twocolumn declaration to achieve this; the \onecolumn declaration reverts the output back to the one-column format. Both the declarations \onecolumn and \twocolumn force a new page to be started. An important difference between the twocolumn option and the \twocolumn declaration is that the latter does not alter the values of any length parameters as the former does.

There are a small number of commands which behave differently when the twocolumn option is chosen, in particular \pagebreak, \newpage and \marginpar. The \marginpar command places marginal notes in the nearest margin, that is to say, in the right-hand margin if the \marginpar command occurs in the right-hand column and in the left-hand margin if the \marginpar command occurs in the left-hand column; whether one- or two-sided printing is in force has no effect on the placement of such marginal notes. The \newpage and \pagebreak commands start new columns rather than new pages, but the \clearpage and \cleardoublepage commands continue to terminate the current page.

The value of the length parameter \columnsep is the width of the gap that separates the two columns of text and the value of \columnseprule is the width of the vertical rule that is placed in the gap between the two columns; the default value of this is zero inches.

11.2 Floats

11.2.1 Some Examples

The greatest differences between one- and two-column output, however, is in the treatment of floats. In two-column output both one- and two-column wide floats

myth	example
antitypical	redemption through vicarious sacrifice
architypical	dragon slaying
atypical	dragon impregnating queen
typical	account of creation

Table 11.1: Some types of myth.

Once upon a time there lived a fierce dragon in the land of Urghh and he terrorized the inhabitants of that green and once pleasant land; but there arose in Urghh a mighty queen who bore the name of Alice who bore the dragon a son ...

Figure 11.1: The beginning of the story.

are available. The `figure` and `table` environments produce floats one-column wide; whereas the `figure*` and `table*` environments produce floats that are two-columns wide. For example, in order to produce Fig. 11.1 you need these commands:

```
\begin{figure}
\hrule
\vspace{4ex}
Once upon a time there lived
a fierce dragon in the land
of Urghh and he terrorized
the inhabitants of that green
and once pleasant land; but
there arose in Urghh a mighty
queen who bore the name of
Alice who bore the dragon
a son \ldots
\vspace{4ex}
\hrule
\caption
```

```
{The beginning of the story.}
\label{JJ}
\end{figure}
```

And to produce Table 11.1 you have to include these commands in your input file:

```
\begin{table*}
\begin{center}
\begin{tabular}{|l|l|}\hline
\multicolumn{1}{|c|}{myth} &
\multicolumn{1}{c|}{example} \\
\hline\hline
antitypical &
redemption through vicarious
sacrifice \\ \hline
architypical &
dragon slaying \\ \hline
atypical &
dragon impregnating
queen \\ \hline
typical &
account of creation
\\ \hline
\end{tabular}
\end{center}
\caption
{Some types of myth.}
\label{KK}
\end{table*}
```

All the options relating to the `table` and `figure` environments described in section 4.9 are also available for the `table*` and `figure*` environments.

11.2.2 Parameters

There are a number of parameters that affect the placement and appearance of floats; first, I look at the effects of the following counters:

bottomnumber is the maximum number of floats that can occur at the bottom of each column which contains both text and floats.

dbltopnumber is the maximum number of two-column floats that can occur at the top of a page that contains text as well as floats.

topnumber is the maximum number of floats that can occur at the top of each column which contains both text and floats.

totalnumber is the maximum number of floats that can occur in a single column.

Note that two-column wide floats cannot be placed at the bottom of the page.

Next, I explain how the meanings of those parameters whose values are floating-point numbers are affected by the choice of the **twocolumn** option:

\topfraction is the amount of each column that can be occupied by floats at its top (if it also contains text).

\bottomfraction is the amount of the column that can be occupied by floats at its bottom (if it also contains text).

\textfraction is the minimum amount of text that can appear in a column.

\floatpageaction is the minimum amount of a floats-only column that has to be taken up by floats.

\dbltopfraction is the amount of each page that can be occupied by two-column wide floats at its top (if it also contains text).

\dblfloatpageaction is the minimum amount of a floats-only page that has to be taken up by two-column wide floats.

Finally, I look at those length parameters that affect the appearance of floats:[1]

\dblfloatsep is the amount of vertical space that is placed between two two-column wide floats on a page that contains both text and floats.

\dbltextfloatsep is the amount of vertical space left between a double-column float and the text either below or above it.

\floatsep is the amount of vertical space left between single-column floats on a page that contains both text and floats.

\intextsep is the amount of vertical space placed above and below a float that occurs in the middle of a text page because the h location option has been chosen.

\textfloatsep is the amount of vertical space left between a single-column wide float and the text either below or above it.

---

[1] Note that these are all *rubber* length parameters; for more information about these see subsection B.1.2. All these length parameters are robust commands that must not be preceded by a \protect command.

A

Mathematical Symbols

A.1 Introduction

There are several categories of mathematical symbols in TeX and the most important of these are shown in the following table:[1]

kind of atom	name	example	command
ordinary	Ord	\gamma	\mathord
large operator	Op	\prod	\mathop
binary operation	Bin	\wedge	\mathbin
relation	Rel	\gg	\mathrel
opening	Open	\{	\mathopen
closing	Close	\}	\mathclose
punctuation	Punct	,	\mathpunct
inner	Inner	{1 \over 2}	\mathinner

I will now describe the symbols belonging to each of these categories in greater detail.

A.2 Ordinary Symbols

In math mode as well as treating the 26 uppercase Roman letters A to Z and the 26 lowercase Roman letters a to z as ordinary symbols TeX also considers the following 18 characters to be ordinary symbols:

$$0 \quad 1 \quad 2 \quad 3 \quad 4 \quad 5 \quad 6 \quad 7 \quad 8 \quad 9 \quad ! \quad ? \quad . \quad | \quad / \quad ` \quad @ \quad "$$

To say that a character is an *ordinary symbol* means that TeX does not insert any extra space when these symbols occur next to each other.[2] Note that the full stop is considered to be an ordinary symbol in math mode and not a punctuation mark. This

---

[1] TeXperts will be well aware that this is a slight simplification. See section 8.2 for more information.
[2] Knuth (1986), p. 132.

ensures that real numbers are correctly typeset in math mode. Thus, $12.72 > x$ is produced by means of the commands `$12.72 > x$`.

When any of the 52 upper- and lowercase letters occur within math brackets—either `$` or `$$`—then they appear in math italic font. This is slightly different from text italic. The letters themselves are slightly larger and the spacing is completely different. This comes out clearly in a word like 'effluent', which in text italic looks like *effluent*, but in math italic appears as $effluent$. The reason for this is that mathematicians typically use single letters for the names of functions and variables, and juxtaposition usually indicates multiplication. Computer scientists, on the other hand, like to use multi-letter identifiers. This can be achieved in TEX by using `${\it effluent}$`.

A.2.1 Lowercase Greek Letters

There are twenty-four letters in the Greek alphabet and their lowercase forms are produced as follows:[3]

α	\alpha	η	\eta	ν	\nu	τ	\tau
β	\beta	θ	\theta	ξ	\xi	υ	\upsilon
γ	\gamma	ι	\iota	o	o	ϕ	\phi
δ	\delta	κ	\kappa	π	\pi	χ	\chi
ϵ	\epsilon	λ	\lambda	ρ	\rho	ψ	\psi
ζ	\zeta	μ	\mu	σ	\sigma	ω	\omega

TEX considers each of these to be an ordinary symbol. Note that omicron is produced by typing 'o' in math mode. Mathematicians also use variants of delta, epsilon, theta, pi, rho and phi. These are produced as follows:

∂	\partial	ϑ	\vartheta	ϱ	\varrho
ε	\varepsilon	ϖ	\varpi	φ	\varphi

Still another variant of epsilon, namely $\in$ produced by the command \in, is used for set membership, but TEX treats this as a relation and not an ordinary operator.

TEX also contains the symbol ς produced by typing **\varsigma**. According to Knuth (1986), p. 434, this—and upsilon—are not letters that are used by mathematicians. They are included in TEX in case someone wants to quote *short* Greek passages. If you want a Greek version of TEX, then you should set up a new font.

---

[3] This—and the following table of variant lowercase Greek letters—is adapted from a table that occurs in Knuth (1986), p. 434.

A.2.2 Uppercase Greek Letters

There are twenty-four letters in the Greek alphabet and their uppercase forms are produced like this:[4]

A	`{\rm A}`	H	`{\rm H}`	N	`{\rm N}`	T	`{\rm T}`
B	`{\rm B}`	Θ	`\Theta`	Ξ	`\Xi`	Υ	`\Upsilon`
Γ	`\Gamma`	I	`{\rm I}`	O	`{\rm O}`	Φ	`\Phi`
Δ	`\Delta`	K	`{\rm K}`	Π	`\Pi`	X	`{\rm X}`
E	`{\rm E}`	Λ	`\Lambda`	P	`{\rm P}`	Ψ	`\Psi`
Z	`{\rm Z}`	M	`{\rm M}`	Σ	`\Sigma`	Ω	`\Omega`

Note that by default "upright" versions of the uppercase Greek letters are produced; this is because these are the most commonly used in mathematics.

A.2.3 Italic Uppercase Greek Letters

A	A	*I*	I	*P*	P
B	B	*K*	K	*Σ*	`{\mit\Sigma}`
Γ	`{\mit\Gamma}`	*Λ*	`{\mit\Lambda}`	*T*	T
Δ	`{\mit\Delta}`	*M*	M	*Υ*	`{\mit\Upsilon}`
E	E	*N*	N	*Φ*	`{\mit\Phi}`
Z	Z	*Ξ*	`{\mit\Xi}`	*X*	X
H	H	*O*	O	*Ψ*	`{\mit\Psi}`
Θ	`{\mit\Theta}`	*Π*	`{\mit\Pi}`	*Ω*	`{\mit\Omega}`

A.2.4 Uppercase Calligraphic Letters

$\mathcal{A}$	`{\cal A}`	$\mathcal{H}$	`{\cal H}`	$\mathcal{O}$	`{\cal O}`	$\mathcal{U}$	`{\cal U}`
$\mathcal{B}$	`{\cal B}`	$\mathcal{I}$	`{\cal I}`	$\mathcal{P}$	`{\cal P}`	$\mathcal{V}$	`{\cal V}`
$\mathcal{C}$	`{\cal C}`	$\mathcal{J}$	`{\cal J}`	$\mathcal{Q}$	`{\cal Q}`	$\mathcal{W}$	`{\cal W}`
$\mathcal{D}$	`{\cal D}`	$\mathcal{K}$	`{\cal K}`	$\mathcal{R}$	`{\cal R}`	$\mathcal{X}$	`{\cal X}`
$\mathcal{E}$	`{\cal E}`	$\mathcal{L}$	`{\cal L}`	$\mathcal{S}$	`{\cal S}`	$\mathcal{Y}$	`{\cal Y}`
$\mathcal{F}$	`{\cal F}`	$\mathcal{M}$	`{\cal M}`	$\mathcal{T}$	`{\cal T}`	$\mathcal{Z}$	`{\cal Z}`
$\mathcal{G}$	`{\cal G}`	$\mathcal{N}$	`{\cal N}`				

A.2.5 Miscellaneous Symbols

The following table of various symbols of type Ord is adapted from one that appears in Knuth (1986), p. 435:

---

[4] This table of uppercase Greek letters is adapted from one that occurs in Knuth (1986), p. 434.

∀	\forall	ℓ	\ell	♭	\flat
∃	\exists	℘	\wp	♯	\sharp
¬	\neg	ℜ	\Re	♮	\natural
⊤	\top	ℑ	\Im	♠	\spadesuit
⊥	\bot	′	\prime	♡	\heartsuit
∅	\emptyset	∇	\nabla	◇	\diamondsuit
ℵ	\aleph	√	\surd	♣	\clubsuit
∞	\infty	‖	| or \Vert	△	\triangle
ℏ	\hbar	∠	\angle	◇	\Diamond
ι	\imath	\	\backslash	□	\Box
ȷ	\jmath	℧	\mho				or \vert
/	/	℘	\%	$	\$
#	\#	‐	_	&	\&

The symbols ◇, □ and ℧ are peculiar to LaTeX and are not to be found in plain TeX.

A.3   Large Operator Symbols

A.3.1   Introduction

The following table of large operator symbols is adapted from one that appears in Knuth (1986), p. 435:

∑	\sum	⋂	\bigcap	⊙	\bigodot
∏	\prod	⋃	\bigcup	⊗	\bigotimes
∐	\coprod	⊔	\bigsqcup	⊕	\bigoplus
∫	\int	⋁	\bigvee	⊎	\biguplus
∮	\oint	⋀	\bigwedge		

When subscripts and superscripts are attached to a control word for a large operator symbol in display style, then they appear under and over the symbol, respectively, as limits. For example, `$$\sum_{i=1}↑{i=n} i↑2,$$` produces:

$$\sum_{i=1}^{i=n} i^2,$$

whereas `$\sum_{i=1}↑{i=n} i↑2$` produces $\sum_{i=1}^{i=n} i^2$ within text. Note that the size of the operator has altered as well.

A.3.2 Log-like Symbols

arccos	\arccos	dim	\dim	log	\log
arcsin	\arcsin	exp	\exp	max	\max
arctan	\arctan	gcd	\gcd	min	\min
arg	\arg	hom	\hom	Pr	\Pr
cos	\cos	inf	\inf	sec	\sec
cosh	\cosh	ker	\ker	sin	\sin
cot	\cot	lg	\lg	sinh	\sinh
coth	\coth	lim	\lim	sup	\sup
csc	\csc	lim inf	\liminf	tan	\tan
deg	\deg	lim sup	\limsup	tanh	\tanh
det	\det	ln	\ln		

These operators fall into two distinct categories depending on how subscripts and superscripts behave in display style. Subscripts and superscripts become limits in display style when attached to the following operators: \det, \gcd, \inf, \lim, \liminf, \limsup, \max, \min, \Pr and \sup.

A.3.3 Defining your own Large Operators

In order to define your own log-like function you have to decide how you want subscripts and superscripts to behave. If you want them to appear as limits in display style, then define your operator as:

```
\def\dom{\mathop{\rm dom}\limits}
```

Otherwise, define it in this way:

```
\def\dom{\mathop{\rm dom}\nolimits}
```

Roscoe and Hoare (1988) contains on p. 181 the formula:

$$\mathop{\rm IF}_{i=1}^{n} b_i P_i = \mathop{\rm IF}_{i=1}^{n} b_i^* P_i.$$

To get this in LaTeX you input

```
$$\IF_{i=1}^n b_i P_i = \IF_{i=1}^n b_i^* P_i.$$
```

where \IF is defined as \def\IF{\mathop{\rm IF}\limits}.

A.4 Binary Operator Symbols

A.4.1 Introduction

A binary operator is something like $+$ or $\sqcap$. It makes a term or expression out of two terms or expressions. It should be contrasted with a binary relation symbol like $>$ or

⊐, since these makes a predicate or proposition out of two terms or expressions. This difference is reflected in how much space separates the operators from their arguments.[5] In the case of a relation, like:

$$x > y,$$

there is a thick amount of separating space. This amount is represented by the command \; and which is about five eighteenths of a quad.[6] In the case of an operator, like:

$$x + y,$$

there is a medium amount of separating space. This amount is represented by the command \: and which is about two nineths of a quad.[7] The following table of binary operator symbols is adapted from one that appears in Knuth (1986), p. 436:

+	+	⊎	\uplus	◇	\diamond
−	-	⊔	\sqcup	◁	\triangleleft
±	\pm	⊓	\sqcap	▷	\triangleright
∓	\mp	·	\cdot	◁	\lhd
×	\times	•	\bullet	▷	\rhd
∗	\ast or *	∘	\circ	⊴	\unlhd
⋆	\star	◯	\bigcirc	⊵	\unrhd
÷	\div	⊙	\odot	△	\bigtriangleup
∧	\wedge	⊕	\oplus	▽	\bigtriangledown
∨	\vee	⊖	\ominus	†	\dagger
∪	\cup	⊗	\otimes	‡	\ddagger
∩	\cap	⊘	\oslash	II	\amalg
\	\setminus	≀	\wr	mod	\bmod

Some of these symbols are not in TEX, namely ◁, ▷, ⊴ and ⊵. This table is complete.

A.4.2   Defining your own Operator Symbols

Say you want to define the symbol ⧺ which some people—for example, Bird (1988)—use for list concatenation. The way to do this is as follows:[8]

    \def\con{\mathbin{+\mkern-8mu+}}

Defining it like this gets the spacing correct:

$$x \mathbin{+\!\!\!+} (y \mathbin{+\!\!\!+} z) = (x \mathbin{+\!\!\!+} y) \mathbin{+\!\!\!+} z.$$

This was produced by means of the following:

    $$x \con (y \con z) = (x \con y) \con z.$$

---

[5] This information comes from Knuth (1986), p. 167.

[6] A quad of space is one em wide.

[7] In TEX this amount of space is represented by \> which in LATEX has a special meaning in the tabbing environment.

[8] The mu (math unit) is a unit of length. There are 18 mu to an em. The mu can only be used in math mode.

A.5 Binary Relation Symbols

A.5.1 Introduction

The following table of binary relation symbols is adapted from one that appears in Knuth (1986), p. 436:

>	`>`	<	`<`	=	`=`
≤	`\leq`	≥	`\geq`	≡	`\equiv`
≺	`\prec`	≻	`\succ`	∼	`\sim`
≼	`\preceq`	≽	`\succeq`	≃	`\simeq`
≪	`\ll`	≫	`\gg`	≍	`\asymp`
⊂	`\subset`	⊃	`\supset`	≈	`\approx`
⊆	`\subseteq`	⊇	`\supseteq`	≅	`\cong`
⊏	`\sqsubset`	⊐	`\sqsupset`	⋈	`\Join`
⊑	`\sqsubseteq`	⊒	`\sqsupseteq`	⋈	`\bowtie`
∈	`\in`	∋	`\ni`	∝	`\propto`
⊢	`\vdash`	⊣	`\dashv`	⊨	`\models`
⌣	`\smile`	⌢	`\frown`	≐	`\doteq`
|	`\mid`	‖	`\parallel`	⊥	`\perp`
:	`:`				

The symbols ⊏, ⊐ and ⋈ are not in plain TEX. Note also that : is treated by TEX as a relation. This ensures the correct spacing in constructs like `$$x := x + 1,$$`, which produces:

$$x := x + 1.$$

In order to get the colon that is used to indicate the type of an object or function, see under punctuation symbols below. To negate any relation symbol simply precede it by `\not`. Thus, `$x \not\equiv y$` gives $x \not\equiv y$.

A.5.2 Arrow Symbols

The following arrow symbols are all considered to be binary relations by TEX and spacing is added accordingly. This table of arrow symbols is adapted from one that appears in Knuth (1986), p. 437:

↑	\uparrow	↓	\downarrow
⇑	\Uparrow	⇓	\Downarrow
↕	\updownarrow	⇕	\Updownarrow
↗	\nearrow	↘	\searrow
↙	\swarrow	↖	\nwarrow
←	\leftarrow	⟵	\longleftarrow
⇐	\Leftarrow	⟸	\Longleftarrow
→	\rightarrow	⟶	\longrightarrow
⇒	\Rightarrow	⟹	\Longrightarrow
↔	\leftrightarrow	⟷	\longleftrightarrow
⇔	\Leftrightarrow	⟺	\Longleftrightarrow
↦	\mapsto	⟼	\longmapsto
↩	\hookleftarrow	↪	\hookrightarrow
↼	\leftharpoonup	⇀	\rightharpoonup
↽	\leftharpoondown	⇁	\rightharpoondown
⇌	\rightleftharpoons	⤳	\leadsto

The symbol ⤳ is not in plain TEX. Note that when preceded by either **\left** or **\right** the commands **\downarrow**, **\Downarrow**, **\uparrow**, **\Uparrow**, **\updownarrow** and **\Updownarrow** produce delimiters whose size depends on what they delimit.

A.6   Delimiters

For more information about delimiters than is contained in this section, see section 7.4 above.

A.6.1   Opening Symbols

The following table is adapted from one that occurs in Knuth (1986), p. 437:

(	(	[	[	{	\{
⟨	\langle	⌊	\lfloor	⌈	\lceil

The symbol { can also be produced by means of the command **\lbrace** and the symbol [can be produced by **\lbrack**.

A.6.2   Closing Symbols

The following table is adapted from one that occurs in Knuth (1986), p. 437:

)	)	]	]	}	\}
⟩	\rangle	⌋	\rfloor	⌉	\rceil

The symbol } can also be prodiced by means of the command **\rbrace** and the symbol] can be produced by **\rbrack**.

A.6.3 Defining your own Bracket-like Symbols

Some people try to use $<$ and $>$ as bracket-like symbols, but the spacing does not work out correctly. If you do want to use these as delimiters, then you have to define them like `\def\lacute{\mathopen{<}}` and `\def\racute{\mathclose{>}}`. Notice the difference in spacing in the following example, where the operators on the left of the $\Longleftrightarrow$ sign have been redefined.

$$<x, y> \Longleftrightarrow \; < x, y > .$$

This was produced by means of the following:

```
$$\lacute x, y \racute \iff < x, y>.$$
```

Compare this with:

$$<x, y> \Longleftrightarrow \langle x, y \rangle,$$

produced by means of the following:

```
$$\lacute x, y \racute \iff \langle x, y \rangle,$$
```

A.7   Punctuation Symbols

When commas and semicolons occur in mathematical formulas TEX puts a thin space after them. It also does this for the colon when the command `\colon` is used. Notice the difference in spacing in the following:

$$f\colon x \rightarrow y \qquad f : x \rightarrow y,$$

which was produced by means of the following:

```
$$f \colon x \rightarrow y \qquad f : x \rightarrow y,$$
```

The following symbols can be used in any mode and—according to Lamport (1986), p. 40—when, used in math mode they are punctuation symbols: † (`\dag`), ‡ (`\ddag`), § (`\S`), ¶ (`\P`), © (`\copyright`) and £ (`\pounds`).

B

Useful Notions

B.1 Lengths and Length Parameters

B.1.1 Lengths

The following absolute units of length are available in TeX: `bp` (big point), `cc` (cicero), `cm` (centimetre), `dd` (didot point), `in` (inch), `mm` (millimetre), `pc` (pica), `pt` (point) and `sp` (scaled point). The following conversions are exact in TeX:

$$72 \text{ big points} = 1 \text{ inch,}$$
$$1 \text{ cicero} = 12 \text{ didot points,}$$
$$2.54 \text{ centimetres} = 1 \text{ inch,}$$
$$1157 \text{ didot points} = 1238 \text{ points,}$$
$$1 \text{ inch} = 72.27 \text{ points,}$$
$$10 \text{ millimetres} = 1 \text{ centimetre,}$$
$$1 \text{ pica} = 12 \text{ points,}$$
$$65536 \text{ scaled points} = 1 \text{ point.}$$

The scaled point is the dimension in terms of which TeX stores all lengths internally.

In addition to these absolute units of length—whose value does not depend on the current size of type—there are also three relative length units available, namely `em`, `ex` and `mu` (mathematical unit), the last of these is only available in math mode. Traditionally, the em was the width of an uppercase letter 'M' and the ex was the height of a lowercase letter 'x', but in the fonts used by TeX they are just font-dependent units of length. In the Computer Modern fonts designed by Knuth the em-dash is always one em wide, the ten digits are each half an em wide and the ordinary parentheses (and) are one em high; furthermore, the letter 'x' is one ex high.

B.1.2   Length Parameters

A *length parameter* is a length command whose value affects the appearance of the output produced by LaTeX. Length parameters are either *rigid* or *rubber*; a rubber one is one whose actual value depends on the context in which it occurs, whereas the value of a rigid length parameter is fixed and will neither stretch nor shrink. For example, the value of the rigid length parameter \textheight is the height of the body region on the output page as produced by LaTeX.

Rigid Length Parameters

The following is a list of LaTeX's rigid length parameters:

\arraycolsep	\headsep	\marginparpush
\arrayrulewidth	\itemindent	\marginparsep
\bibindent	\labelsep	\marginparwidth
\columnsep	\labelwidth	\mathindent
\columnseprule	\leftmargin	\oddsidemargin
\doublerulesep	\leftmargini	\parindent
\evensidemargin	\leftmarginii	\rightmargin
\fboxrule	\leftmarginiii	\tabbingsep
\fboxsep	\leftmarginiv	\tabcolsep
\footheight	\leftmarginv	\textheight
\footnotesep	\leftmarginvi	\textwidth
\footskip	\linewidth	\topmargin
\headheight	\listparindent	\unitlength

In order to change one of these you need to include in your input file or style file an assignment like \arraycolsep=5pt or you can use the \setlength command in this way \setlength{\unitlength}{1mm} or \setlength{\rightmargin}{leftmargin}.

Rubber Length Parameters

The following is a list of LaTeX's rubber length parameters:

\abovedisplayshortskip	\dbltextfloatsep	\partopsep
\abovedisplayskip	\floatsep	\textfloatsep
\baselineskip	\intextskip	\topsep
\belowdisplayshortskip	\itemsep	\topskip
\belowdisplayskip	\parsep	
\dblfloatsep	\parskip	

The way you alter any of these is by means of the following sort of assignment:

    \parskip=12pt plus 4pt minus 2pt

This means that the natural value of the rubber length parameter is 12 points—in TEXese this is known as *natural space*—but it can stretch or expand by up to 4 points and it can shrink or contract by up to 2 points. In assignments to rubber length parameters the plus and minus keywords and their associated lengths are optional; if either is omitted, then TEX assumes a zero point value.

The topic of rubber length or glue—as it is known in TEXese—gets pretty complicated and I think that it would be inappropriate for me to say more about it here; the interested reader is referred to Snow (1992), chapter 10, for a very readable account of the whole topic of glue.

B.2 Environments

There are 34 built-in environments in LATEX though additional ones can be introduced by means of the \newenvironment and \newtheorem declarations and existing ones can be given new meanings by the \renewenvironment declaration.[1] The following is a complete list of the predefined environments:

abstract	flushleft	table
array	flushright	table*
center	itemize	tabular
description	letter	tabular*
displaymath	list	thebibliography
document	math	theindex
enumerate	minipage	trivlist
eqnarray	picture	verbatim
eqnarray*	quotation	verbatim*
equation	quote	verse
figure	sloppypar	
figure*	tabbing	

The general-purpose list environment—and its restricted trivlist version—are used to define some of the other environments, namely the list-like ones which are center, description, enumerate, flushleft, flushright, itemize, quotation, quote, thebibliography and verse.

B.3 Counters and Current \ref Values

A *counter* in LATEX is an integer-valued variable and there are 23 built-in counters though additional ones can be defined by means of the \newcounter command (and

---

[1] Lamport (1986), p. 34, says that corresponding to each declaration there is an environment whose name is obtained by stripping off the initial backslash of the declaration name. I have completely ignored this "feature" as Lamport's account of it is so confused. For example, if it were as simple as he suggests, then why are the environments corresponding to the declarations \centering, \raggedleft and \raggedright called center, flushright and flushleft rather than centering, raggedleft and raggedright?

sometimes using the \newtheorem command creates a new counter). The following is a complete list of LaTeX's predefined counters:

bottomnumber	figure	subparagraph
chapter	footnote	subsection
dbltopnumber	mpfootnote	subsubsection
enumi	page	table
enumii	paragraph	tocdepth
enumiii	part	topnumber
enumiv	secnumdepth	totalnumber
equation	section	

Some of these counters are parameters that influence the placement of floats, namely bottomnumber, dbltopnumber, topnumber and totalnumber. The counter tocdepth controls what goes into the table of contents and secnumdepth influences the numbering of sectional units.

The others are used for numbering various things and these numbers—except in the case of footnotes—can be used for cross-referencing purposes. The value of a counter can be output in various ways. For example, if *ctr* is a counter, then \arabic{*ctr*} outputs the value of *ctr* in the form of an Arabic numeral, whereas \roman{*ctr*} outputs its value in the form of a lowercase Roman numeral, \Roman{*ctr*} outputs its value in the form of an uppercase Roman numeral, \alph{*ctr*} and \Alph{*ctr*} output its value—but only if this lies between 1 and 26 inclusive—as a lowercase and uppercase letter, respectively. Corresponding to each counter *ctr* there is a command \the*ctr* which is the default text output associated with the counter. For example, the page counter keeps the current page number, but the output text that appears on the page is stored in the command \thepage whose default value is \arabic{page}. But the textual output associated with LaTeX's predfined counters is not always in the form of an Arabic numeral as the following table shows:

ctr	\the*ctr*
footnote	\arabic{footnote}
mpfootnote	\alph{mpfootnote}
page	\arabic{page}
part	\Roman{part}

Every \label{*key*} command writes a \newlabel{*key*}{{*text*$_1$}{*text*$_2$}} command to the aux file where *text*$_2$ is the page number of the page on which \label{*key*} appeared and *text*$_1$ depends on the context in which \label{*key*} appeared: inside an enumerate environment it is a label depending on how deeply nested the environment is; following a \caption command inside a figure, figure*, table or table* environment it is the figure or table label; inside an equation or eqnarray environment it is the label of the current formula; and elsewhere it is a label depending on some sectioning command. Note that in both the `book` and `report` document styles all these labels are preceded by the chapter number except those produced by the `enumerate` environment.[2]

When you place a `\pageref{`*key*`}` command in your input, then *text*$_2$ is output; and the presence of a `\ref{`*key*`}` command outputs *text*$_1$.

B.4   Moving Arguments and Fragile Commands

When your input file is being processed by LATEX a number of files in addition to the `dvi` file are written (or overwritten) and some arguments to some LATEX commands contain text and/or commands that are written to those additional files. For example, if your input file contains a `\makeindex` command and a number of `\index{`*text*`}` commands, then the *text* arguments will actually appear in the `idx` file that LATEX writes. Such arguments are known as *moving* arguments. (There are also some cases in which a moving argument does not involve writing information to a file; if a command has a moving argument, this information is included in the glossary.)

LATEX commands are either *fragile* or *robust*: a robust command is one that, if it appears in a moving argument, will be transferred to an additional file exactly as it occurs in that argument; however, in transferring a fragile command problems may occur but these can be avoided by preceding the fragile command with a `\protect` command.

---

[2] Note that this is a slight simplification of what really happens.

C

Glossary

The order of non-alphanumeric characters in this glossary is determined by the order in which they occur in Knuth's typewriter font—which is shown below for those not familiar with it—and the escape character is regarded as invisible for the purposes of ordering (except that \name follows name). Furthermore, no non-alphanumeric character follows an alphanumeric character in the ordering adopted here. Underlining is used to indicate that an argument to a command or environment is a moving one.

	0	1	2	3	4	5	6	7	8	9
0	Γ	Δ	Θ	Λ	Ξ	Π	Σ	Υ	Φ	Ψ
10	Ω	↑	↓	'	ı	¿	ı	ȷ	`	´
20	ˇ	˘	¯	˙	¸	ß	æ	œ	ø	Æ
30	Œ	Ø	␣	!	"	#	$	%	&	'
40	(	)	*	+	,	-	.	/	0	1
50	2	3	4	5	6	7	8	9	:	;
60	<	=	>	?	@	A	B	C	D	E
70	F	G	H	I	J	K	L	M	N	O
80	P	Q	R	S	T	U	V	W	X	Y
90	Z	[	\	]	ˆ	_	'	a	b	c
100	d	e	f	g	h	i	j	k	l	m
110	n	o	p	q	r	s	t	u	v	w
120	x	y	z	{	ǀ	}	˜	¨		

\ is the escape character that starts every command consisting of more than one character.

\␣ produces an inter-word space. (Robust.)

!' produces ¡ in paragraph or LR mode. (Robust.)

\! produces a negative amount of thin horizontal space (normally about minus one sixth of a quad) in math mode. (Robust.)

\\"*char* This produces a dieresis or umlaut (ö) over the following single character *char* in LR or paragraph mode. (Robust.)

#*i* indicates the place in a command or environment definition where a parameter is to go (*i* must lie between 1 and 9 inclusive).

\\# produces # in any mode. (Robust.)

$*form*$ typesets *form* in math mode and text style to produce an in-text formula. It can only occur in paragraph or LR modes and it is equivalent to both \\(*form*\\) and \\begin{math} *form* \\end{math}. (Robust.)

\\$ produces $ in any mode. (Robust.)

$$*form*$$ This can only occur in paragraph mode where it causes *form* to be typeset in math mode using the display style and the result is centred on a line by itself *even if* the fleqn document style option has been chosen.

% Everything that follows this command to the next end-of-line character—including that character—is treated as a comment (and thus ignored by TeX).

\\% produces % in any mode. (Robust.)

& is used in various environments to indicate vertical alignment.

\\& produces & in any mode. (Robust.)

' In math mode this produces a prime, for example, x' produces x'.

\\'*char* This produces an acute accent (ó) over the following single character *char* in LR or paragraph mode, but *not* within the tabbing environment. There use \\a'*char*. (Robust.)

\\(*form*\\) This construct can only occur in LR or paragraph modes where it typesets *form* as an in-text mathematical formula in text style; it is equivalent to both \\begin{math} *form* \\end{math} and $*form*$. Both \\(and \\) are fragile.

\\) See \\(.

*{*i*}{*pre*} An expression that can only occur inside the *preamble* of an array or tabular environment. It is equivalent to *i* copies of *pre*, where *i* is any positive whole number and *pre* is any legitimate combination of preamble commands.

* This discretionary multiplication sign can only occur in math mode where it indicates a place where a mathematical formula can be broken across lines; a multiplication sign × is inserted if the formula is broken across lines, but not otherwise.

+ produces the symbol + in all modes; in math mode this is a binary operator symbol.

\+ Inside the `tabbing` environment this increases the value of *left-tab-margin* by 1. (Fragile.)

\, produces a thin amount of horizontal space (normally about one sixth of a quad) in all modes. Its default value in math mode is actually 3mu. (Robust.)

- produces the binary operator symbol − in math mode; in other modes it produces a hyphen. Use -- for an en-dash and --- for an em-dash in either paragraph or LR mode.

\- Except inside the `tabbing` environment this discretionary hyphen indicates a place in a word where TEX can end a line; if it does this, it inserts a hyphen.

\- Inside the `tabbing` environment this decreases the value of *left-tab-margin* by 1. (Fragile.)

\.*char* This produces a dot accent (ȯ) over the following single character *char* in LR or paragraph mode. (Robust.)

\/ This is the italic correction command which should be used whenever a change from italic or slanted type to one which is neither of them takes place.

: produces the binary relation symbol : in math mode. It should not be used for a punctuation mark in math mode; for that use \colon.

\: produces a medium amount of horizontal space (normally about two nineths of a quad) but only in math mode. Its default value is actually 4mu plus 2mu minus 4mu. Note that in plain TEX this amount of space is indicated by the command \>. (Robust.)

\; produces a thick amount of horizontal space (normally about five eighteenths of a quad) but only in math mode. Its default value is actually 5mu plus 5mu. (Robust.)

< produces the binary relation symbol < in math mode. It should *not* be used there for an angle bracket; for that use \langle. Outside math mode a ¡ symbol is produced; except in the scope of a \tt declaration, when < is produced.

\< Inside the `tabbing` environment this undoes the effect of one previous \+ command. (Fragile.)

= produces the symbol = in all modes; in math mode this is a binary relation symbol.

\= Inside the `tabbing` environment this is used to set tab positions. (Fragile.)

\=*char* This produces a macron accent (ō) over the following single character *char* in LR or paragraph mode, but *not* within the `tabbing` environment. There use \a=*char*. (Robust.)

> produces the binary relation symbol > in math mode. It should *not* be used there for an angle bracket; for that use \rangle. Outside math mode a ¿ symbol is produced; except in the scope of a \tt declaration, when > is produced.

\> Inside the tabbing environment this is used to move to the next tab position. Note that in plain TEX this command is used to produce a medium amount of space in math mode. (Fragile.)

?' produces ¿ in paragraph or LR mode. (Robust.)

\@ Placed before a full stop, exclamation or question mark this command makes the following space into one like that which normally follows these punctuation characters. (It is usually used between an uppercase letter and such a punctuation mark which actually does end a sentence.)

@{*text*} This so-called @-expression can only occur in the preamble of an array, tabular or tabular* environment; it places *text* in every row of the result. It removes any space that would normally be inserted in the row. The *text* argument is a moving one.

@article{*key,field-list*} This kind of entry in a BIBTEX bibliographic database is used for articles or papers that have been published in journals, periodicals or magazines. The *key* and *field-list* parameters are explained in chapter 5.

@book{*key,field-list*} This kind of entry in a BIBTEX bibliographic database is used for books which have a named publisher. The *key* and *field-list* parameters are explained in chapter 5.

@booklet{*key,field-list*} This kind of entry in a BIBTEX bibliographic database is used for a work that has been printed and bound, but which has no indication on it identifying who produced it. The *key* and *field-list* parameters are explained in chapter 5.

@conference{*key,field-list*} This kind of entry in a BIBTEX bibliographic database is used for an article or paper that is published in the proceedings of some conference. (This kind of entry is exactly the same as the @inproceedings type.) The *key* and *field-list* parameters are explained in chapter 5.

@inbook{*key,field-list*} This kind of entry in a BIBTEX bibliographic database is used for chapters—or other parts—of a book. It can even be used just for a collection of pages from a book. The *key* and *field-list* parameters are explained in chapter 5.

@incollection{*key,field-list*} This kind of entry in a BIBTEX bibliographic database is used for chapters—or other parts—of a book which have their own titles. The book in question may have, for example, each chapter written by a different person. The *key* and *field-list* parameters are explained in chapter 5.

`@inproceedings{`*key,field-list*`}` This kind of entry in a BIBTEX bibliographic database is used for an article or paper that is published in the proceedings of some conference. (This kind of entry is exactly the same as the `@conference` type.) The *key* and *field-list* parameters are explained in chapter 5.

`\@listi` A command executed when a `list` environment occurring within the scope of no other `list` environment is opened. It is used to initialize a number of the length parameters affecting the appearance of the list.

`\@listii` A command executed when a `list` environment which occurs within the scope of one other `list` environment is opened. It is used to initialize a number of the length parameters affecting the appearance of the list.

`\@listiii` A command executed when a `list` environment which occurs within the scope of two other `list` environments is opened. It is used to initialize a number of the length parameters affecting the appearance of the list.

`\@listiv` A command executed when a `list` environment which occurs within the scope of three other `list` environments is opened. It is used to initialize a number of the length parameters affecting the appearance of the list.

`\@listv` A command executed when a `list` environment which occurs within the scope of four other `list` environments is opened. It is used to initialize a number of the length parameters affecting the appearance of the list.

`\@listvi` A command executed when a `list` environment which occurs within the scope of five other `list` environments is opened. It is used to initialize a number of the length parameters affecting the appearance of the list.

`@manual{`*key,field-list*`}` This kind of entry in a BIBTEX bibliographic database is used for manuals or other kinds of technical documentation. The *key* and *field-list* parameters are explained in chapter 5.

`@mastersthesis{`*key,field-list*`}` This kind of entry in a BIBTEX bibliographic database is used for a dissertation or thesis written for a Master's degree. The *key* and *field-list* parameters are explained in chapter 5.

`@misc{`*key,field-list*`}` This kind of entry in a BIBTEX bibliographic database is used when something you want to refer to fits nowhere else. The *key* and *field-list* parameters are explained in chapter 5.

`@phdthesis{`*key,field-list*`}` This kind of entry in a BIBTEX bibliographic database is used for a doctoral thesis or dissertation. The *key* and *field-list* parameters are explained in chapter 5.

`@proceedings{`*key,field-list*`}` This kind of entry in a BIBTEX bibliographic database is used for the proceedings of a conference as distinct from a single paper in such a collection. The *key* and *field-list* parameters are explained in chapter 5.

@string{*abbrv=text***}** This can only occur within a bib file where it makes *abbrv* into an abbreviation for *text*, which must be enclosed in double quotes.

@techreport{*key,field-list***}** This kind of entry in a BibTeX bibliographic database is used for a research or technical report produced by an institution such as a school or department in a university or an industrial research laboratory. The *key* and *field-list* parameters are explained in chapter 5.

@unpublished{*key,field-list***}** This kind of entry in a BibTeX bibliographic database is used for a document—such as a typescript—that has a title and an author but has not been published in any way. A samizdat document may belong in this category. The *key* and *field-list* parameters are explained in chapter 5.

\[*form***\]** This construct can only occur in paragraph mode and it there typesets *form* in math mode and then makes it into a displayed equation centered on a line by itself *except* if the **fleqn** document style option has been chosen. In that case the formula is indented from the left margin by the value of the **\mathindent** length parameter. It is equivalent to **\begin{displaymath}***form***\end{displaymath}**. Both **\[** and **\]** are fragile.

\\[*len***]** This command ends a line; if the optional parameter *len* is present, then *len* amount of vertical space is inserted between the lines. (Fragile.)

*[*len***]** Like the **\\[***len***]** command except that the place where this command occurs will never be placed at the end of a page. (Fragile.)

\] See **\[**.

form$_1$**^***form*$_2$ This makes *form*$_2$ into a superscript of *form*$_1$. If *form*$_2$ contains more than one symbol, then curly braces should be placed around it. The control sequence or command **\sp** can be used instead of the caret character. Thus, *form*$_1$**\sp***form*$_2$ is equivalent to *form*$_1$**^***form*$_2$. (Robust.)

\^*char* This produces a circumflex accent (ô) over the following single character *char* in LR or paragraph mode. (Robust.)

form$_1$**_***form*$_2$ This makes *form*$_2$ into a subscript of *form*$_1$. If *form*$_2$ contains more than one symbol, then curly braces should be placed around it. The control sequence or command **\sb** can be used instead of the underline character. Thus, *form*$_1$**\sb***form*$_2$ is equivalent to *form*$_1$**_***form*$_2$. (Robust.)

_ produces _ in any mode. (Robust.)

\`***char* This produces a grave accent (ò) over the following single character *char* in LR or paragraph mode, but *not* within the **tabbing** environment. There use **\a`*char*. (Robust.)

{*scope*} Used for delimiting scope or enclosing mandatory command arguments.

\{ produces { in all modes. In math mode this is an opening symbol. There it can also be produced by the command \lbrace. (Robust.)

| In math mode this produces an ordinary symbol | which can also be produced by \vert; following \left or \right, however, it produces an appropriate delimiter. Outside math mode it produces an em-dash; except in the scope of an \tt declaration, where it produces |. (Robust.)

\| In math mode this produces an ordinary symbol ‖ which can also be produced by \Vert; following \left or \right, however, it produces an appropriate delimiter. (Robust.)

} See {.

\} produces } in all modes. In math mode this is a closing symbol. There it can also be produced by the command \rbrace. (Robust.)

~ produces an inter-word space and inhibits line-breaking.

\~*char* This produces a tilde accent (õ) over the following single character *char* in LR or paragraph mode. (Robust.)

11pt A possible option to the \documentsyle command. It causes the size of type that is used to be an 11 point one, rather than the default 10 point one.

12pt A possible option to the \documentsyle command. It causes the size of type that is used to be a 12 point one, rather than the default 10 point one.

\a'*char* This command is only available within the tabbing environment where it produces an acute accent (ó) over the following single character *char*. (Fragile.)

\a=*char* This command is only available within the tabbing environment where it produces a macron accent (ō) over the following single character *char*. (Fragile.)

\a'*char* This command is only available within the tabbing environment where it produces a grave accent (ò) over the following single character *char*. (Fragile.)

\aa A command only available in paragraph and LR modes for producing the lowercase Scandinavian a-with-circle letter (å). (Robust.)

\AA A command only available in paragraph and LR modes for producing the uppercase Scandinavian a-with-circle letter (Å). (Robust.)

abbrv One of the possible options to the \bibliographystyle command. The entries in the bibliography are arranged alphabetically and each one is labelled by means of a number enclosed in square brackets, like [17]. The option takes its name from the fact that the names of authors, editors, months and journals are abbreviated.

a	\abovedisplayskip + \baselineskip
b	\belowdisplayskip + \baselineskip
c	\abovedisplayshortskip + \baselineskip
d	\belowdisplayshortskip + \baselineskip
e	$\geq$ 2em

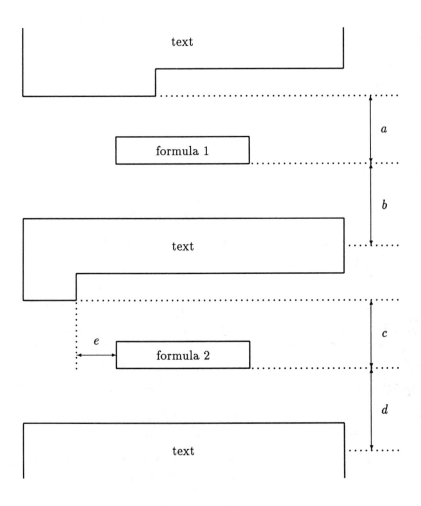

Figure C.1: "Short" and "long" displayed formulas.

{*form*$_1$ \above *len form*$_2$} produces a fraction with a central horizontal line of width *len* and with *form*$_1$ above *form*$_2$. This is a primitive TEX command.

\abovedisplayshortskip A rubber length parameter whose value is the additional vertical space that is placed above a "short" displayed formula, unless the fleqn option to the \documentstyle command has been chosen. (Additional to the value of \baselineskip, that is to say.) A "short" formula is one for which the distance labelled *e* in Fig. C.1 on p. 192 is greater than 2 em, where the length of em is determined by the size of type used in the paragraph preceding the formula. The value of this command is altered by certain declarations that change the size of type being used. (This is a primitive TEX command and these details are included for information only. They are, in any case, a simplification of what really happens. See Knuth (1986), pp. 188–189, and Eijkhout (1992), pp. 202–203, for details.) This is a robust command that must not be preceded by a \protect command.

\abovedisplayskip A rubber length parameter whose value is the additional vertical space that is placed above a "long" displayed formula, unless the fleqn option to the \documentstyle command has been chosen. (Additional to \baselineskip, that is to say.) A "long" formula is one whose left-most point is to the left of the end of the last line of the paragraph preceding it or—if it is to the right of this point—the distance between those points is less than 2 em in the font used in the preceding paragraph. See Fig. C.1 on p. 192, where formula 1 is "long" in this sense. The value of this command is altered by certain declarations that change the size of type being used. (This is a primitive TEX command and these details are included for information only. They are, in any case, a simplification of what really happens. See Knuth (1986), pp. 188–189, and Eijkhout (1992), pp. 202–203, for details.) This is a robust command that must not be preceded by a \protect command. See p. 144 for an example of its use; this is the only circumstance in which you are ever likely to need this command.

abstract An environment used for abstracts in the article and report document styles. It should be placed after the \maketitle command within the document environment in your input file. By default the first line of the abstract is indented but this can be cancelled by using a \noindent command.

\acute A command that produces an accent in math mode. Thus, $\acute x$ produces $\acute{x}$. (Robust.)

\addcontentsline{*ext*}{*sec-unit*}{*entry*} This command writes to the file specified by the *ext* parameter which can be either lof, lot or toc. The argument *sec-unit* controls the nature of what is written: if *ext* is lof, then *sec-unit* must be figure; if *ext* is lot, then *sec-unit* must be table; if *ext* is toc, then *sec-unit* can be either part, chapter (but not in the article document style), section, subsection, subsubsection, paragraph or subparagraph. (Note that *sec-unit* is `section`, for example, and *not* `\section`.) The argument *entry*—which is a moving argument—is the actual text that will appear in the list of figures, list of tables or table of contents. If you want the number of a figure, table or sectional unit to occur in the appropriate list, then instead of just text appearing in *entry* you need to use a `\numberline` command. Note that this takes the place of the text as in the following example:

```
\addcontentsline{lof}{figure}
    {\protect\numberline{12.3}
    {Cricket fielding positions.}}
```

If *entry*—or the corresponding argument in `\numberline`—is too long, then you will get a buffer size exceeded error message.

address A field in an entry in a BIBTEX bibliographic database which holds the address of the publisher of a written work. The less well known the publisher the more information should be included here.

`\address{`*text*`}` A declaration that can only occur in the `letter` document style. It is used for producing the address of the letter's sender. One or more `\\` commands can occur within the argument *text* to force a new line.

`\addtocontents{`*ext*`}{`*text*`}` This command writes *text* to the file specified by the *ext* argument which can be either `lof`, `lot` or `toc`. The moving argument *text* can contain formatting commands as well as ordinary text. If *text* is too long, then you will get a LaTeX buffer size exceeded error message.

`\addtocounter{`*ctr*`}{`*i*`}` This global declaration assigns to the counter *ctr* the result of adding *i* to the current value of *ctr*. (Fragile.)

`\addtolength{`*cmd*`}{`*len*`}` This assigns to the length command *cmd*—which must begin with a backslash—the result of adding *len* to its current value. (Robust.)

`\addvspace{`*len*`}` This normally adds *len* amount of vertical space. However, two such commands in succession, like `\addvspace{`len_1`}\addvspace{`len_2`}` only add len_i amount of space, where len_i is the maximum of len_1 and len_2. This command is used in the definition of many environments and results in the space surrounding nested environments being the same as the space above and below a single environment. (Fragile.)

`\ae` A command only available in paragraph and LR modes for producing the lowercase Latin and Scandinavian vowel ligature (æ). (Robust.)

`\AE` A command only available in paragraph and LR modes for producing the uppercase Latin and Scandinavian vowel ligature (Æ). (Robust.)

`\aleph` produces the ordinary symbol ℵ but only in math mode. (Robust.)

alph One of the available parameters to the `\pagenumbering` global declaration. Page numbers appear as lowercase letters when it is used.

\alph{*ctr*} The value of the counter *ctr*—which must be a positive whole number less than 27—is output as a lowercase letter. (Robust.)

Alph One of the available parameters to the `\pagenumbering` global declaration. Page numbers appear as uppercase letters when it is used.

\Alph{*ctr*} The value of the counter *ctr*—which must be a positive whole number less than 27—is output as an uppercase letter. (Robust.)

alpha One of the possible options to the `\bibliographystyle` command. The entries in the bibliography are arranged alphabetically and each one is labelled by means of a label made up out of the first three letters of the author's name and the last two digits of the year of publication. [Lak76] is an example.

\alpha produces the ordinary symbol α but only in math mode. (Robust.)

\amalg produces the binary operator symbol $\amalg$ but only in math mode. (Robust.)

and separates multiple authors or editors in the `author` and `editor` fields of an entry in a BibTeX bibliographic database.

and␣others This can terminate an author or editor field of an entry in a BibTeX bibliographic database. It appears in the output as '*et al.*'

\and A command that can only occur within the argument to an `\author` declaration. It is used to separate the names of multiple authors.

\angle produces the ordinary symbol $\angle$ but only in math mode. (Robust.)

annote The name of a field in an entry in a BibTeX bibliographic database. It is used for annotations that do not appear in the bibliography produced.

\appendix A declaration that alters the way in which the sectional units of your document are numbered. In the `book` and `report` document styles chapters start being "numbered" alphabetically and in the `article` document style sections start being "numbered" alphabetically. It has no effect on the numbering of parts. Note that it takes no arguments.

\approx produces the binary relation symbol $\approx$ but only in math mode. (Robust.)

arabic One of the available parameters to the `\pagenumbering` global declaration. Page numbers appear as Arabic numerals when it is used.

\arabic{*ctr*} The value of the counter *ctr* is output as an Arabic numeral. (Robust.)

\arccos produces a log-like symbol (arccos) but only in math mode. Subscripts and superscripts never appear as limits attached to the symbol produced. (Robust.)

\arcsin produces a log-like symbol (arcsin) but only in math mode. Subscripts and superscripts never appear as limits attached to the symbol produced. (Robust.)

\arctan produces a log-like symbol (arctan) but only in math mode. Subscripts and superscripts never appear as limits attached to the symbol produced. (Robust.)

\arg produces a log-like symbol (arg) but only in math mode. Subscripts and superscripts never appear as limits attached to the symbol produced. (Robust.)

array An environment that can only be used in math mode where it produces two-dimensional spatial arrangements of predominantly mathematical symbols.

\arraycolsep This rigid length parameter is half the amount of horizontal space left between the columns produced by an array environment. It is a robust command that must not be preceded by a \protect command.

\arrayrulewidth This rigid length parameter is the width of every line that is produced by an array environment. It is a robust command that must not be preceded by a \protect command.

\arraystretch This command has a value which is a floating-point number. It controls the amount of vertical space that occurs between the rows produced in an array, tabular or tabular* environment by multiplying the default width. Its default value is 1 and changing it to 1.25, say, by the \renewcommand or \def declaration makes the rows produced one and a quarter times further apart.

\arrowvert This command is only available in math mode where it has to be preceded by either \left or \right and when it is it produces a delimiter as shown in Table 7.1 on p. 100.

\Arrowvert This command is only available in math mode where it has to be preceded by either \left or \right and when it is it produces a delimiter as shown in Table 7.1 on p. 100.

article One of the things that can take the place of the *doc-style* argument to the \documentstyle command; see chapter 6 for more information.

\ast produces the binary operator symbol * but only in math mode; the character * produces the same symbol. (Robust.)

\asymp produces the binary relation symbol $\asymp$ but only in math mode. (Robust.)

{$form_1$ \atop $form_2$} produces a fraction-like arrangement of symbols without a central horizontal line but with $form_1$ above $form_2$. This is a primitive TeX command.

{*form*$_1$ \atopwithdelims *delim*$_1$ *delim*$_2$ *form*$_2$} produces an arrangement of symbols something like a fraction with *form*$_1$ on top of *form*$_2$, but without a horizontal central line and the whole thing enclosed with *delim*$_1$ on the left and *delim*$_2$ on the right. This is a primitive TeX command which is used to define \brace, \brack and \choose.

author The name of a field in an entry in a BibTeX bibliographic database which contains the name or names of the authors of a work.

\author{*text*} The author or authors of a document are declared by means of this declaration. If more than one author's name appears in *text*, then they should be separated by \and commands. You can use the \\ command inside *text* in order to force a line break and one or more \thanks commands can also appear in *text*. These produce footnotes whose markers are regarded as having zero width. If a \thanks command does not end a line, then it should be followed by a \␣ command in order to insert some inter-word space.

aux This is the file extension of an auxiliary file which contains various sorts of information which is used for cross-referencing purposes.

\b␣*char* or \b{*char*} This produces a bar-under accent (o̠) underneath the following single character *char* in LR or paragraph mode. (Robust.)

\backslash produces the ordinary symbol \ but only in math mode; following either \left or \right, however, it produces a delimiter. (Robust.)

\bar A command that produces an accent in math mode. Thus, $\bar x$ produces $\bar{x}$. (Robust.)

\baselineskip A rubber length parameter whose value—when multiplied by the value of the command \baselinestretch—is the normal distance between the baselines of every two successive lines in a paragraph. (It is, in fact, a primitive TeX command.) The value used for the entire paragraph is that which this command has when the end of the paragraph is reached. Although the value of this command can be a rubber length, Knuth says that giving it a rigid value produces a better looking page. Even when its value is a rigid length, the actual distance between the baselines of successive lines can vary if one of them contains a large symbol. See Knuth (1986), pp. 78–79, for an account of what happens in those circumstances. Note that the value of \baselineskip is altered by declarations (like \tiny and \large) that change the size of type being used. (These details are included for information only. The value of \baselineskip is the responsibility of a document style's designer. If you really must alter the distance between baselines—for example, to produce the appearance of a double-spaced typewritten document—then alter the value of \baselinestretch). This is a robust command that must not be preceded by a \protect command.

\baselinestretch A command whose value is a floating-point number and by default this is 1. The actual distance between the baselines of two successive lines in a paragraph is the value of \baselineskip multiplied by the value of \baselinestretch.

\batchmode If this command is the first command in your input file—coming before even the \documentstyle command—then nothing is written to your terminal and TEX carries on processing as best it can even if errors occur. The log file is still written.

bbl The file extension of a file created or overwritten when BIBTEX is run. It contains the formatting commands that are actually used to produce the bibliography in your output; you can edit this file if you do not like any part of the output it produces.

\begin{env} This command starts the *env* environment. (Fragile.)

\belowdisplayshortskip A rubber length parameter whose value is the additional vertical space that is placed below a "short" displayed formula, unless the fleqn option to the \documentstyle command has been chosen. See the entry for \abovedisplayshortskip for an explanation of what a "short" formula is and see also Fig. C.1 on p. 192. This is a primitive TEX command and it is also a robust command that must not be preceded by a \protect command.

\belowdisplayskip A rubber length parameter whose value is the additional vertical space that is placed below a "long" displayed formula, unless the fleqn option to the \documentstyle command has been chosen. See the entry for \abovedisplayskip for an explanation of what a "long" formula is and see also Fig. C.1 on p. 192. This is a primitive TEX command and it is also a robust command that must not be preceded by a \protect command.

\beta produces the ordinary symbol β but only in math mode. (Robust.)

\bf A declaration that alters the style of the type being used to **bold**. (Robust.)

bib The file extension of a file that contains one or more BIBTEX bibliographic database entries.

\bibindent A rigid length parameter—only available if the openbib option to the \documentstyle command has been chosen—whose value is the amount of indentation used for the second and subsequent lines of entries produced by the thebibliography environment. This is a robust command that must not be preceded by a \protect command.

\bibitem[*text*]{*key*} A command that can only occur within the thebibliography environment. The argument *key* is made up out of letters, numerals and punctuation marks other than a comma. It is used in a \cite command to refer to a work in the bibliography. If *text* is absent, then LATEX generates a numerical label enclosed in square brackets like [31]; otherwise, if *text* is present, then [*text*] is used as the label. Note that *text*—if present—is a moving argument. (Fragile.)

\bibliography{*bib-file-list*} If any \cite{*key*} commands occur in your input file, then BIBTEX looks in the files listed in *bib-file-list* to see if an entry with key *key* occurs there. If it does, the bibliography produced will contain an entry produced from the data contained in the bib file. Only the base names of bib files occur in *bib-file-list* and multiple names are separated by commas.

\bibliographystyle{*bib-style*} This command is used in conjunction with BIBTEX and it determines how the bibliography in your output is going to look. Standard options for the *bib-style* argument are abbrv, alpha, plain and unsrt. Others, such as agsm, dcu or kluwer—used with the harvard option to the \documentstyle command—may be avaliable on your computer system.

\bigcap produces the large operator symbol $\bigcap$ but only in math mode. The symbol produced is slightly larger in displayed formulas than when it occurs as part of an in-text formula. Subscripts and superscripts appear under and over the symbol produced by this command—as limits—when it occurs in a displayed formula. (Robust.)

\bigcirc produces the binary operator symbol $\bigcirc$ but only in math mode. (Robust.)

\bigcup produces the large operator symbol $\bigcup$ but only in math mode. The symbol produced is slightly larger in displayed formulas than when it occurs as part of an in-text formula. Subscripts and superscripts appear under and over the symbol produced by this command—as limits—when it occurs in a displayed formula. (Robust.)

\bigodot produces the large operator symbol $\bigodot$ but only in math mode. The symbol produced is slightly larger in displayed formulas than when it occurs as part of an in-text formula. Subscripts and superscripts appear under and over the symbol produced by this command—as limits—when it occurs in a displayed formula. (Robust.)

\bigoplus produces the large operator symbol $\bigoplus$ but only in math mode. The symbol produced is slightly larger in displayed formulas than when it occurs as part of an in-text formula. Subscripts and superscripts appear under and over the symbol produced by this command—as limits—when it occurs in a displayed formula. (Robust.)

\bigotimes produces the large operator symbol $\bigotimes$ but only in math mode. The symbol produced is slightly larger in displayed formulas than when it occurs as part of an in-text formula. Subscripts and superscripts appear under and over the symbol produced by this command—as limits—when it occurs in a displayed formula. (Robust.)

\bigskip produces vertical space whose height is given by \bigskipamount; it is defined as \vspace{\bigskipamount}. Note that is different from the plain TEX definition. (Fragile.)

\bigskipamount A rubber length whose value is 12pt plus 4pt minus 4pt.

\bigsqcup produces the large operator symbol ⊔ but only in math mode. The symbol produced is slightly larger in displayed formulas than when it occurs as part of an in-text formula. Subscripts and superscripts appear under and over the symbol produced by this command—as limits—when it occurs in a displayed formula. (Robust.)

\bigtriangledown produces the binary operator symbol ▽ but only in math mode. (Robust.)

\bigtriangleup produces the binary operator symbol △ but only in math mode. (Robust.)

\biguplus produces the large operator symbol ⊎ but only in math mode. The symbol produced is slightly larger in displayed formulas than when it occurs as part of an in-text formula. Subscripts and superscripts appear under and over the symbol produced by this command—as limits—when it occurs in a displayed formula. (Robust.)

\bigvee produces the large operator symbol ⋁ but only in math mode. The symbol produced is slightly larger in displayed formulas than when it occurs as part of an in-text formula. Subscripts and superscripts appear under and over the symbol produced by this command—as limits—when it occurs in a displayed formula. (Robust.)

\bigwedge produces the large operator symbol ⋀ but only in math mode. The symbol produced is slightly larger in displayed formulas than when it occurs as part of an in-text formula. Subscripts and superscripts appear under and over the symbol produced by this command—as limits—when it occurs in a displayed formula. (Robust.)

blg This is the file extension of a file that is created or overwritten when BIBTEX is run; it contains all the information that appeared on your terminal when BIBTEX was processing your input file.

\bmod produces the binary operator symbol (mod) but only in math mode. (Robust.)

\boldmath A declaration which cannot be used in math mode but which causes most symbols occurring in math mode following the declaration (or in its scope) to appear in a bold style of type. The only symbols that do not appear bold are: all symbols in script or scriptscript style, the symbols

$$+ \quad : \quad ; \quad ! \quad ? \quad (\quad) \quad [\quad]$$

and the symbols that come in several sizes (like $\sum$ and $\int$) and also large delimiters produced by \left and \right. (Fragile.)

book One of the things that can take the place of the *doc-style* argument to the \documentstyle command; see chapter 6 for more information.

booktitle This is the name of a field in an entry in a BIBTEX bibliographic database. It is used for the titles of works only part of which is being referred to.

\bordermatrix The general form of this plain TEX command is like this:

$$\text{\textbackslash bordermatrix\{}form_{11} \ \& \ form_{12} \ \& \ \dots \ \& \ form_{1n} \ \text{\textbackslash cr}$$
$$form_{21} \ \& \ form_{22} \ \& \ \dots \ \& \ form_{2n} \ \text{\textbackslash cr}$$
$$\vdots$$
$$form_{m1} \& \ form_{m2}\& \ \dots \ \& \ form_{mn}\text{\textbackslash cr\}}$$

It is like \pmatrix except that labels are placed along the top and left-hand side of the parenthesized matrix produced.

\bot produces the ordinary symbol $\perp$ but only in math mode. (Robust.)

\bottomfraction The value of this command is a floating-point number between 0 and 1. Its value specifies how much of the bottom part of each text page can be used for floats. It can be altered by \def or \renewcommand. Its default value is 0.3. If the twocolumn document style option has been chosen, the value of this command only affects single-column floats; there is no analogous command which applies to two-column floats.

bottomnumber The value of this counter is the maximum number of floats, that is to say, tables or figures, that can occur at the bottom of each text page. Its default value is 1. If the twocolumn document style option has been chosen, the value of this counter only affects single-column floats; there is no analogous command which applies to two-column floats.

\bowtie produces the binary relation symbol $\bowtie$ but only in math mode. (Robust.)

\Box produces the ordinary symbol $\square$ but only in math mode. Note that this command is not present in plain TEX. (Robust.)

bp TEX keyword for *big point*, a unit of length, which exactly satisfies the equality 1 in = 72 bp. (Roughly, 1 bp = 0.0139 in = 0.35 mm = 1.004 pt.)

{*form*$_1$ \brace *form*$_2$} produces a fraction-like arrangement of symbols with *form*$_1$ on top of *form*$_2$, but without a central horizontal line and with the whole thing enclosed in curly braces. This is a plain TEX command.

\bracevert This command is only available in math mode where it has to be preceded by either \left or \right and when it is it produces a delimiter as shown in Table 7.1 on p. 100.

{*form*$_1$ \brack *form*$_2$} produces a fraction-like arrangement of symbols with *form*$_1$ on top of *form*$_2$, but without a central horizontal line and with the whole thing enclosed in square brackets. This is a plain TEX command.

\breve A command that produces an accent in math mode. Thus, $\breve x$ produces $\breve{x}$. (Robust.)

\bullet produces the binary operator symbol • but only in math mode. (Robust.)

\c⎵*char* or \c{*char*} produces a cedilla accent (ç) underneath the following single character *char* in LR or paragraph mode. (Robust.)

\cal A declaration that can only be used in math mode to alter the style of type being used to calligraphic (which is also known as script). Only uppercase letters are available in this style of type. (Robust.)

\cap produces the binary operator symbol ∩ but only in math mode. (Robust.)

\caption{*heading*} A command that can only occur inside a figure, figure*, table or table* environment. It produces a numbered caption. If you want to refer to a captioned figure or table, then you need to include a \label command either somewhere in *heading* or else following the \caption command but within the body of the environment. If a list of figures or a list of tables is produced by means of either the \listoffigures or the \listoftables command, then *heading* is the text that will appear in the list of figures or the list of tables produced. Note that *heading* is a moving argument so any fragile commands in it must be preceded by \protect commands. (Fragile.)

\caption[*entry*]{*heading*} This is the same as the \caption{*heading*} command, except that *entry* is the text that will appear in any list of tables or figures produced by a \listoffigures or the \listoftables command. In this form of the command *entry* is a moving argument but *heading* is not. (Fragile.)

cc TEX keyword for *cicero*, a unit of length, which exactly satisfies the equality 1 cc = 12 dd. (Roughly, 1 cc = 0.1777 in = 4.51 mm = 12.84 pt.)

\cc{*text*} A command that can only occur inside a letter environment. It is used for listing any "carbon copies". LATEX generates 'cc:' and *text* follows this. One or more \\ commands can occur in the argument *text* to force a new line.

`\cdot` produces the binary operator symbol · but only in math mode. (Robust.)

`\cdots` produces the ellipsis (· · ·) consisting of three "centred" dots, but only in math mode. (Robust.)

`center` An environment used for centring text (or any box). The command `\\` can be used inside this environment in order to force the end of a line of text. Within this environment LATEX is in paragraph mode.

`\centering` A declaration that causes the text (or box) in its scope to be centred in the body of a page. Note that the TEX command of the same name does something different; its original definition is available as `\@centering`.

`chapter` A field in an entry in a BIBTEX bibliographic database which holds the number of the chapter being referred to.

`chapter` A counter used to control the numbering of chapters. It is initialized to zero and incremented by the `\chapter` command before a number is generated. Values can be assigned to it by means of the `\setcounter` command. (So, if you want, for example, your first chapter to be numbered 0, include the command `\setcounter{chapter}{-1}` in your preamble.)

`\chapter[`*entry*`]{`*heading*`}` A sectioning command which opens a new chapter. It is not available if the `article` document style is being used. If the `report` or `book` document style is being used, then chapters have level number 0. By default chapters are numbered automatically in those document styles. (This can be altered by changing the value of the counter `secumndepth`.) If the optional argument *entry* is absent, then by default *heading* will appear in the table of contents if one is produced. (This can be altered by changing the value of the counter `tocdepth`.) If *entry* is present, then it will appear in the table of contents but *heading* will appear in the body of the document produced. If *entry* is present, then it is a moving argument; but if it is absent, then *heading* is the moving argument. (Fragile.)

`\chapter*{`*heading*`}` A sectioning command which opens a new chapter which is neither numbered nor will it appear in the table of contents. (Fragile.)

`\char`*i* outputs the character from the current font whose code number is *i*. If *i* is in octal, it must be preceded by an opening quote and if *i* is in hexadecimal, it must be preceded by a double quote. This is a primitive TEX command that cannot be used in math mode.

`\check` A command that produces an accent in math mode. Thus, `$\check x$` produces $\check{x}$. (Robust.)

`\chi` produces the ordinary symbol χ but only in math mode. (Robust.)

{*form*₁ \choose *form*₂} produces a fraction-like arrangement of symbols with $form_1$ on top of $form_2$, but without a central horizontal line and with the whole thing enclosed in ordinary parentheses. This is a plain TEX command.

\circ produces the binary operator symbol ∘ but only in math mode. (Robust.)

\circle{*d*} A command that can only occur as an argument to a \put or \multiput command inside a picture environment. Thus, \put(*i*, *j*){\circle{*d*}} places a circle of diameter d on the picture in such a way that its centre is at the point whose coordinates are (i, j). Note that LaTeX can only produce a very restricted class of circles. The largest circle it can draw is 40 points (which is about half an inch). Also, there are only a finite number of diameters available. If there is not one exactly the size you specify, then LaTeX will use the one in its repertoire that is closest to the one you specify. (Fragile.)

\circle*{*d*} is like \circle{*d*} except that the circle produced is a filled-in disk. Note that LaTeX can only produce a very restricted class of disks. The largest disk it can produce has a diameter of 15 points (which is about a fifth of an inch). Also, there are only a finite number of diameters available. If there is not one exactly the size you specify, then LaTeX will use the one in its repertoire that is closest to the one you specify. (Fragile.)

\cite[*text*]{*key-list*} is used for producing references to a bibliography produced by BIBTEX or done yourself. The argument *key-list* is a list of keys—separated by commas—that have been defined either in a bib file or a thebibliography environment. If *text* is present, it is added as an annotation to the reference. (Fragile.)

\cleardoublepage This command—which should only be used in paragraph mode— terminates the current paragraph and the current page. Any unfilled space is placed at the bottom of the page rather than between paragraphs even if you have used the \flushbottom declaration. All figures and tables in "memory" are output. If two-sided printing is in effect, then the next page to have text on it will be a right-handed and odd-numbered one. If using the twocolumn document style option, then the use of \cleardoublepage may cause the right-hand column to be entirely blank. (Fragile.)

\clearpage This command terminates the current paragraph and the current page. It can only be used in paragraph mode. Any unfilled space is placed at the bottom of the page rather than between paragraphs even if you have used the \flushbottom declaration. All figures and tables in "memory" are output. If using the twocolumn document style option, then the use of \clearpage may cause the right-hand column to be entirely blank. (Robust.)

\cline{*i-j*} A command that is only available inside an array, tabular or tabular* environment. Whereas \hline produces a horizontal line across the entire width of the resulting table, this command only produces a line extending across columns *i* to *j* inclusive. Both *i* and *j* must be present, but they can be the same. It must come either after the command that opens the environment, after a \\ command or after another \cline command.

\closing{*text*} A command that can only occur inside a letter environment. It is used for the message that occurs at the end of the letter. For example, *text* could be Yours sincerely.

\clubsuit produces the ordinary symbol ♣ but only in math mode. (Robust.)

cm TEX keyword for *centimetre*, a unit of length, which exactly satisfies the equality 1 in = 2.54 cm. (Roughly, 1 cm = 0.3937 in = 28.45 pt.)

\columnsep A rigid length parameter whose value is the width of the space between the two columns of text in the twocolumn option to the \documentstyle command. This is a robust command that must never be preceded by a \protect command.

\columnseprule A rigid length parameter whose value is the width of the vertical line that separates the two columns of text in the twocolumn option to the \documentstyle command. By default it has a value of 0 inches, that is to say, no visible rule is placed between the columns. This is a robust command that must never be preceded by a \protect command.

\cong produces the binary relation symbol $\cong$ but only in math mode. (Robust.)

\coprod This command—which can only occur in math mode—produces a symbol for a large operator ($\coprod$). The symbol produced is slightly larger in displayed formulas than when it occurs as part of an in-text formula. Subscripts and superscripts appear under and over the symbol produced by this command—as limits—when it occurs in a displayed formula. (Robust.)

\copyright produces the copyright symbol © in all modes. (Robust.)

\cos produces the log-like symbol (cos) but only in math mode. Subscripts and superscripts never appear as limits attached to the symbol produced. (Robust.)

\cosh produces the log-like symbol (cosh) but only in math mode. Subscripts and superscripts never appear as limits attached to the symbol produced. (Robust.)

\cot produces the log-like symbol (cot) but only in math mode. Subscripts and superscripts never appear as limits attached to the symbol produced. (Robust.)

\coth produces the log-like symbol (coth) but only in math mode. Subscripts and superscripts never appear as limits attached to the symbol produced. (Robust.)

\cr This primitive TEX command is used to end lines inside the arguments of the **\bordermatrix, \cases, \displaylines, \eqalign, \eqalignno, \leqalignno, \matrix** and **\pmatrix** commands.

\csc produces the log-like symbol (csc) but only in math mode. Subscripts and superscripts never appear as limits attached to the symbol produced. (Robust.)

\cup produces the binary operator symbol ∪ but only in math mode. (Robust.)

\d␣*char* or **\d{***char***}** produce a dot-under accent (o̧) underneath the following single character *char* in LR or paragraph mode. (Robust.)

\dag produces the dagger symbol † in all modes. (Robust.)

\dagger produces the binary operator symbol † but only in math mode. (Robust.)

\dashbox{*h***}(***i, j***)[***pos***]{***picture-object***}** This command can only appear inside the **picture** environment. It produces a box with a dashed frame drawn around it; the arguments have the same meaning as for the **\makebox** command, *q.v.*; except for *h* which is the length of the dashes and gaps that make up the frame. (Fragile.)

\dashv produces the binary relation symbol ⊣ but only in math mode. (Robust.)

\date{*text***}** (1) This declaration is used to declare *text* to be the date of a document. If it is omitted, then the date on which you ran LATEX on your input file is used as the date of the document. You can use the **** command inside *text* in order to force a line break and one or more **\thanks** commands can also appear in *text*. These produce footnotes whose markers are regarded as having zero width. If a **\thanks** command does not end a line, then it should be followed by a **\␣** command in order to insert some inter-word space. (2) This declaration can also occur in the **letter** document style in order to produce a date of your choice. One or more **** commands can occur in *text*, but in this case no **\thanks** commands can occur.

\dblfloatpagefraction This command only has an effect when the **twocolumn** document style option has been chosen. Its value is a floating-point number between 0 and 1 which specifies the minimum amount of space that must be occupied by double-column floats on a floats-only page. For example, if its value is 0.6, then at least 60% of the page would have to be occupied by double-column floats. It can be altered by **\def** or **\renewcommand**. Its default value is 0.5.

\dblfloatsep If the **twocolumn** option to the **\documentstyle** command has been chosen, then this rubber length parameter affects the placement of two-column wide floats; it is the amount of vertical space that appears between two such floats on a page that contains both text and floats. It is a robust command that should not be preceded by a **\protect** command.

\dbltextfloatsep The value of this rubber length parameter only has an effect if the **twocolumn** document style option has been chosen. It is a rubber length parameter whose value is the amount of vertical space left between a double-column float and the text either below or above it. It is a robust command that must not be preceded by a **\protect** command.

\dbltopfraction The value of this command only has an effect if the **twocolumn** document style option has been chosen. Its value is a floating-point number between 0 and 1 which specifies how much of the top part of each text page can be used for double-column floats. It can be altered by **\def** or **\renewcommand**. Its default value is 0.7.

dbltopnumber The value of this counter only has an effect if the **twocolumn** document style option has been chosen. Its value is the maximum number of two-column floats that can occur at the top of each text page. Its default value is 2.

dd TEX keyword for *didot point*, a unit of length, which exactly satisfies the equality 1157 dd = 1238 pt. (Roughly, 1 dd = 0.0148 in = 0.376 mm = 1.07 pt.)

\ddag produces the double dagger symbol ‡ in all modes. (Robust.)

\ddagger produces the binary operator symbol ‡ but only in math mode. (Robust.)

\ddot A command that produces an accent in math mode. Thus, **$\ddot x$** produces $\ddot{x}$. (Robust.)

\ddots produces the diagonal ellipsis ($\ddots$) consisting of three diagonal dots, but only in math mode. (Robust.)

\def*cmd*#1#2 ... #*i*{*def*} defines *cmd*—which must begin with a backslash—to be a command equivalent to *def*; defined commands can have up to 9 arguments. When a parameterized command is used as *cmd*{*arg₁*}{*arg₂*}...{*argᵢ*}, it is replaced with *def* in which arg_j (for $1 \le j \le i$) has been substituted for #*j*. Be careful not to put spaces or anything else before, between or after the #*j* in the argument list. For a fuller discussion of all its features see chapter 20 of Knuth (1986). This is a primitive TEX command.

\deg produces the log-like symbol (deg) but only in math mode. Subscripts and superscripts never appear as limits attached to the symbol produced. (Robust.)

\delta produces the ordinary symbol δ but only in math mode. To produce the ordinary symbol ∂ use **\partial**. (Robust.)

\Delta produces the ordinary symbol Δ but only in math mode. (Robust.)

description An environment usually used for making glossaries. An **\item**[*text*] command inside it produces *text* in bold type.

\det produces the log-like symbol (det) but only in math mode. Subscripts and superscripts appear under and over the symbol produced—as limits—when it occurs as part of a displayed formula. (Robust.)

\diamond produces the binary operator symbol ⋄ but only in math mode. (Robust.)

\Diamond produces the ordinary symbol ◇ but only in math mode. Note that this command is not present in plain TeX. (Robust.)

\diamondsuit produces the ordinary symbol ◊ but only in math mode. (Robust.)

\dim produces the log-like symbol (dim) but only in math mode. Subscripts and superscripts never appear as limits attached to the symbol produced. (Robust.)

\displaylimits The effect of cmd\displaylimits_$form_1$^$form_2$ in display style (in math mode) is to force $form_1$ to appear as a limit below the symbol produced by cmd and to make $from_2$ appear as a limit above it and in text style $form_1$ appears as a subscript and $form_2$ as a superscript. This is a primitive TeX command.

\displaylines{$form_1$\cr $form_2$\cr ... $form_n$\cr} Each of the $form_i$ is displayed on a line by itself and they are all centred on the line in which they occur. This is a primitive TeX command.

displaymath An environment used for typesetting a mathematical formula so that it appears on a line by itself. The more concise forms \[$form$\] and $$$form$$$ are also available; though the latter construct is unaffected by the choice of the fleqn option to the \documentstyle command. Inside this environment LaTeX is in math mode and display style.

\displaystyle A declaration that can only be used in math mode. It forces TeX to typeset formulas in display style, which is the default style for formulas that occur on a line by themselves. This is a primitive TeX command. (Robust.)

\div produces the binary operator symbol ÷ but only in math mode. (Robust.)

doc File extension used for a file which contains exactly the same macros or commands as the corresponding sty file, but with more explanatory material included as comments.

document The outermost environment in all input files.

\documentstyle[opt-$list$]{doc-$style$} This command must be present in every LaTeX file. It specifies the style of the document. Standard styles are article, report, book and letter, but others may be available on your system. Only one *doc-style* alternative is permitted and the \documentstyle command causes the file *doc-style*.sty to be read. Standard options are 11pt, 12pt, draft, fleqn, leqno, openbib, titlepage, twocolumn and twoside. No spaces should be included in *opt-list* and if more than one option is included, then commas should be used as separators. For each option *opt* present in *opt-list* LATEX either executes the command \ds@*opt* (if it exists) or it reads the file *opt*.sty. Only a small number of commands can come before the \documentstyle command; for example, the \batchmode, \errorstopmode, \nonstopmode and \scrollmode commands.

\dot A command that produces an accent in math mode. Thus, $\dot x$ produces $\dot{x}$. (Robust.)

\doteq produces the binary relation symbol $\doteq$ but only in math mode. (Robust.)

\dotfill This command produces a row of dots—as occurs, for example, in a table of contents—that expands to fill all the available space where it occurs; see Table C.1 on p. 210 for a picture of what it does. (Robust)

\doublerulesep A rigid length parameter whose value is the distance that separates two vertical lines produced by either a | | expression in the *preamble* of an **array**, **tabular** or **tabular*** environment or the distance between two horizontal line produced by two \hline commands. It is robust and must not be preceded by a \protect command.

\downarrow produces the binary relation symbol $\downarrow$ but only in math mode. Following \left and \right, however, it produces an appropriate delimiter. (Robust.)

\Downarrow produces the binary relation symbol $\Downarrow$ but only in math mode. Following \left and \right, however, it produces an appropriate delimiter. (Robust.)

\downbracefill produces an upward pointing curly brace which expands to fill all the horizontal space available; see Table C.1 for a graphical depiction of what it does.

draft A possible option to the \documentstyle command. If chosen, then a solid, rectangular blob of black will appear in the right-hand margin when text juts out into this margin.

\ds@*opt* If *opt* occurs in the list of options to the \documentstyle command, then the command \ds@*opt* is executed—if it is defined—otherwise the commands in the style file *opt*.sty are executed.

dvi File extension used of the device independent file created when the corresponding tex file is processed by LATEX.

edition (A BibTEX field-name.) An indication of which edition is being referred to. For example, 7 or "Thirty-ninth". If a numeral is not used, then an ordinal with an initial uppercase letter should be used.

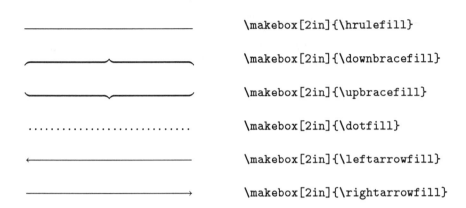

Table **C.1**: Six `fill` commands.

editor (A BIBT_EX field-name.) This holds the name of the editor of a book being referred to (or their names if there are more than one) or the name of the editor of a book—such as the proceedings of a conference—part of which is being referred to (or their names if there are more than one).

\ell produces the ordinary symbol ℓ but only in math mode. (Robust.)

em A font-dependent unit of length which is equal to the width of a quad. It used to be the width of a capital letter 'M', but that may or may not be the case nowadays. It is generally used for horizontal measurements. It is also the width of one \quad, twice the width of an \enskip or an \enspace, and half the width of a \qquad.

\em A declaration that changes the current style of type. Whereas a command like \it always selects italic type and \rm always selects Roman type, what \em selects depends on the context in which it occurs. For example, if \rm is in effect, it is equivalent to \it; if \it is in effect, it is equivalent to \rm. (Robust.)

empty A page style option to the \pagestyle and \thispagestyle declarations. Both the head and the foot of the page are left empty. Although the page number does not occur on any output page, LaTeX still assigns a page number to each page.

\emptyset produces the ordinary symbol $\emptyset$ but only in math mode. (Robust.)

\end{*env*} A command used for ending the *env* environment. (Fragile.)

\encl{*text*} A command that can only occur inside a `letter` environment. It is used for listing any enclosures. LaTeX generates 'encl:' and *text* follows this. One or more \\ commands can occur in the argument *text* to force a new line.

\enskip produces horizontal space which is half an em wide in all modes. A line break can occur where this command appears. This is a plain TEX command.

\enspace produces horizontal space which is half an em wide in all modes. A line break cannot occur where this command appears. This is a plain TEX command.

enumerate An environment used to produce labelled lists. The nature of the labels depends on the level of nesting, but they are generated automatically when the **\item** command—without any arguments—is used.

enumi A counter used to keep track of the labels in an **enumerate** environment which does not appear inside another **enumerate** environment.

enumii A counter used to keep track of the labels in an **enumerate** environment which is nested inside another one.

enumiii A counter used to keep track of the labels in an **enumerate** environment which is nested inside two others.

enumiv A counter used to keep track of the labels in an **enumerate** environment which is nested inside three others.

epsf A non-standard option to the **\documentstyle** command which is used if you want to include an encapsulated PostScript graphic in your output. See section 4.10 for an account of how it works. (The **epsf** macros where written by Tomas Rokicki and revised by Donald Knuth.)

\epsfbox{*file***}** This is only available if the **epsf** option to the **\documentstyle** command has been chosen. It includes the encapsulated PostScript file *file* in your output; see section 4.10 for an example of its use.

\epsffile{*file***}** does exactly the same as **\epsfbox{***file***}** does.

\epsfxsize A rigid length parameter whose value is the width of the box produced by TEX when it reads in an encapsulated PostScript file using the **\epsfbox** (or **\epsffile**) command; it is used to scale the graphic inputted. This command is only available if you have chosen the **epsf** option to the **\documentstyle** command.

\epsfysize A rigid length parameter like **\epsfxsize** except that its value is the height of the box that TEX produces.

\epsilon produces the ordinary symbol ϵ but only in math mode. To produce the ordinary symbol ε use **\varepsilon** and for the binary relation $\in$ use **\in**. (Robust.)

\eqalign{*lhs*$_1$&*rhs*$_1$\cr *lhs*$_2$&*rhs*$_2$\cr ... *lhs*$_n$&*rhs*$_n$\cr} A plain TEX command that can only be used in math mode and display style to produce several displayed formulas aligned on the symbols that follow the ampersands. The formulas *lhs*$_i$ and *rhs*$_i$ are typeset in display style. This command needs to be reinstated—as described in section 8.4—before it can be used.

\eqalignno{*lhs*$_1$&*rhs*$_1$&*en*$_1$\cr *lhs*$_2$&*rhs*$_2$&*en*$_2$\cr ... *lhs*$_n$&*rhs*$_n$&*en*$_n$\cr} This plain TEX command that can only be used in math mode and display style to produce several displayed formulas aligned on the symbols that follow the ampersands. The formulas *lhs*$_i$ and *rhs*$_i$ are typeset in display style. The expressions *en*$_i$—which usually are numerical labels—are placed on the extreme right-hand side of the body region of the page; if any such expressions are omitted, then so should the preceding ampersand. This command needs to be reinstated—as described in section 8.4—before it can be used.

eqnarray (Equation array.) An environment that produces a collection of displayed equations each of which is numbered. (To suppress the numbering use the eqnarray* environment.) Inside this environment LATEX is in math mode. See section 7.8 above for more information.

eqnarray* An environment used for producing a collection of displayed equations none of which is labelled.

\eqno This primitive TEX command is only available in math mode and display style where it produces a label on the right-hand side of the body region.

equation A counter used by both the equation and the eqnarray environments in order to keep track of how it labels displayed formulas.

equation An environment that produces a displayed mathematical formula with a numerical label generated automatically. In the article document style formulas are numbered consecutively throughout the output document starting with (1) and the labels are just single numbers. In the report and book document styles formulas are numbered consecutively throughout each chapter of the output document starting with (X.1), where X is the number of the chapter, and all the labels are made up out of two numbers.

\equiv produces the binary relation symbol $\equiv$ but only in math mode. (Robust.)

\errorstopmode This primitive TEX command makes TEX ask for user input when an error occurs; it is the default run mode. This is one of the few commands that can come before the \documentstyle command in the input file.

\eta produces the ordinary symbol η but only in math mode. (Robust.)

\evensidemargin A rigid length parameter whose value affects the appearance of each even-numbered output page. On left-hand pages—if two-sided printing is in operation—the distance between the left-hand edge of the paper and the left-hand edge of the body is the sum of the value of \evensidemargin and one inch. (See Fig. C.4 on p. 258.) This is a robust command that must never be preceded by a \protect command.

ex A font-dependent unit of length which used to be equal to the height of a lowercase letter 'x', but that may or may not be the case nowadays. It is generally used for vertical measurements.

\exists produces the ordinary symbol ∃ but only in math mode. (Robust.)

\exp produces the log-like symbol (exp) but only in math mode. Subscripts and superscripts never appear as limits attached to the symbol produced. (Robust.)

\extracolsep{*len*} A length parameter that can only occur within the argument to an @-expression which occurs in the preamble of an **array**, **tabular** or **tabular*** environment. It has the effect of putting *len* amount of space to the left of all the following columns and this space is not suppressed by the presence of further @-expressions.

\fbox{*text*} produces $\boxed{text}$ in all modes—but not inside the **picture** environment—with *text* being processed in LR mode. The width of the lines is determined by the value of the \fboxrule length parameter and the width of the space separating the frame from the *text* is given by the length parameter \fboxsep. Thus, the width of the resulting box is the width of the box produced after *text* has been processed plus twice the sum of \fboxrule and \fboxsep. (Robust.)

\fboxrule The value of this rigid length parameter is the width of the horizontal and vertical "framing" rules produced by an \fbox or \framebox command, except inside the **picture** environment. Other commands control the width of lines produced in the **picture** environment.

\fboxsep The value of this rigid length parameter is the amount of space that separates the box produced by processing the *text* argument of an \fbox or \framebox command and the horizontal and vertical rules comprising the "frame" that surrounds it, except inside the **picture** environment. Inside the **picture** environment no surrounding space is left.

figure A counter used in the numbering of floats created by the **figure** and **figure*** environments. It is only incremented if a \caption command has been included inside the environment.

figure An environment which produces a float. If the **twocolumn** document style option has been chosen, then the float produced is only one column wide and the **b** and **h** options for the *pos* argument are unavailable; otherwise, it behaves exactly like the **figure*** environment, *q.v.*

`figure*` An environment which produces a float. If a `\caption` command is present within it, the word 'Figure' and a numerical label are produced automatically. If the `twocolumn` document style option has been chosen, then the float produced is two columns wide. Its general format is:

$$\text{\\begin\{figure*\} } [pos] \; text \; \text{\\end\{figure*\}}$$

The *text* is processed in paragraph mode and a parbox of width `\textwidth` is produced. The optional argument *pos* is a sequence of between one and four different letters chosen from `b`, `h`, `p` and `t`. It affects the position where the float may appear as follows:

b The float may appear at the bottom of a text page.

h The float may be placed in the output in the same relative position to its neighbours as it occurs in the input.

p The float may appear on a floats-only page.

t The float may appear at the top of a text page.

The default value of *pos* is `tbp`.

`\fill` This is a rubber length command which is "infinitely" stretchable.

`\flat` produces the ordinary symbol ♭ but only in math mode. (Robust.)

`fleqn` This document style option causes all displayed equations occurring within the `\[` and `\]` commands and also those occurring inside the `displaymath`, `equation`, `eqnarray` and `eqnarray*` environments to be indented from the left margin by a distance of `\mathindent` rather than being centred, as is the default. Note that this option has no effect on equations occurring within a pair of double dollar signs; these formulas continue to be centred even if the `fleqn` option has been used.

`\floatsep` A rubber length parameter whose value is the amount of vertical space left between floats that appear on the same text page. If the `twocolumn` document style option has been chosen, the value of this command only affects single-column floats; for two-column floats see `\dblfloatsep`. This is a robust command that must not be preceded by a `\protect` command.

`\floatpagefraction` The value of this command is a floating-point number between 0 and 1. Its value specifies the minimum amount of space that must be occupied by floats on a floats-only page. For example, if its value is 0.6, then at least 60% of the page would have to be occupied by floats. It can be altered by `\def` or `\renewcommand`. Its default value is 0.5. If the `twocolumn` document style option has been chosen, the value of this command only affects single-column floats; for two-column floats see `\dblfloatpagefraction`.

\flushbottom This declaration has the effect of making the body on all pages the same height. Extra space is added between paragraphs to achieve this effect when necessary.

flushleft An environment used for producing paragraphs that are not right justified, but have a ragged right edge.

flushright An environment used for producing paragraphs that are not left justified, but have a ragged left edge.

\fnsymbol{*ctr***}** Here *ctr* is a counter whose value must lie between 1 and 9 inclusive. This command can only occur in math mode where it produces the following nine symbols depending on the value of *ctr*: *, †, ‡, §, ¶, ‖, **, †† and ‡‡. For example, the commands:

\newcounter{stone}\setcounter{stone}{4}$\fnsymbol{stone}$

produce §. (Robust.)

\footheight A rigid length parameter whose value affects the appearance of each output page. Its value is the height of the box containing the text in the foot of the page. See Fig. C.4 on p. 258. This is a robust command that must not be preceded by a **\protect** command.

footnote A counter used for the numbering of footnotes. In the **book** and **report** document styles it is initialized to zero at the beginning of each chapter and in the **article** document style it is initialized to zero at the start of the document. It is incremented automatically by both the **\footnote** and **\footnotetext** commands before being used.

\footnote[*i***]{***text***}** This command can be used either in paragraph mode or inside a **minipage** environment in order to produce a footnote. In paragraph mode if the optional numerical argument *i* is missing, then the **footnote** counter is incremented and then used as the number of the footnote. This occurs as a superscript in the body of the page where the **\footnote** command occurs and also at the bottom of the body of the page where *text* also appears. If *i*—which must be a positive whole number—is present, then the counter **footnote** is left unaltered and *i* is used as the footnote number. Inside a **minipage** environment the footnote mark will appear as a letter and the *text* will appear in the bottom part of the box produced. If the number *i* is present, then the corresponding lowercase letter will be used as the footnote mark. Note that this is different from the plain TEX **\footnote** command. (Fragile.)

\footnotemark[*i***]** This command can be used in any mode to produce a footnote mark which appears as a superscript in the body of the page but nowhere else. If *i* is absent, then the counter **footnote** is incremented by one and then that value is used as the footnote mark. If *i*—which must be a positive whole number—is present, then the counter `footnote` is left unaltered and *i* is used as the footnote mark. This command is usually used in conjunction with `\footnotetext`. (Fragile.)

`\footnoterule` Normally when a footnote appears on a page it is separated from the text above by a horizontal line or rule a third of the width of the page. This command produces that effect.

`\footnotesep` A rigid length parameter whose value minus the current length separating baselines gives the amount of space left between footnotes and also just below the horizontal line or rule generated by `\footnoterule`. This is a rigid length command that must not be preceded by a `\protect` command.

`\footnotesize` A declaration that alters the size of type and also selects the roman font of that size. It cannot be used in math mode. Usually the type size selected is just bigger than `\scriptsize` and just smaller than `\small`. (Fragile.)

`\footnotetext[i]{text}` This command can be used in any mode. It behaves exactly like `\footnote` except that no footnote mark appears in the body of the page marking the presence of a footnote. It is usually used in conjunction with `\footnotemark`. (Fragile.)

`\footskip` A rigid length parameter whose value affects the appearance of each output page. Its value is the distance between the bottom of the body and the bottom of the foot. See Fig. C.4 on p. 258. This is a robust command that must never be preceded by a `\protect` command.

`\forall` produces the ordinary symbol ∀ but only in math mode. (Robust.)

`\frac{top}{bot}` A command only available in math mode for producing a fraction with *top* above the fraction line and *bot* below it. (Robust.)

`\frame{picture-object}` This command—which can only appear inside the `picture` environment—puts a "frame" made up out of vertical and horizontal lines around *picture-object* with no separating space. The bottom left-hand corner of the resulting box is the reference point. (Fragile.)

`\framebox[len][pos]{text}` Outside the `picture` environment this processes *text* in LR mode and then "frames" the result as shown in Fig. C.2 on p. 217. (Fragile.)

`\framebox(i, j)[pos]{picture-object}` This form of this command can only appear inside the `picture` environment. The parameters have the same meaning as for the `\makebox` command, *q.v.* The only difference between this command and `\makebox` is that this one produces text with a "frame" made up out of vertical and horizontal lines surrounding it. (Fragile.)

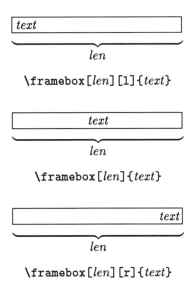

Figure C.2: The effect of the *pos* argument in the \framebox command.

\frenchspacing By default TEX puts more space after punctuation marks like the full stop (period). When the \frenchspacing declaration is in force, however, TEX regards the space following a punctuation mark in exactly the same way that it treats a space between words. (Fragile.)

\frown produces the binary relation symbol ⌢ but only in math mode. (Robust.)

\fussy This declaration influences line breaking. When it is in force—and it is the default—text will sometimes stick out into the right-hand margin and a warning message is displayed on your terminal. It affects the typesetting of any paragraph if it is in force when that paragraph ends.

\gamma produces the ordinary symbol γ but only in math mode. (Robust.)

\Gamma produces the ordinary symbol Γ but only in math mode. (Robust.)

\gcd produces the log-like symbol (gcd) but only in math mode. Subscripts and superscripts appear under and over the symbol produced—as limits—when it occurs as part of a displayed formula. (Robust.)

\ge produces the binary relation symbol $\geq$ but only in math mode; it has exactly the same effect as the command \geq. (Robust.)

\geq produces the binary relation symbol $\geq$ but only in math mode; the command \ge produces exactly the same symbol. (Robust.)

\gets produces the binary relation symbol ← but only in math mode; it has exactly the same effect as the command **\leftarrow**. (Robust.)

glo File extension of a file which is written if a **\makeglossary** command occurs in your input file (and a **\nofiles** command does not occur there). It contains a **\glossaryentry**{*text*}{*p*} command for every **\glossary**{*text*} command that occurs in your input file (and nothing else).

\global Placed before **\def** or an assignment this makes that declaration global, that is to say, its significance transcends any curly braces inside whose scope the declaration occurs. This is a primitive TeX command.

\glossary{*text*} This command causes the command **\glossaryentry**{*text*}{*p*} to be written to a glo file (if one is being written to). Any characters can occur in *text* (but all braces—including **\{** and **\}**—must come in matching pairs) unless the **\glossary** command occurs inside the argument of another command, when *text* can only include letters, numerals and punctuation marks. (Fragile.)

\glossaryentry{*text*}{*p*} This command can only occur in a glo file. It is written there automatically by LaTeX itself whenever a **\glossary**{*text*} command occurs in the input file. (This only happens if a **\makeglossary** command occurs in the preamble of your input file and a **\nofiles** command does not occur there.) The number *p* is the page number of the page in the output where **\glossary**{*text*} occurs.

\gg produces the binary relation symbol ≫ but only in math mode. (Robust.)

\grave A command that produces an accent but only in math mode. Thus, the input **$\grave x$** produces $\grave{x}$. (Robust.)

\H␣char or **\H**{*char*} This produces a long Hungarian umlaut (ö) over the following single character *char* in LR or paragraph mode. (Robust.)

\hat A command that produces an accent in math mode. Thus, **$\hat x$** produces $\hat{x}$. (Robust.)

\hbar produces the ordinary symbol $\hbar$ but only in math mode. (Robust.)

\hbox{*text*} makes a horizontal box; the individual components of the *text* argument are placed next to each other horizontally. This is a primitive TeX command.

\headheight A rigid length parameter whose value affects the appearance of each output page. Its value is the height of the box containing the text in the head of the page. See Fig. C.4 on p. 258. This is a robust command that must never be preceded by a **\protect** command.

headings A page style option to the \pagestyle and \thispagestyle declarations. The document style determines what information goes into the head of the page—usually it is a sectional-unit heading—and the foot is left empty. It is the default page style for the **book** document style.

\headsep A rigid length parameter whose value affects the appearance of each output page. Its value is the distance between the bottom of the head and the top of the body. See Fig. C.4 on p. 258. This is a robust command that must never be preceded by a \protect command.

\heartsuit produces the ordinary symbol $\heartsuit$ but only in math mode. (Robust.)

\hfill This is just an abbreviation for \hspace{\fill}. (Robust.)

\hline A command that is only available inside an **array**, **tabular** or **tabular*** environment. It produces a horizontal line across the entire width of the resulting table. It must come either after the command that opens the environment or after a \\ command.

\hom produces a log-like symbol (hom) but only in math mode. Subscripts and superscripts never appear as limits attached to the symbol produced. (Robust.)

\hookleftarrow produces the binary relation symbol $\hookleftarrow$ but only in math mode. (Robust.)

\hookrightarrow produces the binary relation symbol $\hookrightarrow$ but only in math mode. (Robust.)

howpublished (A BibTeX field-name.) This field is optional for two kinds of publication and it indicates how the item in question was published. The text should start with an initial uppercase letter.

\hrulefill This command produces a horizontal line or rule which expands to fill all the available space where it occurs. See Table C.1 on p. 210 for a picture of what it does. (Robust)

\hspace{*len***}** A command that produces *len* amount of horizontal space which disappears at a line break. (Robust.)

\hspace*{*len***}** A command that produces *len* amount of horizontal space which does not disappear at a line break. (Robust.)

\huge A declaration that alters the size of type and also selects the roman font of that size. It cannot be used in math mode. Usually the type size selected is just bigger than \LARGE and just smaller than \Huge. (Fragile.)

\Huge A declaration that alters the size of type and also selects the roman font of that size. It cannot be used in math mode. Usually the type size selected is the largest available and is just bigger than **\huge**. (Fragile.)

\hyphenation{*word-list***}** This is a global declaration which tells TEX how the words that occur in *word-list* can be hyphenated; words in *word-list* are separated by spaces and hyphens in individual words indicate places where hyphenation is allowed. (Robust.)

\i produces a dotless letter ı in paragraph and LR modes. (Robust.)

idx File extension of a file which is written if a **\makeindex** command occurs in the preamble of your input file (and a **\nofiles** command does not occur there). It contains an **\indexentry{***text***}{***p***}** command for every **\index{***text***}** command that occurs in your input file (and nothing else).

\iff (If and only if.) This command produces the symbol $\Longleftrightarrow$ in math mode; it has exactly the same effect as the commands **\;\Longleftrightarrow\;**; that is to say, the symbol $\Longleftrightarrow$ with extra thick space to its left and right. (Robust.)

\Im produces the ordinary symbol $\Im$ but only in math mode. (Robust.)

\imath produces the ordinary symbol $\imath$ but only in math mode. (Robust.)

in TEX keyword for *inch*, a unit of length, which exactly satisfies the equalities 1 in = 72.27 pt = 25.4 mm.

\in produces the binary relation symbol $\in$ but only in math mode. (Robust.)

\include{*file***}** This command is used in conjunction with **\includeonly{***file-list***}** for producing only part of a large document whose content has been split into several input files. Note that the result of processing *file* will—if it appears at all—always start on a new page and it will terminate as if a **\clearpage** command had been included at the end of *file*.**tex**. (Fragile.)

\includeonly{*file-list***}** This command can only occur in the preamble of your input file. The argument *file-list* is a list of zero or more extensionless filenames. If two or more are present, then they are separated by commas. (*file* refers to *file*.**tex**.) If *file* occurs in *file-list*, the command **\include{***file***}** does not have to occur in the body of the input file. Only the text contained in a *file* that appears in *file-list* occurs in the output produced by LATEX. (Fragile.)

\indent This forces the next line of text that LATEX outputs to be indented the same amount that is the current value of the **\parindent** length parameter. (Robust.)

\index{*text***}** This command causes the command **\indexentry{***text***}{***p***}** to be written to an **idx** file (if one is being written to). Any characters can occur in *text* (but all braces—including \{ and \} must come in matching pairs) unless the \index command occurs inside the argument of another command, when *text* can only include letters, numerals and punctuation marks. (Fragile.)

\indexentry{*text*}{*p*} This command can only occur in an idx file. It is written there automatically by LaTeX itself whenever an \index{*text*} command occurs in the input file. (This only happens if a \makeindex command occurs in the preamble of your input file and a \nofiles command does not occur there.) The number *p* is the page number of the page in the output where \index{*text*} occurs.

\indexspace A command used inside the theindex environment for producing extra vertical space. It is usually used to separate items beginning with different letters of the alphabet.

\inf produces a log-like symbol (inf) but only in math mode. Subscripts and superscripts appear under and over the symbol produced—as limits—when it occurs as part of a displayed formula. (Robust.)

\infty produces the ordinary symbol ∞ but only in math mode. (Robust.)

\input{*file*} This has the same effect as if the contents of the file *file* were present in this part of the input file. If *file* has no extension, then the file *file*.tex is included. The braces are optional.

institution (A BIBTeX field-name.) This holds the name of the institution—for example, "Programming Research Group"—under whose auspices the technical report being referred to was produced.

\int produces the large operator symbol $\int$ but only in math mode. The symbol produced is slightly larger in displayed formulas than when it occurs as part of an in-text formula. Subscripts and superscripts appear under and over the symbol produced by this command—as limits—when it occurs in a displayed formula. (Robust.)

\intextsep A rubber length parameter whose value is the amount of vertical space placed above and below a float that occurs in the middle of a text page because the h location option has been chosen. This is a robust command that must not be preceded by a \protect command.

\iota produces the ordinary symbol ι but only in math mode. In order to produce a dotless lowercase italic letter $\imath$—needed, for example, when you want to combine it with an accent—use \imath. (Robust.)

\it A declaration that alters the style of the type being used to *italic*. (Robust.)

\item[*text*] A command that can only occur inside a small number of environments, namely `enumerate`, `itemize`, `description`, `list`, `theindex` and `trivlist`. Although what it does differs slightly from environment to environment it always indicates the start of a new piece of information. Note that it is different from the plain TEX command of the same name. (Fragile.)

\itemindent A rigid length parameter whose value affects the appearance of the `list` environment as shown in Fig. C.3 on p. 229. This is a robust command that must not be preceded by a \protect command.

itemize An environment used to produce labelled lists where the label does not—by default—change from one use of an \item command to another.

\itemsep A rubber length parameter whose value affects the appearance of the `list` environment as shown in Fig. C.3 on p. 229. This is a robust command that must not be preceded by a \protect command.

\j produces a dotless letter ȷ in paragraph and LR modes. (Robust.)

\jmath produces the ordinary symbol $\jmath$ but only in math mode. (Robust.)

\jobname This gives the first or base name of the main input file that is being processed.

\Join produces the binary relation symbol ⋈ but only in math mode. Note that this command is unavailable in plain TEX. (Robust.)

\jot The value of this rigid length parameter is the amount of additional inter-row vertical space in an `eqnarray` or `eqnarray*` environment.

journal (A BIBTEX field-name.) The name of the journal in which the article being referred to was published. Various abbreviations may be available on your system; check with someone who knows.

\kappa produces the ordinary symbol κ but only in math mode. (Robust.)

\ker produces a log-like symbol (ker) but only in math mode. Subscripts and superscripts never appear as limits attached to the symbol produced. (Robust.)

key (A BIBTEX field-name.) You should not confuse this field-name with the *key* that is used in \cite commands. This is used for sorting the entry when no other field usually used for sorting is present.

\kill This command can only occur within a `tabbing` environment where it ensures that the row it terminates produces no output, but the values of any tab stops are retained. It also sets *next-tab-stop* to be the same as *left-margin-tab* and begins a new line.

\l A command only available in paragraph and LR modes for producing a lowercase Polish suppressed-l (ł). (Robust.)

\L A command only available in paragraph and LR modes for producing an uppercase Polish suppressed-l (Ł). (Robust.)

\label{*key*} This command is used for cross-referencing purposes. It associates *key*—which can only consist of letters, numerals and punctuation marks—with the current \ref value. Although fragile, this command does not have to be preceded by a \protect command when it occurs in the argument of a sectioning or a \caption command.

\labelitemi A command that holds the symbol used to label items in the outermost or top-level occurrence of an itemize environment. By default the symbol used—in the **article, report, book** and **letter** document styles—is • ($\bullet$). Its "value" can be altered by either a \def or \renewcommand declaration.

\labelitemii This contains the symbol used to label the items of an itemize environment that occurs within one other itemize environment. By default the symbol used—in the **article, report, book** and **letter** document styles—is − ({\bf --}). The "value" of this can be altered either by a \def or a \renewcommand declaration.

\labelitemiii A command that holds the symbol used to label the items of an itemize environment that occurs within the scope of two other itemize environments. By default the symbol used—in the **article, report, book** and **letter** document styles—is ∗ ($\ast$). The "value" of this can be altered either by a \def or a \renewcommand declaration.

\labelitemiv This contains the symbol used to label the items of an itemize environment that occurs within the scope of three other itemize environments. By default the symbol used—in the **article, report, book** and **letter** document styles—is · ($\cdot$). The "value" of this can be altered either by a \def or a \renewcommand declaration.

\labelsep A rigid length parameter whose value affects the appearance of the list environment as shown in Fig. C.3 on p. 229. This is a robust command that must not be preceded by a \protect command.

\labelwidth A rigid length parameter whose value affects the appearance of the list environment as shown in Fig. C.3 on p. 229. This is a robust command that must not be preceded by a \protect command.

\lambda produces the ordinary symbol λ but only in math mode. (Robust.)

\Lambda produces the ordinary symbol Λ but only in math mode. (Robust.)

\land (logical and) produces the binary operation symbol ∧ but only in math mode; it has exactly the same effect as the command **\wedge**. (Robust.)

\langle produces the opening symbol ⟨ but only in math mode. (Robust.)

\large A declaration that alters the size of type and also selects the roman font of that size. It cannot be used in math mode. Usually the type size selected is just bigger than **\normalsize** and just smaller than **\Large**. (Fragile.)

\Large A declaration that alters the size of type and also selects the roman font of that size. It cannot be used in math mode. Usually the type size selected is just bigger than **\large** and just smaller than **\LARGE**. (Fragile.)

\LARGE A declaration that alters the size of type and also selects the roman font of that size. It cannot be used in math mode. Usually the type size selected is just bigger than **\Large** and just smaller than **\huge**. (Fragile.)

\LaTeX produces the logo LaTeX.

\lbrace produces the opening symbol { but only in math mode; it has exactly the same effect as the command **\{**. (Robust.)

\lceil produces the opening symbol ⌈ but only in math mode. (Robust.)

\ldots This command—which is available in all modes—produces an ellipsis (...) consisting of three "low" dots. (Robust.)

\le produces the binary relation symbol ≤ but only in math mode; it has exactly the same effect as the command **\leq**. (Robust.)

\leadsto produces the binary relation symbol ⤳ but only in math mode. Note that this command is unavailable in plain TeX. (Robust.)

\left*delim₁* *form* **\right***delim₂* A construct only available in math mode and there only in display style. The formula *form* is processed and then delimiters are chosen of the correct size to fit around it. Both **\left** and **\right** have to be present, but a full stop can take the place of either *delim₁* or *delim₂* which results in no output. Both **\left** and **\right** are robust.

\leftarrow produces the binary relation symbol ← but only in math mode. The command **\gets** produces exactly the same symbol. (Robust.)

\Leftarrow produces the binary relation symbol ⇐ but only in math mode. (Robust.)

\leftarrowfill produces an arrow pointing left which expands to fill all the horizontal space available; see Table C.1 on p. 210 for a graphical depiction of what it does.

\lefteqn{*form***}** A command that can only occur within an `eqnarray` or `eqnarray*` environment. It is used for splitting long formulas that will not fit on a single line. The argument *form* is processed in math display style.

\leftharpoondown produces the binary relation symbol ↼ but only in math mode. (Robust.)

\leftharpoonup produces the binary relation symbol ↽ but only in math mode. (Robust.)

\leftmargin A rigid length parameter whose value affects the horizontal distance between the left margin of the enclosing environment and the left margin of the current `list` environment as shown in Fig. C.3 on p. 229. If a `list` environment occurs within the scope of no other `list` environment, then by default **\leftmargin** is assigned the value **\leftmargini**; if a `list` environment occurs within the scope of one other `list` environment, then by default **\leftmargin** is assigned the value **\leftmarginii**; ...; if a `list` environment occurs within the scope of five other `list` environments, then by default **\leftmargin** is assigned the value **\leftmarginvi**; and further nestings are not allowed. This is a robust command that must not be preceded by a **\protect** command.

\leftmargini A rigid length parameter whose value is used for setting the width of certain left margins, for example, in the `list` environment. See **\leftmargin**. This is a robust command that must not be preceded by a **\protect** command.

\leftmarginii A rigid length parameter whose value is used for setting the width of certain left margins, for example, in the `list` environment. See **\leftmargin**. This is a robust command that must not be preceded by a **\protect** command.

\leftmarginiii A rigid length parameter whose value is used for setting the width of certain left margins, for example, in the `list` environment. See **\leftmargin**. This is a robust command that must not be preceded by a **\protect** command.

\leftmarginiv A rigid length parameter whose value is used for setting the width of certain left margins, for example, in the `list` environment. See **\leftmargin**. This is a robust command that must not be preceded by a **\protect** command.

\leftmarginv A rigid length parameter whose value is used for setting the width of certain left margins, for example, in the `list` environment. See **\leftmargin**. This is a robust command that must not be preceded by a **\protect** command.

\leftmarginvi A rigid length parameter whose value is used for setting the width of certain left margins, for example, in the `list` environment. See **\leftmargin**. This is a robust command that must not be preceded by a **\protect** command.

\leftrightarrow produces the binary relation symbol ↔ but only in math mode. (Robust.)

\Leftrightarrow produces the binary relation symbol ⇔ but only in math mode. (Robust.)

\leq produces the binary relation symbol ≤ but only in math mode. Alternatively, the command **\le** can be used to produce the same symbol. (Robust.)

\leqalignno{*lhs$_1$&rhs$_1$&en$_1$*\cr *lhs$_2$&rhs$_2$&en$_2$*\cr ... *lhs$_n$&rhs$_n$&en$_n$*\cr} This is a plain TEX command that can only be used in math mode and display style to produce several displayed formulas aligned on the symbols that follow the ampersands. The formulas *lhs$_i$* and *rhs$_i$* are typeset in display style. The expressions *en$_i$*—which are usually numerical labels—are placed on the extreme left-hand side of the body region of the page; if any such expressions are omitted, then so should the preceding ampersand. This command needs to be reinstated—as described in section 8.4—before it can be used.

leqno One of the standard options that is available to the **\documentstyle** command. By default formulas numbered automatically by LaTEX have their labels positioned on the right of the output page; including this option transfers them to the left-hand side of the page.

\leqno This primitive TEX command is only available in math mode and display style where it produces a label on the left-hand side of the body region.

letter A standard document style parameter to the **\documentstyle** command.

letter An environment that can only occur within the **letter** document style. It is used for producing letters. One or more **letter** environments can occur in the same input file. Its general format is:

$$\text{\textbackslash begin\{letter\}\{\underline{text_1}\}\ text_2\ \textbackslash end\{letter\}}$$

Note that *text$_1$* here is a moving argument, so any fragile commands in it need to be preceded by a **\protect** command. This argument is used for the address of the recipient of the letter. One or more \\ commands can occur in *text$_1$* in order to force a new line. Note also that *text$_1$* is not an optional argument. You will get an error message if it is omitted. The whole **letter** environment is a moving argument.

\lfloor produces the opening symbol ⌊ but only in math mode. (Robust.)

\lg produces a log-like symbol (lg) but only in math mode. Subscripts and superscripts never appear as limits attached to the symbol produced. (Robust.)

\lgroup This command is only available in math mode where it produces a delimiter that looks like a large left parenthesis; it must be preceded, however, by either **\left** or **\right**.

\lhd produces the binary operator symbol ◁ but only in math mode. Note that this command is unavailable in plain TEX. (Robust.)

\lim produces a log-like symbol (lim) but only in math mode. Subscripts and superscripts appear under and over the symbol produced—as limits—when it occurs as part of a displayed formula. (Robust.)

\liminf produces a log-like symbol (lim inf) but only in math mode. Subscripts and superscripts appear under and over the symbol produced—as limits—when it occurs as part of a displayed formula. (Robust.)

\limits The effect of cmd**\limits**_$form_1$^$form_2$ in math mode is to make $form_1$ appear as a limit underneath the symbol produced by cmd and $form_2$ to appear as a limit over it. This effect is produced both in text and display styles. This is a primitive TEX command.

\limsup produces a log-like symbol (lim sup) but only in math mode. Subscripts and superscripts appear under and over the symbol produced—as limits—when it occurs as part of a displayed formula. (Robust.)

\line A command that can only occur as the argument to a **\put** or **\multiput** command inside a `picture` environment. The command:

$$\text{\put}(i,j)\{\text{\line}(p,q)\{l\}\}$$

draws an arrow which starts at the point (i, j) and whose projection on the x-axis is l units. (The only exception to this occurs when we want to produce a vertical line, in which case l gives the actual length of the line produced.) The slope of the line is given by (p, q), that is to say, it goes p units in the x direction for every q units it goes in the y direction. Both p and q must be whole numbers between -6 and $+6$, inclusive, with no common divisor. Note that the LATEX **\line** command is completely different from the plain TEX command of the same name. (Fragile.)

\linebreak[i] The optional numerical argument i can be either 0, 1, 2, 3, or 4. If it is absent or its value is 4, then the **\linebreak** command marks the position of the end of a line. The output is right justified—unless some other command or declaration has suppressed right justification—with the word that came before the **\linebreak** command occurring at the extreme right of the line on which it occurs. (This may cause an underfull **\hbox** warning message.) If the numerical argument i is 0, then TEX can end the line at that point, but the presence of the command neither encourages nor discourages this. If the numerical value of i is 1, 2 or 3, then this encourages TEX to make a line break at that point and the higher the number the stronger the encouragement. (Fragile.)

\linethickness{len} This declaration only affects the thickness of vertical and horizontal lines in a `picture` environment. It makes them len wide.

\linewidth The value of this rigid length parameter—which must never be altered—is the current width of lines. It is changed when certain environments—such as `quotation`—are used. This is a robust command that must not be preceded by a `\protect` command.

list A general-purpose environment for producing lists of information. Optionally, the items in the list can be labelled in a variety of ways. A number of parameters control the organization and appearance of the list; see Fig. C.3 on p. 229 for the effect of these. (The length parameter `\parindent` is also included in that diagram as this may influence the choice of values for some of the other parameters.) The general format of the `list` environment is:

$$\begin{list}\{text_1\}\{dec\text{-}list\} \; text_2 \; \end{list}$$

where *text*$_1$ is what will be generated by an `\item` command which does not have an optional argument, *dec-list* is a sequence of assignments to some of the length parameters that appear in Fig. C.3 on p. 229—any length parameter that is not given a value in this way is initialized by an assignment in one of `@listi, ...,` `@listv` or `@listvi` (the choice depends on the level of nesting) which is carried out before *dec-list*—and *text*$_2$ is the information to be displayed; one or more `\item` commands can occur in *text*$_2$. Note that a `\usecounter` command can occcur in *dec-list* if you want the automatically generated labels to be numbered in an increasing sequence.

\listoffigures This command produces a list of figures at the place in the input file where it occurs. You need to run LaTeX at least twice to get a correct list of figures. It causes a `lof` file to be written or overwritten except if you have included a `\nofiles` command.

\listoftables This command produces a list of tables at the place in the input file where it occurs. You need to run LaTeX at least twice to get a correct list of tables. It causes a `lot` file to be written or overwritten except if you have included a `\nofiles` command.

\listparindent A rigid length parameter whose value affects the appearance of the `list` environment as shown in Fig. C.3 on p. 229. This is a robust command that must not be preceded by a `\protect` command.

\ll produces the binary relation symbol $\ll$ but only in math mode. (Robust.)

\llap This plain TeX command prints text overlapping to the left; it is used, for example, inside the argument of the `\displaylines` command to place labels on the extreme right-hand side of the body region.

\lmoustache This command is only available in math mode where it produces a strange looking delimiter as shown in Table 7.1 on p. 100; note that it has to be preceded by either `\left` or `\right`.

a	\topsep + \parskip or \topsep + \parskip + \partopsep		
b	\itemsep + \parsep	f	\leftmargin
c	\parsep	g	\listparindent
d	\labelwidth	h	\rightmargin
e	\labelsep	i	\parindent

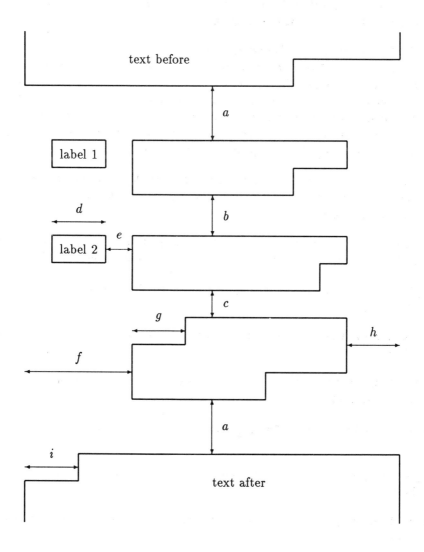

Figure C.3: Parameters of the list environment.

\ln produces a log-like symbol (ln) but only in math mode. Subscripts and superscripts never appear as limits attached to the symbol produced. (Robust.)

\lnot (logical not) produces the ordinary symbol ¬ but only in math mode; it has
exactly the same effect as the command \neg. (Robust.)

\load{*size*}{*style*} This command loads a font whose size is given by *size* and whose
style is given by *style*, where *size* is one of \tiny, \scriptsize, \footnotesize,
\small, \normalsize, \large, \Large, \LARGE, \huge or \Huge; and *style* is
one of \bf, \it, \sc, \sf, \sl or \tt.

lof The file extension of a file which is only created or overwritten if your input
file contains a \listoffigures command (and does not contain a \nofiles
command). The lof file contains the information necessary to produce a list
of figures for your document. This information comes from every \caption
command which occurs within the scope of a figure or figure* environment in
your input file. The list of figures is produced by the \listoffigures command
if a lof file exists when you process your input file.

log File extension of a file created when you run LaTeX which contains all the information that appeared on your terminal while LaTeX was running and also some
additional information.

\log produces a log-like symbol (log) but only in math mode. Subscripts and superscripts never appear as limits attached to the symbol produced. (Robust.)

\longleftarrow produces the binary relation symbol ⟵ but only in math mode.
(Robust.)

\Longleftarrow produces the binary relation symbol ⟸ but only in math mode.
(Robust.)

\longleftrightarrow produces the binary relation symbol ⟷ but only in math
mode. (Robust.)

\Longleftrightarrow produces the binary relation symbol ⟺ but only in math
mode. (Robust.)

\longmapsto produces the binary relation symbol ⟼ but only in math mode. (Robust.)

\longrightarrow produces the binary relation symbol ⟶ but only in math mode.
(Robust.)

\Longrightarrow produces the binary relation symbol ⟹ but only in math mode.
(Robust.)

\lor (logical or) produces the binary operation symbol ∨ but only in math mode; it has exactly the same effect as the command \vee. (Robust.)

lot The file extension of a file which is only created or overwritten if your input file contains a \listoftables command (and does not contain a \nofiles command). The lot file contains the information necessary to produce a list of tables for your document. This information comes from every \caption command which occurs within a table or table* environment in your input file. The list of tables is produced by the \listoftables command if a lot file exists when you process your input file.

\makebox[*len*][*pos*]{*text*} Outside the picture environment this is like \framebox, *q.v.*, except that no "frame" is produced. (Fragile.)

\makebox(*i, j*)[*pos*]{*picture-object*} This form of this command can only occur inside the picture environment. It is explained in subsection 10.2.1.

\makeglossary This command can only occur in the preamble of your input file. It causes a glo file to be written which contains the \glossaryentry commands generated by any \glossary commands that appear in your input file. A \nofiles declaration in the preamble suppresses the writing (or overwriting) of the glo file.

\makeindex This command can only occur in the preamble of your input file. It causes an idx file to be written which contains the \indexentry commands generated by any \index commands that appear in your input file. A \nofiles declaration in the preamble suppresses the writing (or overwriting) of the idx file.

\makelable{*text*} This generates the label produced by the \item command using the *text* argument.

\makelabels A command that takes no arguments which can only occur in the preamble of a letter document style. It causes a list of all the recipient addresses to be produced on a new page following all the letters generated. These can be photocopied onto sticky labels if so desired.

\maketitle A command that produces a title in the **article**, **report** and **book** document styles. In the latter two the title occurs on a page by itself, whereas in the **article** document style the title is put at the top of the first page of output. Some text and all or part of the abstract may appear on the same page. The \maketitle command—if it occurs in the input file at all—must come within the document environment. If it is used, it must be preceded by both \title and \author declarations and may be preceded by a \date declaration.

\mapsto produces the binary relation symbol ↦ but only in math mode. (Robust.)

\marginpar[*text₁*]{*text₂*} This command produce a marginal note. If the optional argument *text₁* is absent, then *text₂* will appear as a marginal note. If the optional argument *text₁* is present, then *text₂* will appear as a marginal note if the current location of marginal notes is in the right-hand margin and *text₁* will appear as a marginal note if the current location of marginal notes is in the left-hand margin. (Fragile.)

\marginparpush The value of this rigid length parameter affects the appearance of marginal notes on the output page. Its value is the minimum distance separating two successive marginal notes. This is a robust command that must never be preceded by a \protect command.

\marginparsep The value of this rigid length parameter affects the appearance of marginal notes on the output page. Its value is the distance between the outer edge of the body and the inner edge of marginal notes. (When one-sided printing is in effect the default is that the outer edge of the body is the right one on all pages and the inner edge of marginal notes is the left one. When two-sided printing is in effect the default is that the outer edge of the body is the right one on odd pages and the left one on even pages and the inner edge of marginal notes is the left one on odd pages and the right one on even pages. These defaults can be altered by means of the \reversemarginpar declaration.) This is a robust command that must never be preceded by a \protect command.

\marginparwidth A rigid length parameter whose value affects the appearance of marginal notes on the output page. Its value is the width of the parbox containing a marginal note. This is a robust command that must never be preceded by a \protect command.

\markboth{*text₁*}{*text₂*} Used in conjunction with the myheadings style option to either the \pagestyle or \thispagestyle declaration this command—in two-sided printing—makes *text₁* into the running head on even-numbered pages and *text₂* into the running head on odd-numbered pages. (Fragile.)

\markright{*text*} Used in conjunction with the myheadings style option to either the \pagestyle or \thispagestyle declaration this command—in one-sided printing—makes *text* into the running head on all pages except the first. (Fragile.)

math An environment used for typesetting a mathematical formula so that it does not appear on a line by itself, that is to say, it is used for producing in-text formulas. The more concise forms \(*form*\) and $*form*$ are also available. Inside the math environment LaTeX is in math mode and formulas are typeset in text style.

\mathindent A rigid length parameter whose value is the distance by which displayed formulas are indented from the left-hand edge of the body of a page when the

fleqn document style option has been chosen. This is a robust command that must never be preceded by a \protect command.

\mathstrut This plain TEX command is only available in math mode where it produces an invisible vertical rule the same height as a parenthesis but with no width.

\matrix The general form of this plain TEX command is like this:

$$\text{\textbackslash matrix}\{form_{11} \ \& \ form_{12} \ \& \ ... \ \& \ form_{1n} \ \text{\textbackslash cr}$$
$$form_{21} \ \& \ form_{22} \ \& \ ... \ \& \ form_{2n} \ \text{\textbackslash cr}$$
$$\vdots$$
$$form_{m1} \& \ form_{m2} \& \ ... \ \& \ form_{mn} \text{\textbackslash cr}\}$$

It can only be used in math mode where it produces a matrix without any enclosing brackets of any sort.

\max produces a log-like symbol (max) but only in math mode. Subscripts and superscripts appear under and over the symbol produced—as limits—when it occurs as part of a displayed formula. (Robust.)

\mbox{*text*} A command that can be used in any mode. The argument *text* is processed in LR mode and under no circumstances will the result be broken across lines. Any declarations in force when an \mbox command occurs affect the processing of *text* if LATEX is in LR or paragraph mode; if it is in math mode, then the processing of *text* is affected by those declarations in effect when LATEX moved into math mode. For example, {\it when $17 > \mbox{age}$} produces *when* $17 > age$. (Robust.)

\medskip produces vertical space whose height is given by \medskipamount; it is defined as \vspace{\medskipamount}. Note that is different from the plain TEX definition. (Fragile.)

\medskipamount A rubber length whose value is 6pt plus 2pt minus 2pt.

\mho produces the ordinary symbol ℧ but only in math mode. Note that this command is not present in plain TEX. (Robust.)

\mid produces the binary relation symbol | but only in math mode. (Robust.)

\min produces a log-like symbol (min) but only in math mode. Subscripts and superscripts appear under and over the symbol produced—as limits—when it occurs as part of a displayed formula. (Robust.)

minipage An environment used for producing a parbox, that is to say, a box whose contents are processed in paragraph mode. Its general format is:

\begin{minipage}[*pos*]{*len*} *text* \end{minipage}

where *len* is the width of the box produced and the optional parameter *pos* can be either b or t. The option b makes the bottom line of the box produced share the same baseline as current line of text and the option t makes the top line of the box produced share the same baseline as the current line of text.

minus *len* A TeX keyword used in assigning rubber length values; *len* represents the amount by which the natural value of the target length argument can shrink.

\mit A declaration that alters the style of the type being used to math italic. (This can only be used in math mode.)

\mkern*len* This primitive TeX command is only available in math mode where it generates *len* amount of space where *len* must be given in terms of the mathematical unit (mu). Whether the space is horizontal or vertical depends on the context where the command occurs.

mm TeX keyword for *millimetre*, a unit of length, which exactly satisfies the equality 10 mm = 1 cm. (Roughly, 1 mm = 0.03937 in = 2.854 pt.)

\models produces the binary relation symbol $\models$ but only in math mode. (Robust.)

month (A BibTeX field-name.) Use either jan, feb, mar, apr, may, jun, jul, aug, sep, oct, nov or dec.

\mp produces the binary operator symbol $\mp$ but only in math mode. (Robust.)

mpfootnote A counter used for the numbering of footnotes inside a **minipage** environment which is initialized to zero when the environment is opened. It is incremented automatically by both the \footnote and \footnotetext commands before being used. Although the value of this counter must be a positive whole number, it appears as the corresponding lowercase letter.

mu TeX keyword for *mathematical unit*; a font-dependent unit of length which can only be used in math mode; 18 mu = 1 em, where the length of the em comes from the font in family 2 in the current style. (See, for example, chapter 23 of Eijkhout (1992) for more information about this.)

\mu produces the ordinary symbol μ but only in math mode. (Robust.)

\multicolumn{*i*}{*pre*}{*text*} This command is used to produce material in a row of the tabular, tabular* or array environments in a way different from that specified in the preamble. The argument *i* is a positive whole number which indicates how many columns this command affects. *pre* is similar to the preamble of the `tabular` or `array` environments except that fewer expressions are allowed and *text* is what is to appear. A `\multicolumn` command must either begin a row or immediately follow an ampersand.

`\multiput`$(i,j)(m,n)${t}{*picture-object*} This command can only occur within the `picture` environment, where it is equivalent to the following t commands:

> `\put`(i,j){*picture-object*}
> `\put`$(i+m,j+n)${*picture-object*}
> `\put`$(i+2m,j+2n)${*picture-object*}
> $\vdots$
> `\put`$(i+(t-1)m,j+(t-1)n)${*picture-object*}

LATEX does not have a very large memory, so there is a maximum number of repetitions allowed and it is about 100.

myheadings A page style option to the `\pagestyle` and `\thispagestyle` declarations which allows you to customize what information you want to appear in the head of the page. (The foot is left empty.) See `\markboth` and `\markright` for how to get information into the head.

`\nabla` produces the ordinary symbol ∇ but only in math mode. (Robust.)

`\natural` produces the ordinary symbol $\natural$ but only in math mode. (Robust.)

`\ne` produces the binary relation symbol $\neq$ but only in math mode; it has exactly the same effect as the command `\neq`. Both are equivalent to `\not=`. (Robust.)

`\nearrow` produces the binary relation symbol $\nearrow$ but only in math mode. (Robust.)

`\neg` produces the ordinary symbol $\neg$ but only in math mode. It can also be produced by `\lnot` (logical not). (Robust.)

`\neq` produces the binary relation symbol $\neq$ but only in math mode; it has exactly the same effect as the command `\ne`. Both are equivalent to `\not=`. (Robust.)

`\newcommand`{*cmd*}[*i*]{*def*} This non-global declaration defines *cmd*—which must not have been defined already—to be a new command. *cmd* must begin with a backslash and must not begin with `\end`. The optional parameter *i* must be a positive whole number between 1 and 9. The number used indicates how many arguments the command you are defining has. The actual definition of the command you are defining is *def*. If the formal parameter #*j* occurs in *def*, then the *j*th actual parameter when the command *cmd* is used is substituted for it. (Fragile.)

\newcounter{*ctr₁***}[***ctr₂***]** This global declaration makes ctr_1—which must consist entirely of letters and must not be the name of an existing counter—into a counter which is initialized to zero. The command **\the***ctr₁* is automatically defined to be **\arabic{***ctr₁***}**. This declaration cannot be used in a file whose name occurs as a parameter in an **\include** command. If ctr_2—which must be the name of an existing counter—is present, then ctr_1 is set to zero whenever ctr_2 is incremented by either **\stepcounter** or **\refstepcounter**. (Fragile.)

\newenvironment{*env***}[***i***]{***def₁***}{***def₂***}** This declaration defines *env* to be a new environment, where *env* must be a fresh name consisting entirely of letters. Furthermore, there must be no command called *****env* defined. The optional parameter *i* must be a positive whole number between 1 and 9. The number used indicates how many arguments the environment being defined has. The parameter def_1 contains a list of those commands executed when LaTeX encounters **\begin{***env***}** and def_2 is the list of commands executed when **\end{***env***}** is encountered. The braces around def_1 and def_2 are part of the syntax of this declaration and do not delimit the scope of any declarations in def_1 or def_2. If the parameter *i* is present, then the environment is opened by means of the command:

> **\begin{***env***}{***arg₁***}...{***argᵢ***}**

and this is the same as def_1 being executed with arg_j substituted for any occurrence of **#***j* in it (for $1 \leq j \leq i$). Note that **#***j* cannot occur in def_2. (Fragile.)

\newfont{*cmd***}{***font***}** This declaration turns the fresh command name *cmd* into a robust declaration—available only in paragraph and LR modes—whose effect is to make *font* the current font. (Fragile.)

\newlength{*cmd***}** This declaration makes *cmd*—which must begin with a backslash and which must not have been defined previously—a length command and initializes its value to zero inches. (Fragile.)

\newline This forces a line break at the end of the current paragraph. (Fragile.)

\newpage This command forces the current paragraph and the current page to be terminated. If the **twocolumn** document style option has been chosen, then this command terminates the current paragraph and the current column. (Robust.)

\newsavebox{*cmd***}** This declares *cmd*—which must be a fresh command name beginning with a backslash—to be a storage bin. It is used in conjunction with **\savebox** or **\sbox**. (Fragile.)

\newtheorem{*env₁***}[***env₂***]{***text***}[***ctr***]** This global declaration defines env_1 to be a new environment; the name env_1 can only consist of letters and must not be the name of any existing counter or environment. At most one of the optional arguments env_2 and *ctr* can be present. The argument *text* contains the word or phrase that will appear—by default in bold—whenever the environment env_1 is used. If neither env_2 nor ctr is present, then a counter also called env_1 is created and each invocation of the environment env_1 will produce output that is numbered consecutively and will start from 1. If ctr—which must be the name of a counter—is present, then a counter also called env_1 is created and the numbers produced by a use of the environment env_1 will look like $i.j$ where i is the value of ctr and j is the number of this particular invocation of the environment. If env_2—which must be the name of an environment created by an earlier \newtheorem declaration—is present, then invocations of both env_1 and env_2 will be numbered consecutively in the same numerical series. (Fragile.)

\ni produces the binary relation symbol ∋ but only in math mode. The command \owns can also be used for this symbol. (Robust.)

\noalign{*text*} A primitive TEX command used to put *text* between the rows of an arrangement of information produced by TEX commands; do *not* use it with LATEX's array environment, for example. It is commonly used to put more space between the rows produced, for example, by the \cases command; it could be used like this \noalign{\smallskip}.

\nocite{*key-list*} Used for including items in a bibliography produced by BIBTEX that you do not actually refer to. The parameter *key-list* is a list of keys—separated by commas—that have been defined in a bib file; the corresponding entries are placed in the bibliography produced. To get a listing of everything in a bib file include a \nocite{*} command somewhere in the document environment. (Fragile.)

\nofiles When LATEX is run a number of subsidiary files are or may be created, namely the aux, glo, idx, lof, lot and toc files. (For example, if your original file is called *file*.tex, then the auxilary file is called *file*.aux.) If you include the \nofiles declaration in the preamble of your input file—the only place it can occur—then none of these subsidiary files are written to. In particular, if any of them already exist, then they are not overwritten.

\noindent Normally, paragraphs are indented slightly from the left edge of the body of text on a page. (The width of the indentation is given by the length parameter \parindent.) This normal indentation can be suppressed by means of the \noindent command. It is useful sometimes, for example, right at the beginning of the abstract and quotation environments. (Robust.)

\nolinebreak[*i*] The optional numerical argument i can be either 0, 1, 2, 3, or 4. If it is absent or its value is 4, then the \nolinebreak command marks a place which will under no circumstances be placed at the end of a line. If the numerical argument i is 0, then TEX can end the line at that point, but the presence of the command neither encourages nor discourages this. If the numerical value of i is

1, 2 or 3, then this discourages TeX from making a line break at that point and the higher the number the stronger the discouragement. (Fragile.)

\nolimits The effect of *cmd*\nolimits_*form*$_1$^*form*$_2$ in math mode is to make *form*$_1$ appear as a subscript to the symbol produced by *cmd* and *form*$_2$ to appear as a superscript to it. This effect is produced both in text and display style. This is a primitive TeX command.

\nonumber This command can only occur inside the eqnarray environment. It has the effect of preventing an equation number being produced for any row in which it occurs.

\nonfrenchspacing By default TeX puts more space after punctuation marks like the full stop (period). Using the \nonfrenchspacing declaration returns you to this default treatment of spacing if it has been changed by a prior use of \frenchspacing. (Fragile.)

\nonstopmode This primitive TeX command ensures that the processing of your file will not stop if an error occurs, though an emergency stop will take place if user input is requested; it is one of the few commands that can come before the \documentstyle command in the input file.

\nopagebreak[*i*] The optional numerical argument *i* can be either 0, 1, 2, 3, or 4. If it is absent or its value is 4, then the \nolinebreak command marks a place which will under no circumstances be placed at the end of a page. If the numerical argument *i* is 0, then TeX can end the page at that point, but the presence of the command neither encourages nor discourages this. If the numerical value of *i* is 1, 2 or 3, then this discourages TeX from making a page break at that point and the higher the number the stronger the discouragement. If the twocolumn document style option has been chosen, then this command effects the ending of a column rather than that of a page. (Fragile.)

\normalmarginpar This declaration makes marginal notes appear in the default margin. (See \marginpar for what the default margins are.)

\normalsize A declaration that alters the size of type and also selects the roman font of that size. It cannot be used in math mode. Usually the type size selected is just bigger than \small and just smaller than \large. (Fragile.)

\not A command only available in math mode which is used to negate the following symbol by putting a slash through it. Thus, \not\equiv produces $\not\equiv$. (Robust.)

note (A BibTeX field-name.) Any additional information that you want to appear in the bibliography that is produced, such as note = "Edited by John Worrall and Elie Zahar". Note that the first word should have an initial uppercase letter.

\nu produces the ordinary symbol ν but only in math mode. (Robust.)

number (A B<small>IB</small>T<small>E</small>X field-name.) The number of the work being referred to.

\numberline{*sec-unit*}{*text*} can only appear as an argument to \addcontentsline, *q.v.* (Fragile.)

\nwarrow produces the binary relation symbol $\nwarrow$ but only in math mode. (Robust.)

\o A command only available in paragraph and LR modes for producing a lowercase Scandinavian o-with-slash-l (ø). (Robust.)

\O A command only available in paragraph and LR modes for producing an uppercase Scandinavian o-with-slash-l (Ø). (Robust.)

\oddsidemargin A rigid length parameter whose value affects the appearance of the output page. On right-hand pages if two-sided printing is in operation and on all pages if one-sided printing is in operation the distance between the left-hand edge of the paper and the left-hand edge of the body is the sum of the value of \oddsidemargin and one inch. See Fig. C.4 on p. 258. This is a robust command that must never be preceded by a \protect command.

\odot produces the binary operator symbol $\odot$ but only in math mode. (Robust.)

\oe A command only available in paragraph and LR modes for producing a lowercase French ligature (œ). (Robust.)

\OE A command only available in paragraph and LR modes for producing an uppercase French ligature (Œ). (Robust.)

\oint produces the large operator symbol $\oint$ but only in math mode. The symbol produced is slightly larger in displayed formulas than when it occurs as part of an in-text formula. Subscripts and superscripts appear under and over the symbol produced by this command—as limits—when it occurs in a displayed formula. (Robust.)

\omega produces the ordinary symbol ω but only in math mode. (Robust.)

\Omega produces the ordinary symbol Ω but only in math mode. (Robust.)

\ominus produces the binary operator symbol $\ominus$ but only in math mode. (Robust.)

\onecolumn This is a non-global declaration, that is to say, it obeys T<small>E</small>X's usual scoping rules, that first starts a new page by executing the command \clearpage and then continues by typesetting the input in a one-column format.

openbib An option to the \documentstyle command. Normally, when you produce a bibliography using the thebibliography environment the second and subsequent lines of each entry begin immediately below the start of the first line (with the label in the "margin"). If you prefer the second and subsequent lines to be indented, then use this option. The rigid length parameter \bibindent controls the size of indentation.

\opening{*text*} A command that can only occur inside a letter environment. It is used for the letter's opening. Note that you must include the word Dear as part of *text* if you want this to appear in the letter produced.

\oplus produces the binary operator symbol $\oplus$ but only in math mode. (Robust.)

organization (A BibTeX field-name.) The sponsors of a conference or the organization associated with a technical manual.

\oslash produces the binary operator symbol $\oslash$ but only in math mode. (Robust.)

\otimes produces the binary operator symbol $\otimes$ but only in math mode. (Robust.)

\oval(*p,q*)[*part*] A command that can only occur in the argument of a \put or \multiput command inside the picture environment; it is explained in section 10.4.

{*form*$_1$ \over *form*$_2$} produces a fraction with a central horizontal line and with *form*$_1$ on top of *form*$_2$. This is a primitive TeX command.

\overbrace{*form*} produces $\overbrace{form}$ but only in math mode. In a displayed formula a superscript places a label over the brace. (Robust.)

\overleftarrow{*form*} produces $\overleftarrow{form}$ but only in math mode.

\overline{*form*} produces $\overline{form}$ but only in math mode. (Robust.)

\overrightarrow{*form*} produces $\overrightarrow{form}$ but only in math mode.

\owns produces the binary relation symbol $\ni$ but only in math mode; it has exactly the same effect as the command \ni. (Robust.)

p{*len*} An expression that can only occur within the *preamble* of an array or tabular environment. Each entry in the column corresponding to this expression will be typeset in a parbox of width *len*; in effect, as if it were the argument *text* in a \parbox[t]{*len*}{*text*} command. As the command \\ is used to separate rows in the array and tabular environments, it can only occur within *text* in special circumstances, namely inside an environment like array, minipage or tabular, inside the *text* argument of a \parbox or in the scope—which must be explicitly indicated with curly braces—of a \centering, \raggedright or \raggedleft declaration.

\P produces the "paragraph" symbol ¶ in all modes. (Robust.)

page A counter which contains the value of the *current* page. Unlike other counters it is incremented *after* the page number is generated. It is, therefore, initialized to one and not to zero.

\pagebreak[*i*] The optional numerical argument *i* can be either 0, 1, 2, 3, or 4. If it is absent or its value is 4, then the **\pagebreak** command marks the position of the end of a page. The output is right justified—unless some other command or declaration has suppressed right justification—with the word that came before the **\pagebreak** command occurring at the extreme right of the line on which it occurs. (This may cause an underfull **\hbox** warning message.) If the numerical argument *i* is 0, then TEX can end the page at that point, but the presence of the command neither encourages nor discourages this. If the numerical value of *i* is 1, 2 or 3, then this encourages TEX to make a page break at that point and the higher the number the stronger the encouragement. If the **twocolumn** document style option has been chosen, then this command effects the ending of a column rather than that of a page. (Fragile.)

\pagenumbering{*num-style*} This global declaration specifies how page numbers will appear. The parameter *num-style* can be either **arabic** (for Arabic numerals), **roman** (for lowercase Roman numerals), **Roman** (for uppercase Roman numerals), **alph** (for lowercase letters) and **Alph** (for uppercase letters). The default value is **arabic**. The **\pagenumbering** global declaration redefines **\thepage** to be ***num-style*{page}** (Fragile.)

\pageref{*key*} This command is used for cross-referencing purposes. It produces as output the page number on which the corresponding **\label{*key*}** command occurred. (Fragile.)

pages (A BIBTEX field-name.) The range of page numbers or a page number or several of these. For example, "679--703", "33--45, 60--63" or "35, 40--43, 70".

\pagestyle{*page-style*} A declaration that obeys the standard TEX scoping rules. It determines the appearance of each page of the final output document. There are four standard page styles, namely **plain**, **empty**, **headings** and **myheadings**. That is to say, *page-style* can be any of these. (Fragile.)

\par This command has the same effect as if you had left a blank line. (Robust.)

paragraph A counter used to control the numbering of paragraphs. It is initialized to zero and incremented by the **\paragraph** command before a number is generated. Values can be assigned to it by means of the **\setcounter** command. The value of this counter is reset to zero by the **\chapter**, **\section**, **\subsection** and **\subsubsection** commands.

\paragraph[*entry*]{*heading*} A sectioning command which opens a new paragraph. Paragraphs have level number 4 in the `article`, `report` and `book` document styles. By default paragraphs are not numbered automatically in those document styles. (This can be altered by changing the value of the counter `secumndepth`.) By default *heading* will not appear in the table of contents if one is produced, but this can be altered by changing the value of the counter `tocdepth`. If paragraph headings do appear in the table of contents, then *heading* is used, unless the optional argument *entry* is present, when that is used instead. If *entry* is present, then it is a moving argument, but if it is absent, then *heading* is the moving argument. (Fragile.)

\paragraph*{*heading*} A sectioning command which opens a new paragraph which is neither numbered nor will it appear in the table of contents. (Fragile.)

\parallel produces the binary relation symbol ‖ but only in math mode; the commands \| and \Vert produce the same sign, but as an ordinary symbol. (Robust.)

\parbox[*pos*]{*len*}{*text*} This command processes *text* in paragraph mode and puts the result into a parbox whose width is given by the *len* argument. The optional argument *pos* can be either b or t. The option b makes the bottom line of the box produced share the same baseline as the current line of text and the option t makes the top line of the box produced share the same baseline as the current line of text. The list-like environments `center`, `description`, `enumerate`, `flushleft`, `flushright`, `itemize`, `quote`, `quotation`, `thebibliography` and `verse`, any environment declared by a \newtheorem declaration and the `tabular` environment *cannot* occur in the argument *text*; nor can any footnote-making commands. (Fragile.)

\parfillskip The value of this rigid length parameter is the amount of horizontal blank space that appears in the last line of paragraphs; see Krieger and Schwarz (1989), section 3.8, "Justification of Paragraphs", for more information. This is a primitive TEX command.

\parindent A rigid length parameter whose value is the width of the indentation at the beginning of a normal paragraph. In a parbox its value is set to zero inches. You can change its value—for example, by means of the \setlength command—anywhere. This is a robust command that must never be preceded by a \protect command.

\parsep This rubber length parameter determines the amount of vertical space that is placed between paragraphs of a single item within the `list` environment; see Fig. C.3 on p. 229 for a graphical depiction of what it does. It is a robust command that should not be preceded by a \protect command.

\parskip A rubber length parameter whose value is the additional vertical space that is inserted between consecutive paragraphs—additional, that is to say, to the amount of vertical space that normally separates consecutive lines within paragraphs; for this see **\baselineskip**. Note that **\parskip** is a rubber length whose natural value is zero inches. Its value can be changed anywhere—for example, by means of the **\setlength** command—but it should always be a rubber or stretchable length. This is a robust command that must never be preceded by a **\protect** command.

part A counter used to control the numbering of parts. It is initialized to zero and incremented by the **\part** command before a number is generated. Values can be assigned to it by means of the **\setcounter** command.

\part[*entry*]{*heading*} A sectioning command which opens a new part. It is allowed when the document style is either **article**, **report** or **book**. Parts have level number 0 in the **article** document style, but in the **report** and **book** styles they have level number -1. By default parts are numbered automatically in those document styles. (This can be altered by changing the value of the counter **secumndepth**.) If the optional argument *entry* is absent, then by default *heading* will appear in the table of contents if one is produced. (This can be altered by changing the value of the counter **tocdepth**.) If *entry* is present, then it will appear in the table of contents but *heading* will appear in the body of the document produced. If *entry* is present, then it is a moving argument, but if it is absent, then *heading* is the moving argument. (Fragile.)

\part*{*heading*} A sectioning command which opens a new part which is neither numbered nor will it appear in the table of contents. (Fragile.)

\partial produces the ordinary symbol ∂ but only in math mode. In order to get the ordinary symbol δ use **\delta**. (Robust.)

\partopsep This is a rubber length parameter whose value is the additional vertical space added before and after a **list** environment if a blank line occurs just before the environment is opened. See Fig. C.3 on p. 229. This is a robust command that must not be preceded by a **\protect** command.

pc TEX keyword for *pica*, a unit of length, which exactly satisfies the equality 1 pc = 12 pt. (Roughly, 1 pc = 0.166 in = 4.22 mm.)

\perp produces the binary relation symbol $\perp$ but only in math mode; the command **\bot** produces the same sign, but as an ordinary symbol. (Robust.)

\phi produces the ordinary symbol ϕ but only in math mode. In order to get the ordinary symbol φ use **\varphi**. (Robust.)

\Phi produces the ordinary symbol Φ but only in math mode. (Robust.)

\pi produces the ordinary symbol π but only in math mode. In order to get the ordinary symbol ϖ use \varpi. (Robust.)

\Pi produces the ordinary symbol Π but only in math mode. (Robust.)

picture An environment used for producing simple line drawings. See chapter 10 for full details of its use.

plain A page style option to the \pagestyle and \thispagestyle declarations. A page number is placed in the foot of the page and the head is left empty. It is the default page style for both the article and report document styles.

plain A possible argument to the \bibliographystyle command. The bibliography produced is sorted alphabetically and labelled by numbers such as [17].

plus *len* A TeX keyword used in assigning rubber length values; *len* represents the amount by which the natural value of the target length parameter can stretch.

\pm produces the binary operator symbol $\pm$ but only in math mode. (Robust.)

\pmatrix The general form of this plain TeX command is like this:

$$\text{\textbackslash pmatrix\{}form_{11}\ \&\ form_{12}\ \&\ \ldots\ \&\ form_{1n}\ \text{\textbackslash cr}$$
$$form_{21}\ \&\ form_{22}\ \&\ \ldots\ \&\ form_{2n}\ \text{\textbackslash cr}$$
$$\vdots$$
$$form_{m1}\&\ form_{m2}\&\ \ldots\ \&\ form_{mn}\text{\textbackslash cr\}}$$

It is like \matrix except that large parentheses are placed around the matrix produced.

\pmod This command can only be used in math mode where it produces a parenthesized "modulo" expression. For example, $m_1 \equiv m_2 \pmod{n}$ produces $m_1 \equiv m_2 \pmod{n}$. (Robust.)

\poptabs A command only available within a tabbing environment where it restores the tab settings stored by a previous \pushtabs command.

\pounds produces the pounds symbol £ in all modes. (Robust.)

\Pr produces a log-like symbol (Pr) but only in math mode. Subscripts and superscripts appear under and over the symbol produced—as limits—when it occurs as part of a displayed formula. (Robust.)

\prec produces the binary relation symbol $\prec$ but only in math mode. (Robust.)

\preceq produces the binary relation symbol $\preceq$ but only in math mode. (Robust.)

\prime produces the ordinary symbol ′ but only in math mode. Note that S' is really $S^\prime$. (Robust.)

\prod produces the large operator symbol ∏ but only in math mode. The symbol produced is slightly larger in displayed formulas than when it occurs as part of an in-text formula. Subscripts and superscripts appear under and over the symbol produced by this command—as limits—when it occurs in a displayed formula. (Robust.)

\propto produces the binary relation symbol ∝ but only in math mode. (Robust.)

\protect Every fragile command that occurs inside a moving argument must be preceded by this command. (Robust, of course.)

\ps{*text*} A command that can only occur inside a `letter` environment. It is used to produce a postscript to a letter. Note that the letters 'PS' are *not* generated by LaTeX. Hence, there is no need for a separate \pps command.

\psi produces the ordinary symbol ψ but only in math mode. (Robust.)

\Psi produces the ordinary symbol Ψ but only in math mode. (Robust.)

pt TeX keyword for *point*, a unit of length, which exactly satisfies the equality 1 in = 72.27 pt. (Roughly, 1 pt = 0.0138 in = 0.35 mm.)

publisher (A BibTeX field-name.) The name of the publishing house. For example, `"Oxford University Press"` or `"Springer"`.

\pushtabs A command only available within a `tabbing` environment where it saves the current tab settings (which can be restored by a \poptabs command).

\put$(i, j)${*picture-object*} This command can only occur within the `picture` environment, where it places the *picture-object* at the location in the picture whose x-coordinate is i and whose y-coordinate is j. Each picture object has a reference point associated with it and the coordinates (i, j) indicate the exact location of this reference point. (Almost anything can be considered as being a picture object, but certain things are used more frequently than others.)

\qquad This plain TeX command produces horizontal space two ems wide in all modes.

\quad This plain TeX command produces one em of horizontal space in all modes.

quotation An environment used for quotations that can only occur in paragraph mode. Inside the environment LaTeX is in paragraph mode. The first line of paragraphs are indented and also the first line after the start of the environment but this can be suppressed by using a \noindent command. Vertical space between paragraphs is the same as normal. The left and right margins of the resulting parbox are indented equally from the normal margins by an equal amount.

quote An environment used for short quotations that can only be used in paragraph mode. Inside the environment LaTeX is in paragraph mode. The first line of a new paragraph is not indented but extra vertical space is inserted between paragraphs. The left and right margins of the resulting parbox are indented equally from the normal margins by an equal amount.

\raggedbottom This declaration allows the height of the body to vary slightly from page to page, the inter-paragraph vertical space being kept constant.

\raggedleft A declaration used for producing paragraphs that are not left justified, but have a ragged left edge.

\raggedright A declaration used for producing paragraphs that are not right justified, but have a ragged right edge.

\raisebox{len_1}[len_2][len_3]{$text$} The argument *text* is processed in LR mode and the resulting box is raised a distance of len_1 above the current baseline. If len_2 is present, then the box produced appears to extend a distance len_2 above the baseline. If len_3 is present, then the box produced appears to extend a distance len_3 below the baseline. (Fragile.)

\rangle produces the closing symbol $\rangle$ but only in math mode. (Robust.)

\rbrace produces the closing symbol $\}$ but only in math mode; it has exactly the same effect as the command **\}**. (Robust.)

\rceil produces the closing symbol $\rceil$ but only in math mode. (Robust.)

\Re produces the ordinary symbol $\Re$ but only in math mode. (Robust.)

\ref{key} This command is used for cross-referencing purposes. It produces as output the **\ref** value which was associated with *key* by a **\label{key}** command. (Fragile.)

\refstepcounter{ctr} The value of the counter *ctr* is increased by 1 and all counters within it are reset to zero. Furthermore, the current **\ref** value is declared to be the text generated by **\the**ctr.

\renewcommand{cmd}[i]{def} This declaration is just like **\newcommand**, *q.v.*, except that *cmd* must be the name of an already-defined command. (Fragile.)

\renewenvironment{env}[i]{def_1}{def_2} is similar to **\newenvironment**, *q.v.*, except that *env* must be the name of an already existing environment. (Fragile.)

report This can take the place of *doc-style* in the **\documentstyle** command; see chapter 6 for more information.

\reversemarginpar This declaration makes marginal notes appear in the opposite margin to the default one.

\rfloor produces the closing symbol ⌋ but only in math mode. (Robust.)

\rgroup This command is only available in math mode where it produces a delimiter that looks like a large right parenthesis; it has to be preceded, however, by either \left or \right.

\rhd produces the binary operator symbol ▷ but only in math mode. Note that this command is unavailable in plain TeX. (Robust.)

\rho produces the ordinary symbol ρ but only in math mode; to get the ordinary symbol ϱ use \varrho. (Robust.)

\right See \left.

\rightarrow produces the binary relation symbol → but only in math mode. The command \to produces the same symbol. (Robust.)

\Rightarrow produces the binary relation symbol ⇒ but only in math mode. (Robust.)

\rightarrowfill produces an arrow pointing right which expands to fill all the horizontal space available; see Table C.1 on p. 210 for a graphical depiction of what it does.

\rightharpoondown produces the binary relation symbol ⇁ but only in math mode. (Robust.)

\rightharpoonup produces the binary relation symbol ⇀ but only in math mode. (Robust.)

\rightleftharpoons produces the binary relation symbol ⇌ but only in math mode. (Robust.)

\rightmargin A rigid length parameter whose value affects the appearance of the list environment as shown in Fig. C.3 on p. 229. It is a ribust command that must not be preceded by a \protect command.

\rlap This plain TeX command prints text overlapping to the right; it is used inside the argument of the \displaylines command to place labels on the extreme left-hand side of the body region.

\rm A declaration that alters the style of the type being used to roman. (Robust.)

\rmoustache This command is only available in math mode where it produces the strange looking delimiter shown in Table 7.1 on p. 100; note that it has to be preceded by either \left or \right.

roman One of the available parameters to the **\pagenumbering** global declaration. Page numbers appear as lowercase Roman numerals when it is used.

\roman{*ctr***}** The value of the counter *ctr* is output as a lowercase Roman numeral. (Robust.)

Roman One of the available parameters to the **\pagenumbering** global declaration. Page numbers appear as uppercase Roman numerals when it is used.

\Roman{*ctr***}** The value of the counter *ctr* is output as an uppercase Roman numeral. (Robust.)

\rule[*len₁***]{***len₂***}{***len₃***}** This command produces a rectangular blob of width *len₂* and height *len₃* which is placed a distance of *len₁* above or below the current baseline (depending on whether *len₁* is positive or negative). By default the value of *len₁* is 0 millimetres. (Fragile.)

\samepage This declaration is used to get the material that occurs within its scope to appear on a single page. Pagebreaks can be forced or encouraged within its scope by using **\pagebreak** commands. (Fragile.)

\S produces the "section" symbol § in all modes. (Robust.)

\savebox{*cmd***}[***len***][***pos***]{***text***}** Outside the **picture** environment this declaration processes *text* in LR mode and the resulting box is placed in the storage bin associated with *cmd*, which must begin with a backslash and must previously have been declared by means of a **\newsavebox** command. The width of the box produced can be specified by means of the optional *len* parameter, which must be a length (for example, **2.3in**). If a width is specified, *text* is centred horizontally in the box produced; unless *pos* is present. If *pos* is **l**, then *text* is placed next to the left edge of the box produced; and if *pos* is **r**, then it is placed next to the right edge. (Fragile.)

\savebox{*cmd***}(***i, j***)[***pos***]{***picture-object***}** This form of this command can only occur inside a **picture** environment. The parameters (i, j), *pos* and *picture-object* have exactly the same meaning as in the case of the **\makebox** command. The parameter *cmd* is the name of the storage bin that must have been introduced previously by means of a **\newsavebox** command and *cmd* must begin with an initial back slash. (Fragile.)

\sb This is an alternative way to get subscripts. Both **x_{83}** and **$x\sb{83}$** produce x_{83}.

\sbox{*cmd***}{***text***}** Outside the **picture** environment this declaration processes *text* in LR mode and the resulting box is placed in the storage bin associated with *cmd*, which must begin with a backslash and must previously have been declared by means of a **\newsavebox** command. (Robust.)

\sc A declaration that alters the style of the type being used to SMALL CAPITALS. (Robust.)

school (A BIBTEX field-name.) The name of a department or school to which a thesis was submitted.

\scriptscriptstyle A declaration that can only be used in math mode. It forces TEX to typeset formulas in scriptscript style. This is the default style, for example, for subscripts and superscripts to subscripts and superscripts within in-text and displayed formulas, that is to say, second-order subscripts and superscripts. This is a primitive TEX command. (Robust.)

\scriptsize A declaration that alters the size of type and also selects the roman font of that size. It cannot be used in math mode. Usually the type size selected is just bigger than **\tiny** and just smaller than **\footnotesize**. (Fragile.)

\scriptstyle A declaration that can only be used in math mode. It forces TEX to typeset formulas in script style. This is the default style, for example, for subscripts and superscripts within in-text and displayed formulas. As well as causing a smaller size of type to be used, the spacing around symbols for relations and binary operators is different. This is a primitive TEX command. (Robust.)

\scrollmode This primitive TEX command ensures that the processing of your file will neither stop if an error occurs nor if user input is requested, though an emergency stop will take place if an attempt is made to **\input** a non-existent file. This is one of the few commands that can come before the **\documentstyle** command in the input file.

\searrow produces the binary relation symbol ↘ but only in math mode. (Robust.)

\sec produces a log-like symbol (sec) but only in math mode. Subscripts and superscripts never appear as limits attached to the symbol produced. (Robust.)

secnumdepth A counter whose value indicates which sectional units are numbered. All sectional units with level numbers less than or equal to the value in this counter are numbered.

section A counter used to control the numbering of sections. It is initialized to zero and incremented by the **\section** command before a number is generated. Values can be assigned to it by means of the **\setcounter** command. In the case of the **report** and **book** document styles the value of the counter **section** is reset to zero by means of the **\chapter** command. Thus, the first section of chapter X is always X.1.

\section[*entry*]{*heading*} A sectioning command which opens a new section. Sections have level number 1 in the **article**, **report** and **book** document styles. By default sections are numbered automatically in those document styles. (This can be altered by changing the value of the counter `secumndepth`.) If the optional argument *entry* is absent, then by default *heading* will appear in the table of contents if one is produced. (This can be altered by changing the value of the counter `tocdepth`.) If *entry* is present, then it will appear in the table of contents but *heading* will appear in the document produced. If *entry* is present, then it is a moving argument, but if it is absent, then *heading* is the moving argument. (Fragile.)

`\section*{`*heading*`}` A sectioning command which opens a new section. The heading produced is neither numbered nor will it appear in the table of contents. (Fragile.)

`series` (A BibTeX field-name.) Some books are published in series; the name of such a series appears here.

`\setcounter{`*ctr*`}{`*i*`}` This global declaration assigns the value *i* to the counter *ctr*. (Fragile.)

`\setlength{`*cmd*`}{`*len*`}` This assigns to the length command *cmd*—which must begin with a backslash—the value *len*. (Robust.)

`\setminus` produces the binary operator symbol \ but only in math mode; the command `\backslash` produces the same sign, but as an ordinary symbol. (Robust.)

`\settowidth{`*cmd*`}{`*text*`}` This assigns to the length command *cmd*—which must begin with a backslash—the natural width of the result of processing *text* in LR mode. (Robust.)

`\sf` A declaration that alters the style of the type being used to sans serif. (Robust.)

`\sharp` produces the ordinary symbol ♯ but only in math mode. (Robust.)

`\shortstack[`*pos*`]{`*col*`}` This command is usually used to produce a piece of text running vertically down the page. Items in *col* are separated by \\ commands and *pos* can either be `l` (for positioning row items flush left), `r` (for positioning row items flush right) or the default `c` (for centring row items). If used in the `picture` environment, the reference point is at the bottom left-hand corner of the box produced. (Fragile.)

`\sigma` produces the ordinary symbol σ but only in math mode; to get the ordinary symbol ς use `\varsigma`. (Robust.)

`\Sigma` produces the ordinary symbol Σ but only in math mode. (Robust.)

`\signature{`*text*`}` A declaration that can only occur in the `letter` document style. It is used for indicating that *text* is the sender of the letter. One or more \\ commands can occur within the argument *text* in order to force a new line.

\sim produces the binary relation symbol $\sim$ but only in math mode. (Robust.)

\simeq produces the binary relation symbol $\simeq$ but only in math mode. (Robust.)

\sin produces a log-like symbol (sin) but only in math mode. Subscripts and super-scripts never appear as limits attached to the symbol produced. (Robust.)

\sinh produces a log-like symbol (sinh) but only in math mode. Subscripts and superscripts never appear as limits attached to the symbol produced. (Robust.)

\sl A declaration that alters the style of the type being used to *slanted*. (Robust.)

\sloppy This declaration influences line breaking. When it is in force text will rarely stick out into the right-hand margin, but a lot of space may be inserted between words. It affects the typesetting of any paragraph if it is in force when that paragraph ends.

sloppypar An environment which typesets the material within it in paragraph mode with the \sloppy declaration in force.

\small A declaration that alters the size of type and also selects the roman font of that size. It cannot be used in math mode. Usually the type size selected is just bigger than \footnotesize and just smaller than \normalsize. (Fragile.)

\smallskip produces vertical space whose height is given by \smallskipamount; it is defined as \vspace{\smallskipamount}. Note that this differs from the plain TeX definition. (Fragile.)

\smallskipamount A rubber length whose value is 3pt plus 1pt minus 1pt.

\smash{*text*} typesets *text* normally but TeX treats the result as if it had a height and a width of zero inches. This is a plain TeX command.

\smile produces the binary relation symbol $\smile$ but only in math mode. (Robust.)

sp TeX keyword for *scaled point*, a unit of length used internally by TeX, which exactly satisfies the equality 1 pt = 2^{16} sp (= 65,536 sp).

\sp This is an alternative way to get superscripts. Both x^{75} and $x\sp{75}$ produce x^{75}.

\space When used in the argument of the \typeout command, this produces a single space on the terminal.

\spadesuit produces the ordinary symbol $\spadesuit$ but only in math mode. (Robust.)

\sqcap produces the binary operator symbol $\sqcap$ but only in math mode. (Robust.)

\sqcup produces the binary operator symbol $\sqcup$ but only in math mode. (Robust.)

\sqrt[*n*]{*form*} produces $\sqrt[n]{form}$ if *n* is present and $\sqrt{form}$ if it is absent, but only in math mode. (Fragile.)

\sqsubset produces the binary relation symbol $\sqsubset$ but only in math mode. Note that this command is unavailable in plain TeX. (Robust.)

\sqsubseteq produces the binary relation symbol $\sqsubseteq$ but only in math mode. (Robust.)

\sqsupset produces the binary relation symbol $\sqsupset$ but only in math mode. Note that this command is unavailable in plain TeX. (Robust.)

\sqsupseteq produces the binary relation symbol $\sqsupseteq$ but only in math mode. (Robust.)

\ss A command only available in paragraph and LR modes for producing a German 'es-zet' or sharp s (ß). (Robust.)

\stackrel{*top*}{*bot*} This command can only be used in math mode where it produces a symbol for a binary relation in which *top* is placed over *bot*. Note that *top* is processed in the same style as superscripts. For example, the input $\stackrel{\wedge}{=}$ produces $\stackrel{\wedge}{=}$. (Robust.)

\star produces the binary operator symbol $\star$ but only in math mode. (Robust.)

\stepcounter{*ctr*} The value of the counter *ctr* is increased by 1 and all counters within it are reset to zero.

\stop When an error occurs one of the options available to you is to enter I\stop (without any spaces) and this terminates the processing of your input file.

\stretch{*fpn*} A rubber length whose natural length is zero inches and whose stretchability is *fpn* times \fill, where *fpn* is a floating-point number which can be either positive or negative. (Robust.)

\strut This plain TeX command is available in all modes where it produces an invisible vertical rule whose height is the value of \baselineskip and which has no width.

sty File extension used of a style file such as report.sty or repl1.sty which contains a collection of macros or commands.

\subitem Used within the theindex environment this produces an indented entry.

\subsubitem A command used within the theindex environment to produce an entry which is indented more than those produced by \subitem commands.

subparagraph A counter used to control the numbering of subparagraphs. It is initialized to zero and incremented by the \subparagraph command before a number is generated. Values can be assigned to it by means of the \setcounter command. The value of the counter subparagraph is reset to zero by the \chapter, \section, \subsection, \subsubsection and \paragraph commands.

\subparagraph[*entry*]{*heading*} A sectioning command which opens a new subparagraph. Subparagraphs have level number 5 in the article, report and book document styles. By default subparagraphs are not numbered automatically in those document styles. (This can be altered by changing the value of the counter secumndepth.) By default *heading* will not appear in the table of contents if one is produced, but this can be altered by changing the value of the counter tocdepth. If subparagraph headings do appear in the table of contents, then *heading* is used, unless the optional argument *entry* is present, when that is used instead. If *entry* is present, then it is a moving argument, but if it is absent, then *heading* is the moving argument. (Fragile.)

\subparagraph*{*heading*} This sectioning command opens a new paragraph which is neither numbered nor will it appear in the table of contents. (Fragile.)

subsection A counter used to control the numbering of subsections. It is initialized to zero and incremented by the \subsection command before a number is generated. Values can be assigned to it by means of the \setcounter command. The value of the counter subsection is reset to zero by both the \chapter and \section commands.

\subsection[*entry*]{*heading*} A sectioning command which opens a new subsection. Subsections have level number 2 in the article, report and book document styles. By default subsections are numbered automatically in those document styles. (This can be altered by changing the value of the counter secumndepth.) If the optional argument *entry* is absent, then by default *heading* will appear in the table of contents if one is produced. (This can be altered by changing the value of the counter tocdepth.) If *entry* is present, then it will appear in the table of contents but *heading* will appear in the body of the document produced. If *entry* is present, then it is a moving argument, but if it is absent, then *heading* is the moving argument. (Fragile.)

\subsection*{*heading*} A sectioning command which opens a new subsection which is neither numbered nor will it appear in the table of contents. (Fragile.)

\subset produces the binary relation symbol $\subset$ but only in math mode. (Robust.)

\subseteq produces the binary relation symbol $\subseteq$ but only in math mode. (Robust.)

subsubsection A counter used to control the numbering of subsubsections. It is initialized to zero and incremented by the \subsubsection command before a number is generated. Values can be assigned to it by means of the \setcounter command. The value of the counter subsubsection is reset to zero by the \chapter, \section and \subsection commands.

\subsubsection[*entry*]{*heading*} A sectioning command which opens a new subsubsection. Subsubsections have level number 3 in the article, report and book document styles. By default subsubsections are numbered automatically in the article style, but they are not numbered automatically in the report or book styles. (This can be altered by changing the value of the counter secumndepth.) By default *heading* will appear in the table of contents in the article style if one is produced, but it will not appear in either the report or the book styles. (This can be altered by changing the value of the counter tocdepth.) If subsubsection headings do appear in the table of contents, then *heading* is used, unless the optional argument *entry* is present, when that is used instead. If *entry* is present, then it is a moving argument, but if it is absent, then *heading* is the moving argument. (Fragile.)

\subsubsection*{*heading*} A sectioning command which opens a new subsubsection which is neither numbered nor will it appear in the table of contents. (Fragile.)

\succ produces the binary relation symbol $\succ$ but only in math mode. (Robust.)

\succeq produces the binary relation symbol $\succeq$ but only in math mode. (Robust.)

\sum produces the large operator symbol $\sum$ but only in math mode. The symbol produced is slightly larger in displayed formulas than when it occurs as part of an in-text formula. Subscripts and superscripts appear under and over the symbol produced by this command—as limits—when it occurs in a displayed formula. (Robust.)

\sup produces a log-like symbol (sup) but only in math mode. Subscripts and superscripts appear under and over the symbol produced—as limits—when it occurs as part of a displayed formula. (Robust.)

\supset produces the binary relation symbol $\supset$ but only in math mode. (Robust.)

\supseteq produces the binary relation symbol $\supseteq$ but only in math mode. (Robust.)

\surd produces the ordinary symbol $\surd$ but only in math mode. (Robust.)

\swarrow produces the binary relation symbol $\swarrow$ but only in math mode. (Robust.)

\symbol{*i*} This produces the character in the current font with number *i*. Thus, {\tt \symbol{92}char} produces \char. If *i* is preceded by ', it is considered to be an octal number and if by ", then it is considered to be a hexadecimal number. (Robust.)

\t␣*char*₁ *char*₂ or \t{*char*₁ *char*₂} This produces a tie-after accent (o͡o) over the following two characters *char*₁ and *char*₂ in LR or paragraph mode. (Robust.)

tabbing An environment used for aligning information without the option of including either horizontal or vertical rules. See sections 4.12 and 9.1 for more information.

\tabbingsep When the \' command is used within the **tabbing** environment, text is pushed to the left and the value of this rigid length parameter is the distance left between the text and the left margin (or an appropriate tab position). This is a robust command that should never be preceded by a \protect command.

\tabcolsep This rigid length parameter is half the amount of horizontal space left between the columns produced by a **tabular** or **tabular*** environment. This is a robust command that must not be preceded by a \protect command.

table A counter used in the numbering of floats created by the **table** and **table*** environments. It is only incremented if a \caption command has been included inside the environment.

table An environment which produces a float. If a \caption command is present inside it, then the word 'Table' and a numerical label are produced automatically; otherwise, it behaves like the **figure** environment, *q.v.*

table* An environment just like the **table** environment, except that if the **twocolumn** document style option has been chosen, then the resulting float is two columns wide.

\tableofcontents This command produces a table of contents at the place in the input file where it occurs. You need to run LaTeX at least twice to get a correct table of contents. It causes a **toc** file to be written or overwritten unless you have included a \nofiles command.

tabular The **tabular** environment can occur in any mode and its general form is:

\begin{tabular}[*pos*]{*preamble*} *row-list* \end{tabular}

The optional *pos* argument controls the vertical positioning of the box produced. By default alignment is on the centre of the box, but a t option aligns on the top row and a b option aligns on the bottom row. The *preamble* specifies how the columns of the table are going to be formatted, as explained in subsection 4.8.1. The *row-list* element consists of one or more *row* components which are separated by \\ commands. Each *row* will usually contain $i - 1$ ampersands where i is the number of columns that the table contains. (Note that if a row contains some \multicolumn commands, then fewer ampersands may be required.) Following a \\ command you can include one or more \hline commands. If two \hline commands occur next to one another, then the vertical space separating them is given by the rigid length parameter \doubleseprule. If you want a line to appear at the bottom of your table, then the final \hline command must be preceded by a \\ command, but the \\ command should be left out if not followed by a \hline command.

tabular* The general format of the tabular* environment is:

\begin{tabular*}{*len*}[*pos*]{*preamble*} *row-list* \end{tabular*}

where *pos*, *preamble* and *row-list* are exactly as for the tabular environment, but *len* gives the width of the box produced. Care must be taken to ensure that the material placed in each row is exactly of this width; usually rubber length commands like \hfill are used for this purpose.

\tan produces a log-like symbol (tan) but only in math mode. Subscripts and superscripts never appear as limits attached to the symbol produced. (Robust.)

\tanh produces a log-like symbol (tanh) but only in math mode. Subscripts and superscripts never appear as limits attached to the symbol produced. (Robust.)

\tau produces the ordinary symbol τ but only in math mode. (Robust.)

\TeX produces the logo TeX.

\textfloatsep A rubber length parameter whose value is the amount of vertical space left between a float and the text either below or above it. If the twocolumn document style option has been chosen, the value of this command only affects single-column floats; for two-column floats see \dbltextfloatsep. This is a robust command that must not be preceded by a \protect command.

\textfraction A command whose value is a floating-point number between 0 and 1 which represents the minimum amount of a text page, that is to say, one which contains both text and floats, that must be occupied by text. For example, if \textfraction is 0.6, then at least 60% of each text page must be occupied by things that are not floats. It can be altered by \def or \renewcommand. Its default value is 0.2.

\textheight A rigid length parameter whose value affects the appearance of each output page. Its value is the normal height of the body of a page. See Fig. C.4 on p. 258. This is a robust command that must never be preceded by a \protect command.

\textstyle A declaration that can only be used in math mode. It forces TeX to typeset formulas in text style. This is the default style for in-text formulas. It can be used in subscripts and superscripts, for example, in order to force the use of larger symbols and to force them to be typeset in text style. This is a primitive TeX command. (Robust.)

\textwidth A rigid length parameter whose value affects the appearance of each output page. Its value is the normal width of the body of a page. See Fig. C.4 on p. 258. This is a robust command that must never be preceded by a \protect command.

\thanks{*text*} A command that can only occur inside the argument of either an \author, \date or \title declaration. It is used to produce a footnote and *text* occurs as the footnote produced. The markers produced are regarded as having zero width. If a \thanks command does not end a line, then it should be followed by a \␣ command in order to insert some inter-word space. Too many \thanks commands—that is to say, more than nine—will cause a 'Counter too large' error message. Note that *text* is a moving argument.

\the*ctr* The \newcounter{*ctr*} command makes *ctr* into a counter, but in order for the value of *ctr* to be output it has to be converted into text, for example, by the \arabic or \Roman commands. Whenever you introduce a new counter LaTeX automatically creates a new command \the*ctr* which produces text output and by default \the*ctr* is defined to be \arabic{*ctr*}. For example, the commands:

```
\newcounter{instinct}
\setcounter{instinct}{7}
\theinstinct
```

produce 7; and the commands

```
\setcounter{instinct}{11}
\def\theinstinct{\Alph{instinct}}
\theinstinct
```

produce K. In the case of LaTeX's built-in counters what \the*ctr* produces varies widely; see section B.3 for more information. (Robust.)

thebibliography Environment used for do-it-yourself bibliographies.

theindex Environment used for producing an index; the output appears in a two-column format.

\theta produces the ordinary symbol θ but only in math mode; to get the ordinary symbol ϑ use \vartheta. (Robust.)

\Theta produces the ordinary symbol Θ but only in math mode. (Robust.)

\thicklines A declaration used to select the thicker of the two standard thicknesses of lines and circles in the **picture** environment. (Robust.)

\thinlines A declaration used to select the thinner of the two standard thicknesses of lines and circles in the **picture** environment. (Robust.)

a	`\topmargin` $+$ 1 in	f	`\footheight`
b	`\headheight`	g	`\oddsidemargin` $+$ 1 in
c	`\headsep`	g	`\evensidemargin` $+$ 1 in
d	`\textheight`	h	`\textwidth`
e	`\footskip` $-$ `\footheight`		

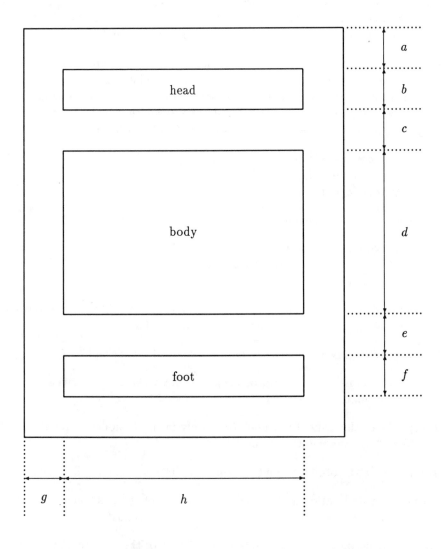

Figure C.4: Parameters affecting the appearance of the output page.

\thispagestyle{*page-style*} A declaration similar to \pagestyle, except that it only affects the current page. The parameter *page-style* can be either plain, empty, headings or myheadings. (Fragile.)

\tiny A declaration that alters the size of type and also selects the roman font of that size. It cannot be used in math mode. Usually the type size selected is the smallest available and just smaller than \scriptsize. (Fragile.)

\tilde A command that produces an accent in math mode. Thus, $\tilde x$ produces $\tilde{x}$. (Robust.)

\times produces the binary operator symbol $\times$ but only in math mode. (Robust.)

title (A BibTeX field-name.) The title of a book or article or whatever.

\title{*text*} This declaration is used to declare *text* to be the title in the article, report and book document styles. (The actual title is produced by a \maketitle command within the document environment.) You can use the \\ command inside *text* in order to force a line break and one or more \thanks commands can also appear in *text*. These produce footnotes whose markers are regarded as having zero width. If a \thanks command does not end a line, then it should be followed by a \␣ command in order to insert some inter-word space.

titlepage A document style option which can only be used if the article document style has been chosen. It forces the title and the abstract—if present—each to appear at the top of a new page.

\to produces the binary relation symbol $\rightarrow$ but only in math mode; it has exactly the same effect as the command \rightarrow. (Robust.)

toc The file extension of a file which is only created or overwritten if your input contains a \tableofcontents command (and does not contain a \nofiles command). The toc file contains the information necessary to produce a table of contents for your document. The information comes from all those sectioning commands in your input file whose level number is less than or equal to the value of the counter tocdepth. The table of contents is produced by the \tableofcontents command if a toc file exists when you process your input file.

tocdepth A counter whose value controls which sectional unit headings will appear in the table of contents if there is one. All headings of sectional units with level numbers less than or equal to the value of this counter will appear in the table of contents.

\today This command causes the date of the day on which you created a dvi file from your input file to be included in that dvi file. The date is in the American format, for example, July 4, 1992. It can only be used in LR or paragraph mode. (Robust.)

\top produces the ordinary symbol ⊤ but only in math mode. (Robust.)

\topfraction The value of this command is a floating-point number greater than zero and less than or equal to one. Its value specifies how much of the top part of each text page can be used for floats. It can be altered by \def or \renewcommand. Its default value is 0.7. If the twocolumn document style option has been chosen, the value of this command only affects single-column floats; for two-column floats see \dbltopfraction.

\topmargin A rigid length parameter whose value affects the appearance of each output page. The distance between the top edge of the paper and the top of the page's head is the sum of the value of \topmargin and one inch. See Fig. C.4 on p. 258. This is a robust command that must never be preceded by a \protect command.

topnumber The value of this counter is the maximum number of floats, that is to say, tables or figures, that can occur at the top of each text page. Its default value is 2. If the twocolumn document style option has been chosen, the value of this counter only affects single-column floats; for two-column floats see dbltopnumber.

\topsep A rubber length parameter used by the list environment to control the appearance and organization of the list generated. See Fig. C.3 on p. 229 for details of its effect. This is a robust command that must never be preceded by a \protect command.

\topskip A rubber length parameter whose value is the minimum distance between the top of the body and the bottom of the first line of text. Its effect is rather like that of \baselineskip, except that it only affects the first line on the page. This is a robust command that must never be preceded by a \protect command.

totalnumber The value of this counter is the maximum number of floats that can appear on a text page. Its default value is 3.

\triangle produces the ordinary symbol △ but only in math mode. (Robust.)

\triangleleft produces the binary operator symbol ◁ but only in math mode. (Robust.)

\triangleright produces the binary operator symbol ▷ but only in math mode. (Robust.)

trivlist An environment which is a restricted form of the list environment. It inherits the values of all parameters in force when the environment opens, except that \leftmargin, \labelwidth and \itemindent are set to zero inches and \parsep is set to the current value of \parskip. Lamport (1986), p. 168, writes, 'Every \item command [within the trivlist environment] must have an optional argument.' Apparently, he is unaware that this statement is self-contradictory.

\tt A declaration that alters the style of the type being used to typewriter. (Robust.)

twocolumn A document style option which makes two columns of text appear on every page. See chapter 11 for more information.

\twocolumn[*text*] This is a global declaration, that is to say, one whose scope is not delimited by curly braces, that first starts a new page by executing the command \clearpage and then typesets the following input in a two-column format. If the optional parameter *text* is present, then it is typeset as a single-column parbox that extends across the entire width of the text body. (Fragile.)

twoside A possible option to the \documentstyle command. It causes odd- and even-numbered pages to be treated differently. For example, the default width of the left margin is different and the moving heads on odd- and even-numbered pages are different (if present at all). It is the default option for the book document style.

type (A BibTeX field-name.) There are many varieties of technical reports; here, you should state which one the work you are referring to is.

\typein[*cmd*]{*text*} This command outputs *text* onto the terminal you are using and it also writes it to the log file. After outputting *text* it stops the processing of your input file until you input something from your keyboard—which input is terminated by a carriage return character. If *cmd* is absent, then your input is processed as if it occurred in your input file where the \typein command occurs. If *cmd* is present and not already defined, then it is defined to be what you input. (Fragile.)

\typeout{*text*} This command outputs *text* onto the terminal you are using and it also writes it to the log file. The argument *text* is a moving one. Preceding a command name in *text* with \protect causes that command name to be output. A command name in *text* defined by either the \newcommand or \renewcommand declaration is replaced by its definition. (Fragile.)

\u␣*char* or \u{*char*} This produces a breve accent (ŏ) over the following single character *char* in LR or paragraph mode. (Robust.)

\unboldmath A declaration that reverses the effect of a previous \boldmath declaration. (Fragile.)

\underbrace{*form*} produces $\underbrace{form}$ but only in math mode; in a displayed formula a subscript places a label below the brace. (Robust.)

\underline{*form*} produces <u>*form*</u> in any mode. (Fragile.)

\unitlength A rigid length parameter whose value determines the length of the unit used for positioning and drawing picture objects in the picture environment. For example, placing the command \unitlength=1mm just before a picture environment makes the unit of length one millimetre. Its default value is 1 point. This is a robust command which must never be preceded by a \protect command.

\unlhd produce the binary operator symbol ⊴ but only in math mode; note that this symbol is unavailable in plain TEX. (Robust.)

\unrhd produce the binary operator symbol ⊵ but only in math mode; note that this symbol is unavailable in plain TEX. (Robust.)

unsrt A possible argument to the \bibliographystyle command. The entries in the bibliography produced occur in the order of their first citation and are labelled by numbers like [31].

\uparrow produces the binary relation symbol ↑ but only in math mode. Following either \left or \right, however, this command produces a delimiter whose size depends on what it delimits. (Robust.)

\Uparrow produces the binary relation symbol ⇑ but only in math mode. Following either \left or \right, however, this command produces a delimiter whose size depends on what it delimits. (Robust.)

\upbracefill produces a downward pointing curly brace which expands to fill all the horizontal space available; see Table C.1 on p. 210 for a graphical depiction of what it does.

\updownarrow produces the binary relation symbol ↕ but only in math mode. Following either \left or \right, however, this command produces a delimiter whose size depends on what it delimits. (Robust.)

\Updownarrow produces the binary relation symbol ⇕ but only in math mode. Following either \left or \right, however, this command produces a delimiter whose size depends on what it delimits. (Robust.)

\uplus produces the binary operator symbol ⊎ but only in math mode. (Robust.)

\usebox{*cmd*} This produces the contents of the storage bin *cmd*. (Robust.)

\usecounter{*ctr*} A declaration that can only occur in the *dec-list* argument to the list environment; it is used for numbering the items of the list automatically.

\upsilon produces the ordinary symbol υ but only in math mode. (Robust.)

\Upsilon produces the ordinary symbol Υ but only in math mode. (Robust.)

\v␣*char* or **\v{*char*}** This produces a háček (ǒ) accent over the following single character *char* in LR or paragraph mode. (Robust.)

\value{*ctr*} This command is used if you want to set the value of one counter equal to another; for example, **\setcounter{war}{\value{equation}}** has the result that the value of **war** is the same as that of **equation**. (The counter **war** must have been introduced previously by means of a **\newcounter{war}** command.) It is a robust command which should never be preceded by a **\protect** command.

\varepsilon produces the ordinary symbol ε but only in math mode. To get the ordinary symbol ϵ use **\epsilon** and to produce the binary relation $\in$ use **\in**. (Robust.)

\varphi produces the ordinary symbol φ but only in math mode. To get the ordinary symbol ϕ use **\phi**. (Robust.)

\varpi produces the ordinary symbol ϖ but only in math mode. To get the ordinary symbol π use **\pi**. (Robust.)

\varrho produces the ordinary symbol ϱ but only in math mode. To get the ordinary symbol ρ use **\rho**. (Robust.)

\varsigma produces the ordinary symbol ς but only in math mode. To get the ordinary symbol σ use **\sigma**. (Robust.)

\vartheta produces the ordinary symbol ϑ but only in math mode. To get the ordinary symbol θ use **\theta**. (Robust.)

\vbox{*text*} produces a vertical box; if several things occur in *text*, then they are placed on top of one another. This is a primitive TeX command.

\vdash produces the binary relation symbol $\vdash$ but only in math mode. (Robust.)

\vdots A command only available in math mode for producing an ellipsis $\vdots$ consisting of three vertical dots. (Robust.)

\vec A command that produces an accent in math mode. Thus, **$\vec x$** produces $\vec{x}$. (Robust.)

\vector A command that can only occur as the argument to a **\put** or **\multiput** command inside a **picture** environment. The commands:

$$\text{\textbackslash put}(i,j)\{\text{\textbackslash vector}(p,q)\{l\}\}$$

draw an arrow which starts at the point (i, j) and whose projection on the x-axis is l units. (The only exception to this occurs when we want to produce a vertical line, in which case l gives the actual length of the line produced.) The slope of the line is given by (p, q), that is to say, it goes p units in the x direction for every q units it goes in the y direction. Both p and q must be whole numbers between -4 and $+4$, inclusive, with no common divisor. (Fragile.)

\vee produces the binary operator symbol ∨ but only in math mode; the command **\lor** (logical or) produces the same symbol. (Robust.)

\verb_char text char_ This outputs _text_ in typewriter font exactly as it appears in your input file. The parameter _char_ can be any single visible character—except a space or a letter or a *—that does not occur in _text_. A space between _char_ and _text_ or _text_ and _char_ appears in the output. No newline character should occur in _text_. Lamport (1986), p. 66, says that a **\verb** command should not occur in the argument of any other command but may occur in an environment; I have found, however, that **\verb** can occur in the arguments of some other commands—such as the **\index** command—and cause no problems.

\verb*_char text char_ Like the **\verb** command except that spaces in _text_ appear as ␣ characters in the output.

verbatim An environment used for producing text exactly as it appears in your input file using the typewriter style of type. Special characters and LaTeX commands do not have their usual meaning inside this environment. They are output as they appear. The only exception being the **\end{verbatim}** command. (Note that no space can occur between **\end** and **{verbatim}**.) This environment cannot occur in the argument to any other command, though it can occur inside another environment.

verbatim* An environment the same as **verbatim** except that spaces in the input file appear as '␣' in the output document.

verse An environment which can be used for displaying poetry. The left and right margins are indented by the same amount. Lines within a stanza are terminated by the **** command and stanzas are separated by means of one or more blank lines.

\vert produces the ordinary symbol | but only in math mode; it has exactly the same effect as the command |. Following either **\left** or **\right**, however, this command produces a delimiter whose size depends on what it delimits. (Robust.)

\Vert produces the ordinary symbol ‖ but only in math mode; it has exactly the same effect as the command **\|**. Following either **\left** or **\right**, however, this command produces a delimiter whose size depends on what it delimits. (Robust.)

\vfill This is just an abbreviation for **\par\vspace{\fill}**. (Fragile.)

\vline This command can only occur within an **array** or **tabular** environment where it produces a vertical line whose height is that of the row in which it occurs. (Robust.)

volume (A BibTeX field-name.) The volume number of a journal or the volume number of a book or conference proceedings that is one of a series.

\vspace{*len***}** This command adds vertical space of height *len* in the output document unless a page break occurs within its "scope". If the **\vspace** command occurs in the middle of a paragraph, then the current line is finished before the space is added. (Fragile.)

\vspace*{*len***}** Like **\vspace{***len***}** except that vertical space of height *len* is added even if a page break occurs within its "scope". (Fragile.)

\wedge produces the binary operator symbol $\wedge$ but only in math mode; the command **\land** (logical and) produces the same symbol. (Robust.)

\widehat A command that produces an accent in math mode which can vary in size. Its largest form appears in **$\widehat{xyz}$** which produces $\widehat{xyz}$. (Robust.)

\widetilde A command that produces an accent in math mode which can vary in size. Its largest form appears in **$\widetilde{xyz}$** which produces $\widetilde{xyz}$. (Robust.)

\wp produces the ordinary symbol $\wp$ but only in math mode. (Robust.)

\wr produces the binary operator symbol $\wr$ but only in math mode. (Robust.)

\xi produces the ordinary symbol ξ but only in math mode. (Robust.)

\Xi produces the ordinary symbol Ξ but only in math mode. (Robust.)

year (A BibTeX field-name.) The year associated with a work that you are referring to. Usually, something like 1976, but the standard BibTeX style can handle text like "Circa 1600" whose last four non-punctuation characters are numerals.

\zeta produces the ordinary symbol ζ but only in math mode. (Robust.)

Bibliography

Abel, N. H. (1826). Untersuchungen über die reihe $1 + \frac{m}{1}x + \frac{m.(m-1)}{2}x^2 + \frac{m.(m-1)(m-2)}{2.3}x^3 \ldots$, *Journal für Reine und Argewandte Mathematik* **1**: 311–339.

Benson, D. J. (1991). *Representations and Cohomology: Basic Representation Theory of Finite Groups and Associative Algebras*, Vol. 1, Cambridge University Press, Cambridge. Cambridge Studies in Advanced Mathematics, vol. 30. Editorial board: D. J. H. Garling, D. Gorenstein, T. tom Dieck and P. Walters.

Bird, R. S. (1988). Lectures on constructive functional programming, Technical Monograph PRG–69, Oxford University Computing Laboratory, (Programming Research Group).

Borde, A. (1992). *TEX by Example: A Beginner's Guide*, Academic Press, New York.

Buerger, D. J. (1990). *LATEX for Engineers and Scientists*, McGraw-Hill, New York.

Butkovskiy, A. G. (1982). *Green's Functions and Transfer Functions Handbook*, Ellis Horwood, Chichester. Translated from the Russian by L. W. Longdon.

Carroll, L. (1970). *The Annotated Alice*, Penguin Books, Harmondsworth, UK. Revised edition with an introduction and notes by Martin Gardner.

Carroll, N. (1988). *Mystifying Movies: Fads and Fallacies in Contemporary Film Theory*, Columbia University Press, New York.

Carroll, N. (1990). *The Philosophy of Horror or Paradoxes of the Heart*, Routledge, New York and London.

Curry, H. B. and Feys, R. (1974). *Combinatory Logic*, Vol. 1, North-Holland, Amsterdam. First published in 1958.

Diller, A. (1988). *Compiling Functional Languages*, Wiley, Chichester.

Diller, A. (1990). **Z**: *An Introduction to Formal Methods*, Wiley, Chichester.

Eijkhout, V. (1992). *TEX by Topic: A TEXnician's Reference*, Addison-Wesley, Reading, MA.

Euclid (1956). *The Thirteen Books of Euclid's Elements*, Vol. I, Introduction and Books I, II, 2nd edn, Dover Publications, Inc., New York. Translated from the text of Heiberg with introduction and commentary by Sir Thomas L. Heath. Originally written about 300 BC.

Florescu, R. R. and McNally, R. T. (1989). *Dracula: Prince of Many Faces: His Life and his Times*, Little, Brown, Boston, MA.

Frege, G. (1980). *Philosophical and Mathematical Correspondence*, Basil Blackwell, Oxford. Edited by Gottfried Gabriel, Hans Hermes, Friedrich Kambartel, Christian Thiel and Albert Veraart. Abridged for the English edition by Brian McGuinness and translated by Hans Kaal.

Gardner, M. (1988a). *Hexaflexagons and Other Mathematical Diversions: The First* Scientific American *Book of Mathematical Puzzles and Recreations*, University of Chicago Press, Chicago and London. Originally published in 1959.

Gardner, M. (1988b). *Time Travel and Other Mathematical Bewilderments*, W. H. Freeman, New York.

Gjertsen, D. (1989). *Science and Philosophy: Past and Present*, Penguin Books, Harmondsworth, UK.

Hallett, M. (1979a). Towards a theory of mathematical research programmes (I), *British Journal for the Philosophy of Science* **30**: 1–25.

Hallett, M. (1979b). Towards a theory of mathematical research programmes (II), *British Journal for the Philosophy of Science* **30**: 135–159.

Hart, H. (1983). *Hart's Rules for Compositiors and Readers at the University Press Oxford*, 39th edn, Oxford University Press, Oxford. First published in 1893.

Heath, S. (1981). *Questions of Cinema*, Indiana University Press, Bloomington, IN.

Hindley, J. R. and Seldin, J. P. (1986). *Introduction to Combinators and λ-calculus*, Cambridge University Press, Cambridge. London Mathematical Society Student Texts, Vol. 1.

Hofstadter, D. R. (1979). *Gödel, Escher, Bach: An Eternal Golden Braid*, The Harvester Press, Hassocks, UK. Harvester Studies in Cognitive Science. General editor: Margaret A. Boden.

Knuth, D. E. (1986). *The TEXbook*, Addison-Wesley, Reading, MA.

Krieger, J. and Schwarz, N. (1989). *Introduction to TEX*, Addison-Wesley, Reading, MA.

Lakatos, I. (1976). *Proofs and Refutations: The Logic of Mathematical Discovery*, Cambridge University Press, Cambridge. Edited by John Worrall and Elie Zahar.

Lakatos, I. (1978). *Mathematics, Science and Epistemology: Philosophical Papers*, Vol. 2, Cambridge University Press, Cambridge. Edited by John Worrall and Gregory Currie.

Lamport, L. (1986). LATEX: *A Document Preparation System*, Addison-Wesley, Reading, MA.

Lem, S. (1991). The time-travel story and related matters of science-fiction structuring, in *Microworlds: Writings on Science Fiction and Fantasy*, Mandarin, London, pp. 136–160.

Littlewood, J. E. (1986). *Littlewood's Miscellany*, Cambridge University Press, Cambridge. Edited by B. Bollobás.

MacLane, S. and Birkhoff, G. (1967). *Algebra*, Collier–Macmillan, London.

Munkres, J. R. (1991). *Analysis on Manifolds*, Addison-Wesley, Redwood City, CA. This book was prepared using the TEX typesetting language.

Ore, O. (1988). *Number Theory and its History*, Dover, New York. First published in 1948.

Patterson, E. M. and Rutherford, D. E. (1965). *Elementary Abstract Algebra*, Oliver and Boyd, Edinburgh and Oxford, University Mathematical Texts.

Popper, K. R. (1973). *The Open Society and its Enemies: The Spell of Plato*, Vol. 1, Routledge & Kegan Paul, London. First published in 1945.

Popper, K. R. (1974). *The Open Society and its Enemies: The High Tide of Prophecy: Hegel, Marx, and the Aftermath*, Vol. 2, Routledge & Kegan Paul, London. First published in 1945.

Prawitz, D. (1965). *Natural Deduction: A Proof-theoretical Study*, Almqvist and Wiksell, Stockholm. Acta Universitatis Stockholmiensis; Stockholm Studies in Philosophy 3.

Quirk, R., Greenbaum, S., Leech, G. and Svartvik, J. (1985). *A Comprehensive Grammar of the English Language*, Longman, London and New York.

Roscoe, A. W. and Hoare, C. (1988). The laws of Occam programming, *Theoretical Computer Science* **60**: 177–229.

Sindermann, C. J. (1982). *Winning the Games Scientists Play*, Plenum Press, New York.

Snow, W. (1992). *TEX for the Beginner with LATEX Notes*, Addison-Wesley, Reading, MA.

Spivak, M. (1986). *The Joy of TEX: A Gourmet Guide to Typesetting with the AMS-TEX Macro Package*, American Mathematical Society, Providence, RI.

Thagard, P. (1992). *Conceptual Revolutions*, Princeton University Press, Princeton, NJ.

Whitehead, G. W. (1978). *Elements of Homotopy Theory*, Springer-Verlag, New York.

Wilson, C. (1984). *A Criminal History of Mankind*, Granada, London.

Index

The order of non-alphanumeric characters here is determined by the order in which they occur in Knuth's typewriter font which is shown on p. 185 for those not familiar with it. The escape character is regarded as invisible for the purposes of ordering (except that \name follows *name*). A reference like '17n' means that the idea occurs in a footnote on p. 17 and '27&n' means that the idea occurs both on p. 27 and also in a footnote on that page. In the case of commands, references are only given to examples of their use; so not all LaTeX commands will be found here, unlike the glossary.